Psychology AS:

The Teacher's Companion for AQA 'A'

GW00660634

Michael Griffin

•

Rosalind Geillis

•

Consultant editor

Cara Flanagan

United Kingdom: Folens Publishers, Waterslade House, Thame Rd, Haddenham, Buckinghamshire HP17 8NT.

www.folens.com

Ireland: Folens Publishers, Greenhills Road, Tallaght, Dublin 24.

Email: info@folens.ie

Editor:	Geoff Tuttle
Project development:	Rick Jackman (Jackman Publishing Solutions Ltd)
Concept design:	Patricia Briggs
Layout artist:	MTC
Illustrations:	MTC
Software architecture and design:	Haremi Ltd
Cover design:	Patricia Briggs, Chris Cardwell and Jump To!
Cover photographer:	Chris Cardwell
Cover image of cat:	courtesy of Clifton Photographic Company

First edition published 2004 by Nelson Thornes
Second edition first published 2009 by Folens Limited

The authors and publisher would like to thank the following for permission to reproduce copyright material:

p.1, © This image is copyright of Nicola Bilic/Fotolia; p.2, © James Steidl/Fotolia; p.2 and p.177, © Pascal Cossardeaux/Fotolia; p.3, © Kirsty Pargeter/Fotolia; p.4, © Yang MingQi/Fotolia and © AKS/ Fotolia; p.5, © Luminis/Fotolia; p.66, © Adrian Frost; p.88, p.89 and p.125, © NiDerLander/Fotolia; p.99, © Candan/Fotolia; p.114, © Blue Wren/Fotolia; p.115, © Velusariot/Fotolia, © Fabrice Rousselot/ Fotolia, © Konstantinos Kokkinis/Fotolia; p.128, © Ioannis Kounadeas/Fotolia; p.133, © Mills21/Fotolia, © Wong Sze Fei/Fotolia, © Jonathan Larsen/Fotolia; p.136, © Marco Bonan/Fotolia, © Brandon Seidel/ Fotolia, © Rachael Arnott/Fotolia; p.137, © Paty Cullen/Fotolia; p.140, © Paul Hill/Fotolia; p.149, © Katarzyna Malecka/Fotolia, © Lorelyn Medina/Fotolia, © Antonis Papantoniou/Fotolia; p.194, © Ioannis Kounadeas/Fotolia; p.200, © Johan Swanepoel/Fotolia, © Beboy/Fotolia, © Bluekat/Fotolia; p.203, © Broker/Fotolia, © Kameel/Fotolia, © Nigel Monckton/Fotolia, © Carole Mineo/Fotolia, © JLV Image Works/Fotolia; p.210, © Andrzej Tokarski/Fotolia, © Ioannis Kounadeas/Fotolia; p.228, © Joe Gough/Fotolia; p.236, © Raphtong/Fotolia; p.238, © Eishier/Fotolia; p.258, © Patrick Hermans/Fotolia, © Kirsty Pargeter/Fotolia, © Kreefax/Fotolia, © Markokg/Fotolia; p.260, © Monika Adamczyk/Fotolia, © Higyou/Fotolia, © Michael Nivelet/Fotolia; p. 203, p.260 and p.261, © Cool Graphics/Fotolia; p.269, © Goran Bogicevic/Fotolia, © Liv Friis-larsen/Fotolia; p.270, © Christos Georghiou/Fotolia, © Bilderbox/ Fotolia, © Eray Haciosmanoglu/Fotolia.

Sections 1 and 3, Handouts 1–9, © This icon is copyright of © rolffimages/Fotolia; Sections 2 and 3, Handouts 40–70 - © Photocreo/Fotolia; Handouts 71–109 - © Willee Cole/Fotolia; Handouts 110–138 - © Ruslan Gilmanshin/Fotolia; Handouts 169–187 - © Marc Dietrich/Fotolia.

Complete Companion book (material on pages 79, 93, 147, 148, 157 and 268).

'Blacky the Dog' on page 81 was adapted from an original drawing by Gerald Blum.

Every effort has been made to contact copyright holders of material used in this publication. If any copyright holder has been overlooked, we should be pleased to make any necessary arrangements.

British Library Cataloguing in Publication Data.
A catalogue record for this publication is available from the British Library.

ISBN 978-1-85008-295-8

NOTES

Acknowledgements

Where does one begin to give praise and recognition for the birth of a book? This book—*In Good Taste*—has come about as the result of the input and contributions of many wonderful people.

First and foremost, Richard Paul Evans opened the door for the "book inside me."

At the same time, Robert G. Allen shared his enormous talent and knowledge.

Together these two men inspired and taught me how to live my dream, so I began writing. Both *NY Times* bestselling authors with a combined forty-five years of writing experience, they became my mentors and assisted in bringing *In Good Taste* to print.

In the process of writing this book, I was introduced to the most remarkable book producer one could ever hope for—Karen Christoffersen has perceptive insight and intuitiveness which she used at lightning speed. I will forever be grateful for all the endless working hours and her own personal hours she dedicated to making this a beautiful book.

I give credit and thanks for the cover and interior page layout design to Paul Killpack (also a fellow Paradise transplant coincidentally). He did a wonderful job in making the book attractive. I suspect I will never know how much work he did in the background without any recognition— a modest, consistent worker.

Thanks go to my California and Utah friends who have given me great recipes and shared their lives with mine. They had good suggestions and support throughout the writing of this book.

My family, of course, knows how much I love and appreciate them and that their support is not measurable. Although my daughter, Lori, could probably put a price on the many hours she did editing and counseling on vegetarian inquiries. And thanks to John, my husband, who ate cereal a lot while I was working into the wee hours of the mornings.

I can never hope to repay any of these people for their efforts, but I hope they know my story will always begin and end with them. Just as *In Good Taste* will become many people's Family History Cookbook and a legacy in their families for generations, my story of the creation of *In Good Taste* will also go down in my family history and will be told for generations to come.

My sole desire for each reader is that you will capture your family recipe treasures in your own new Family History Cookbook.

—Nancy J. Miles

CONTENTS

DEDICATIONS

Michael:

To my gorgeous, long-suffering fiancée Alana! Thank you for putting up with my endless hours of work, and supporting me in all the lovely ways that you do! Love you! Also to all the fantastic teachers I've had the pleasure of working with so far at Keele, and Arthur Terry.

Rosalind:

To Diane Read, Bill Myers and all the Keele PGCE tutors.

INTRODUCTION

Mike Griffin

Mike Griffin: Both Rosalind and I have found this introduction very difficult! I am, after all, only in my second year of teaching, and I am well aware that many people using this resource pack will have had many more years experience than me! That said, I have been incredibly lucky during my short teaching career and have come across some inspirational teachers and outstanding ideas –which I continue to 'borrow' and adapt for my own lessons. Initially, I did my PGCE at Keele University in 2006-2007, which was an incredibly good foundation to start on. The course tutor, Yvonne Hill, gave us a fantastic introduction to teaching techniques and really encouraged us to critically reflect on our 'pedagogy' (I eventually looked this word up in the dictionary!). During that year I absorbed an amazing amount of creative ideas from Yvonne as well as from the other brilliant student teachers around me (Si, Emma, Jim, Gemma, Neil, etc. You know who you are!). Ros interviewed and selected me for my first job (thanks Ros!) at Arthur Terry School in Sutton Coldfield, where I have been ever since. The quality of ideas and teaching staff around me is exceptional, and many more ideas from Arthur Terry have been adapted and found their way into this resource pack. I have to confess that I would not describe myself as the most 'creative' person, or even the most 'creative' teacher. However, I would say my strength lies in collating teaching ideas, adapting them, and applying them in my classroom (I hope this doesn't sound like a job application letter!). After all, why 'reinvent the wheel'? Think about how many great ideas we come across day to day but forget to use. This led me to producing a *Psychology Teacher's Toolkit* with the help of colleagues and Internet forums. Some of you may have downloaded this from www.psychexchange.com. Ultimately, it was this 'toolkit' which led to the publishers asking me to co-author this resource pack – so I hope that is some justification as to why you are reading ideas from a 2nd year teacher! I sincerely hope many of them will be useful for your classroom.

Ros Geillis

Ros Geillis: I think this little introduction has been the hardest section to write! After much staring at a blank screen, writing a sentence then promptly deleting it, drinking yet another coffee, I realised this is exactly how I felt when I first began teaching Psychology. I knew what information I wanted to share with my class (or in this case you, the reader), I knew the amount of time (or space) I had available, yet I found myself searching for a means of communication. As a PGCE student, and during my NQT year, I was lucky enough to meet wonderful people who not only exposed me to a range of teaching ideas but encouraged me to develop my own activities. From these people I learnt that one of the most valuable resources you have are your fellow teachers; watching each other teach, applying activity ideas from another subject to yours, adapting and developing ideas, as well as devising your own, helps you quickly build a bank of resources. Since then I have been lucky enough to work at a school that encourages its staff to share good practice and provides opportunities to work with outside agencies as well as mark A-levels for the exam boards. I am now subject leader of social science but still remember one of the best pieces of advice I received as an NQT: to 'take risks' in terms of providing learning experiences. A number of the activities in this book involve students moving around the room, pictures, stickers and teaching topics to each other. I hope you and your students enjoy them.

Cara Flanagan

Cara Flanagan: My role in this excellent resource pack is a small one, as advisor and subject editor. I have a long history as a teacher, senior examiner and author, and hope that I have been able to use the associated knowledge to polish up the gems that Mike and Ros have produced. The pack owes some debt to the original *AS Teacher's Companion* (co-authored by myself, Sara Berman and Adrian Frost) – lots of the ideas have formed the basis for new handouts and lesson plans but a great deal is new.

WHAT YOU GET!

The written materials start with a Table of Contents which will show you where to find everything. This is organised according to the sections of the specification, subdivided into topics. The pack itself is divided into three sections.

Section 1: General topics

This covers topics such as how to facilitate self- and peer-assessment, how to encourage your students to elaborate their evaluative commentary, and how to approach the specification. Full details of the general topics are given in the Table of Contents.

Section 2: Lesson notes

Notes about the different activities, their rationale and how you might organise them. Links are given to handouts, and simple keys are used to highlight provision for different learning styles and ability differentiation.

Section 3: Handouts

Ready-to-run, photocopiable material.

TABLE OF CONTENTS

Section 1: General topics

Table of contents

Section 2: Lesson notes and Section 3: Handouts

Cognitive psychology: Memory

Developmental psychology: Early social development

Table of contents

Research methods

Table of contents

Biological psychology: Stress

Table of contents

Social psychology: Social influence

Table of contents

Individual differences: Psychopathology (abnormality)

SECTION 1

General topics

1 GETTING STARTED

1.1 WHAT I WISH I'D KNOWN!

In the beginning

Moving from PCGE student to NQT then life as a 'grown-up' teacher has been a steep learning curve. I (RCG) have been lucky to receive advice, ideas and inspiration from a range of colleagues, training courses as well as from listening to my students. The following contains a list of things I've learnt and wish I'd known at the beginning of my teaching career.

Most students don't really like reading

I find my students lovely people who have a great interest in Psychology until it involves reading a textbook! Often on being confronted with a passage their immediate response is 'I don't know the answer'. When faced with such classes, I try not to jump in with the answer but encourage them to take five minutes to study the text, then ask if they are still unsure. Sometimes drawing little doodles in the margin of a passage helps draw their attention to relevant sections and provide a guide to the meaning of the paragraph. Following advice from a colleague I have also discussed with the class what we want to find out from the passage, and displayed these objectives on the board, before they begin reading the text.

Students hate making mistakes

I currently teach, and have met them in the past, students who hate to have crossing out in their work. I refer to them affectionately as my 'neat freaks'. They really dislike matching tasks and try to do nothing until we go over the answers to avoid making a mistake. I try to encourage an atmosphere where it's OK to make mistakes (I frequently do with my spelling!). It also helps if the neat freaks complete the task in pencil with plenty of erasers handy, or spare copies of the sheet are readily available for them to produce a final 'neat' version.

Students need instructions everywhere

To avoid the 'I don't know what to do' whinge I tend to go overboard; instructions are given verbally, displayed on the board or in PowerPoint and on the worksheet. That way no one can use the excuse 'I didn't know what to do' to avoid settling down to the task at hand.

Students tend to give basic AO2 points...

...but find it really difficult to remember to expand the evaluations they make. I tell my students a few developed points are better then a list of basic statements. Using ladders, burgers and evaluation trains (see page 10, page 10, and page 26 respectively) has helped students expand their AO2 points so they make effective comments.

Students need structure at every stage

Lesson objectives are displayed at the start of the lesson for students to record in their folder contents sheet. This helps them understand the point of the lesson, acts as a revision checklist at the end of the topic and ticks the Ofsted box too. Writing frames are provided for the 12-mark questions. Initially these are given to the students but as they move through the course, frames are developed as a class, in small groups and finally as an individual. When marking students' responses to exam questions a mini mark scheme is included (taken from AQA's website) with the grade boundary they reached highlighted and targets related to the next grade boundary.

Students like novelty

My students don't always remember when I ask them about a study by name but do remember the activity. For example, if I ask about Baddeley's 1975 study, I'm met with confused looks and rummaging through folders. The clue 'you remember when we stuck the stickers on the continuum' often jogs their memory. I tend to think the more variety in lessons, the more cues they have to organise the information and assist recall. It also stops them, and me, getting bored. I get a more enthusiastic response to writing activities if they are a bit different, involve filling in boxes and other shapes, are accompanied with a picture or require peer involvement.

2 USEFUL IDEAS FOR PSYCHOLOGY TEACHERS

2.1 EMERGENCY STARTERS AND PLENARIES

It is an easy trap that we all fall into – you use a starter or plenary which works really well; the students are enthusiastic and engaged in the lesson material, but as a result, you use that starter or plenary at least 10 times in the next three weeks! The students no longer greet your activity with eagerness, instead you detect groans of discontent in the room…. 'Not again sir!'

I (MWG) am sure we have all been there! I think many teachers, myself included, have a tendency to forget all the great ideas we have used in the past, holding on to new ones with a firm grip until we are able to think of something else.

The most useful thing I ever did as a teacher (well, as a PGCE student) was to compile a compendium of starters, plenaries, and main lesson activities as I used them, or as I heard ideas from other teachers. Some of you may even have the booklet I produced, *The Psychology Teachers' Toolkit*, which is available on the resource sharing website www.psychexchange.co.uk. Now, whenever I am struggling to think of an idea to teach a new topic, I only have to delve into the toolkit for inspiration. As a relatively new teacher (this being my second year), I am certain that my lesson planning workload has reduced massively!

So my advice is this – create your own! Use an exercise book and just jot down successful activities as you use them. It really does save time in the long run.

Here are some ideas to get you started…

Question Raffle – At the start or end of the lesson, ask each student to write on a piece of paper a question related to the topic and/or lesson objectives. Fold up the questions, place them in a hat and ask the students to pick out a question, and answer it in front of the class. Nice and simple, and minimal work required from yourself!

Blankety Blank – Ever asked students to read part of a sheet or textbook and been frustrated by how little they have taken in? Try setting a time limit and warning them that they will be tested on that information shortly afterwards. Lift quotes from the text they have read and blank out keywords/variables, etc., to see if they can remember what those keywords were. This activity works even better if you can create a PowerPoint which mirrors the old game show!

Psychology Jackanory – To start off a lesson, why not consider reading your students a children's story relevant to your lesson. For example, *The Emperors New Clothes* is useful for thinking about majority and minority influence. Last year, I even had one group sat on the floor with cushions to recreate their primary school circle time – they loved it!

Odd One Out – Display four pictures, keywords or concepts on a PowerPoint or whiteboard and ask students to select which one they think is the odd one out and justify why. You can either deliberately manipulate the odd one out to test knowledge, or purposefully not include an obvious odd one out so that students can make their own links/comparisons between different things.

Quick Sentence – Very easy. Ask a student for a number between say, 20 and 40. Whatever number they select, the students must summarise the lesson in exactly that number of words. Another idea easier on your workload!

Roll up! Roll up! – Display the numbers 1 to 6 on your whiteboard with six corresponding keywords, psychologists, theories or other. Ask individual students to roll a dice and then say all they can about the topic which corresponds to the number they rolled. If you like your gimmicks (which I unashamedly do) then consider purchasing a large inflatable dice for your classroom!

Jerry Springer – Explain that at the end of his shows, Jerry Springer always does a summing up. It usually starts with the phrase 'So… what have we learnt here today? We have learnt that….' Ask the students to complete their Jerry Springer summing up of the lesson. You can then ask some students to read theirs out. Again, for those of the 'gimmick' persuasion, consider buying a humorous Jerry Springer style wig for this moment – the cheaper the better!

I have learnt that…. – You and your students may be familiar with the game 'My Granny went to the shops and she bought….' This plenary is a variation of that game. Students must write down one thing they have learnt that lesson. Then, the teacher selects one person who must say 'I have learnt that….(then whatever they have written down)….'. Then the teacher should select a second student who must state what they learnt, but also what the first person learnt. The teacher should then select a third student who must state what they learnt, what the second student learnt, and then the first. And so on…! This promotes active listening in students, and if my experience is anything to go by, it can require some practice!

Pictionary – Give students a key word, theory or psychologist, and ask them to attempt to draw this in a visual form that other class members would be able to guess. This could be set up as a whole class activity, or a small group competition.

Mixed Bag – On an A4 sheet of paper write a series of plenary statements such as: 'What information is important to remember from this lesson?', 'What are the three key words relevant to this lesson?', 'How could I have improved my work?', 'How could I use the knowledge/skills from this lesson in my other subjects?', 'How can I relate what we have learnt in this lesson to my own life?', and 'How valuable has my contribution to this lesson been and why?' Cut these statements/questions out and ask students to pick one at random at the end of the lesson. They could then feedback their answers to the rest of the class.

Post-it Continuum – This is particularly useful for lessons where you are evaluating a study. Display a continuum on the whiteboard, e.g. low ecological validity to high ecological validity. Give each student a post-it note and ask them to place it on the continuum in relation to the study along with a justification of why they have placed it on the continuum in the position they did. You could even introduce a two-dimension continuum if you are feeling particularly daring!

You Say We Pay – Based on the daytime TV show! Seat a student at the front of the class and display a picture/keyword behind them related to the work you have been doing. Select a different student to describe it to them without using the keyword. See how many the student at the front of the class can successfully guess with the help of their classmates within a given time limit.

2.2 COLLABORATIVE LEARNING

Despite all the warnings and all the training, it did take me (MWG) a long time to realise that group work in my lessons entailed the following: diligent students in the group doing most of the work, the drama students doing most of the feeding back to class, and many other students anonymous in the middle!

Whether we are using small groups for discussions, presentations or more creative work, it can be difficult to ensure that *all* students are on task, and *all* students are learning as a result of the task set.

The trick to making sure group work is successful is by ensuring the tasks you devise are based on the following principles:

- Students are dependent on each other in order to complete the task successfully.
- Students are also individually accountable for the work they have done.
- Students participate equally.

With these aims in mind, here are some simple ideas for structuring your group work:

Random numbers – When setting a discussion question, ask the students to number themselves in their groups. Then make it clear that when you ask the group to feedback their answer, you will choose a number from the group and that person will have to feedback. This ensures that all group members are involved in the discussion and need to pay close attention to what is being said. In addition, it ensures that more gifted students will need to 'teach' their higher order arguments to the weaker students, so that they are able to feedback that idea.

Group statements – Set your students a discussion question. Individually, students should write their response to that question and elaborate their answers as fully as possible. Following this, students should share their statements with members of their group. Finally, the group should write a group statement which reflects the opinions, arguments and ideas of the group as a whole. This prevents the strongest and most confident students from taking over the activity and writing the statement without input from weaker/less confident students.

Snowballing – Ask students individually to write down three ideas in response to a question. For example, 'list three evaluation points for Asch's study'. This works better if you give them a short time limit – say 2 minutes. After those 2 minutes are over, tell students to share their ideas with the person on their left and write down any new ideas they hadn't thought of – give them another 2 minutes to do this. Then repeat the process with students who sit across from them. Hopefully, by the end of the activity they should have picked up different ideas from the students around them, as well as having had the opportunity to share theirs.

Student dimension line – Display some sort of continuum on your PowerPoint or whiteboard. For example, Zimbardo's Prison Experiment was ethical – strongly agree, to strongly disagree. Ask your students to stand along that line to indicate their opinion on this matter. As the teacher, you can now use this line to structure group work. For example, you could 'fold' the line so that the person who most 'strongly agrees' ends up facing the person who most 'strongly disagrees'. Students can then discuss their ideas with the students opposite them (e.g., think, pair, share – see below). Alternatively, you could use a 'systematic sample(!)' - go along the line giving students numbers and then asking them to sit in groups, ensuring that your groups are mixed by having people who 'strongly agree', 'agree', 'disagree' and 'strongly disagree' with the original statement. This idea works particularly well when the original question you set is something like: 'To what extent do you understand ethical issues?' Constructing a dimension line like this also means you can sort your students into differentiated or mixed-ability groups.

Think, pair, share – I am sure many people have heard of this technique already, it is perhaps the most well-known collaborative learning structure. Set your students some kind of discussion question and give them a few moments of thinking time to individually gather their thoughts. Then students should share their ideas with the person next to them. In the feedback phase of this activity, ask students to feedback their partner's ideas as opposed to their own. This encourages active listening and clear communication.

2.3 ASSESSMENT FOR LEARNING – PEER– AND SELF–ASSESSMENT

Where am I? Where do I want to be? How can I get there?

These three questions underlie the reason teachers seem to spend a large part of their free time hunched over reams of lined paper with a white knuckle grip on a red pen. Of course students need to experience exam questions as a form of assessment but we hope the following ideas help add a little variety.

Assessing/reviewing objectives and or class tasks

Objective Venn diagrams – Identify three objectives for the lesson or class task. Display a Venn diagram to the class similar to the one shown here, making sure each objective is clearly displayed. Give each student a sticky note and tell them to write their name on it and place it on the Venn diagram to show which objectives they feel they have achieved. You could also ask students to give a justification for their choice.

This assessment method encourages students to reflect on their own learning and quickly demonstrates where the class is as a whole. If the majority of students do not meet one objective, it may indicate that the area needs to be addressed in a different manner. Differentiation could also

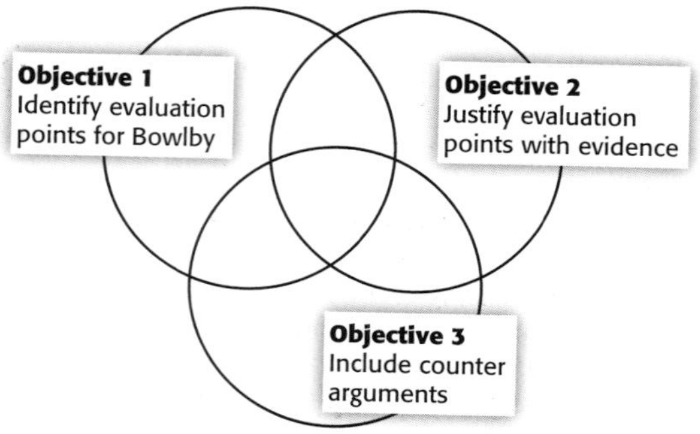

be addressed with all students aiming to achieve the first objective while more able students are challenged to meet more than one objective.

Objective podiums – This assessment technique is similar to the Venn diagrams but uses a slightly different format. After completing a task (e.g., essay, poster, presentation), a podium is displayed alongside clear criteria to show students what they have to do to achieve well on that task. Students then place their work or their name on a sticky label on the podium number which they feel most accurately reflects their attainment.

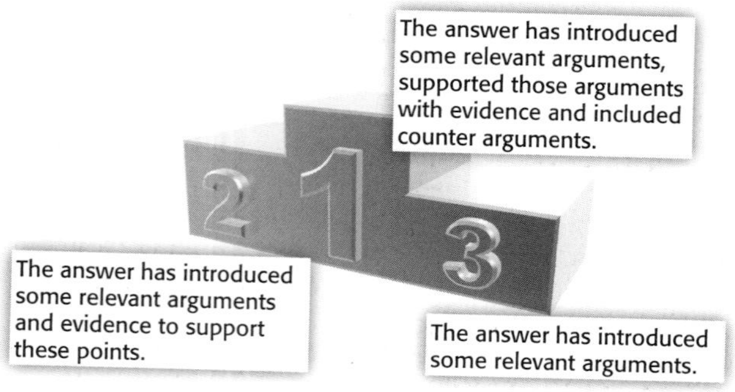

The answer has introduced some relevant arguments, supported those arguments with evidence and included counter arguments.
2
1
3
The answer has introduced some relevant arguments and evidence to support these points.
The answer has introduced some relevant arguments.

Create your own objectives – Instead of imposing objectives for a class task on your students, why not allow them to brainstorm the objectives? For example, tell them they are going to produce a poster on 'stress and the workplace'. Ask them what they feel would make a good poster and the criteria the class should use to peer- or self-assess those posters afterwards.

Bloom's taxonomy stairs – Bloom's taxonomy orders different tasks into levels of thinking. This provides a good way of differentiating class tasks when reviewing work or when devising a class activity. If you wish to use Blooms as an assessment task at the end of the lesson, ask students to write their name on a sticky label and place it on the

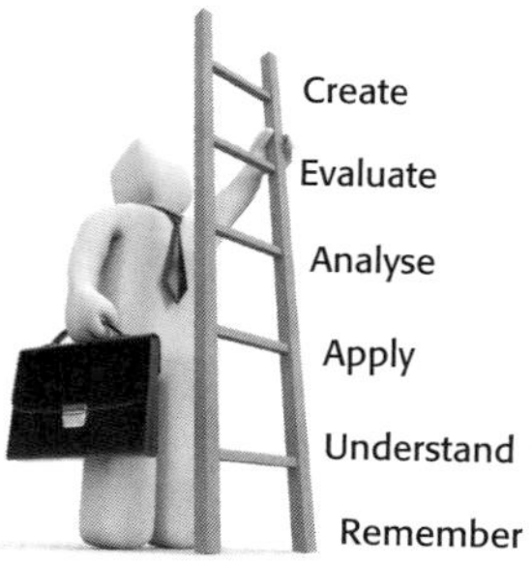

step they feel they have achieved during that lesson. This relies on you creating enough opportunities in the lesson to enable students to achieve the higher order thinking skills if they are capable. You could give students a passage of information and ask them to decide how they wish to use the information. They could then decide which level of thinking they utilised.

Smileys – At the start of each lesson we ask students to write down the title and the aim of the lesson on an index page – see **Handouts 1 and 2**. At the end of the lesson students then have to indicate to what extent they feel they achieved that aim – with a happy face, a neutral face, or an unhappy face. The benefit of these index pages is that they also help students (particularly the lads!) to organise their folders.

Assessing extended writing

Highlights – Asking students to self or peer assess extended pieces of writing is difficult because they generally tend to over mark. This may be because the task has little structure, or they do not fully understand the mark scheme, or cannot identify the relevant components for each element of the mark scheme. One way to help students with this is to give them guidance in deconstructing the extended writing, so they can assess it in bite-sized chunks. Exactly how you ask students to deconstruct the text will depend on your aims and mark scheme. The example below relates to *'Discuss research into the effects of failure to form attachment (privation)'* 8 marks, found on page 63 of *Complete Companion*, and **Handout 63** of this teacher resource pack.

1 Highlight description/knowledge of research into the effects of failure to form attachments for both Alice and Tom's answers.

2 Highlight evaluation/discussion of research into the effects of failure to form attachments in both Alice and Tom's answers.
3 Underline irrelevant information for 'failure to form attachments' if there is any.
4 Circle any description of results and conclusions included.
5 Mark knowledge/understanding out of 4 (consider detail, accuracy and relevance).
6 Mark evaluation/discussion out of 4 (consider effectiveness, elaboration and expression of ideas).

Fold over – Ask your students to fold an A4 lined sheet of paper as shown on the right. Set your students an extended writing question. Students should write their answer on the wider portion of the paper. When everyone has finished, ask the class what details/arguments should have been included in the answer. Students either review their own work or swap with a partner and add any missed details into the narrow column of the paper (see image on the right).

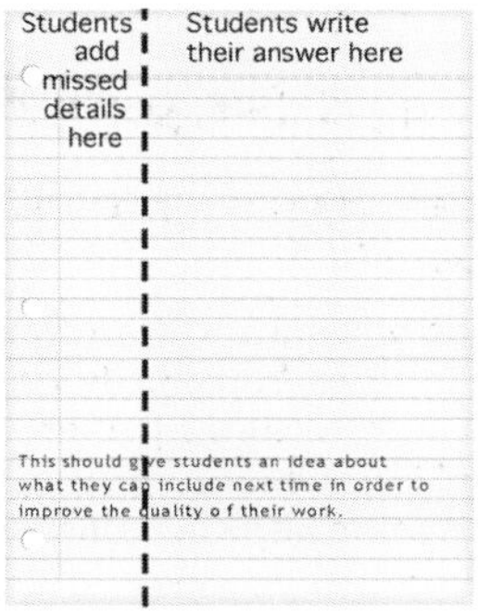
Students add missed details here
Students write their answer here
This should give students an idea about what they can include next time in order to improve the quality of their work.

Self-assessment form – Unfortunately, students often do not check through their essays! We make students hand in their essays with a self-assessment form – see **Handout 3**. This forces students to consider the success of their essay by asking them to rate certain criteria between 1 (strongly agree) and 3 (disagree). This handout could also be used for peer assessment.

2.4 A FEW ICT TRICKS

Here are just a few ideas you could use to 'jazz up' your lessons!

Rolling shows – These can be created using PowerPoint, and essentially consist of a slideshow of images. They are very useful to use when students are coming into lessons. When played with relevant music, they create a good atmosphere and let students know that from the moment they walk into your classroom, they are in a learning environment.

Find a series of images related to the content of the lesson. Insert an image on each slide of your PowerPoint. You could also insert questions for the students to read. When you have finished inserting your images/text, select <Slide Show> from the top menu bar, and then <Slide Transition> from the drop down menu – this should open a menu to the right-hand side of the window. Here you can select which animation you would like to be used to change from one slide to another – I find that 'fade' looks the most professional. Untick the option <On mouse click> and instead select the tick box <Automatically after> and then set the transition to every 5 seconds (or other). Make sure you click the <Apply to all slides> box beneath this. Lastly, select <Slide Show> once again from the top menu bar, and then <Set up show> from the drop down menu. Clicking the tick box for <Loop continuously until 'ESC'> will ensure that your slideshow will cycle through the images until you want it to stop.

Randomiser – This is another technique that can be used with PowerPoint and enables you to select students randomly, for example to answer a question, or to sort them into groups. Enter your students' names into PowerPoint, with one name on each slide. When you have finished this, follow the procedure outlined above for 'Rolling Shows' exactly, except this time, set the transition between slides to be every 0 seconds – this is important to make the process random as you will see later. To stop the slideshow on one of the names simply press 'S' on your keyboard, this will stop the slideshow. To select another name, simply press 'S' again to start the slideshow.

Although I have suggested doing this with names, it can also be used to 'randomise' questions, key terms, and even essay titles.

Templates – Another PowerPoint idea. PowerPoints can often look dull and generic, but it is difficult to make them look more exciting without sacrificing your work-life balance! A simple way around this is to design one 'fancy' template which you use for all future PowerPoints. Spend some time designing a 'title' slide – for example, I include a lesson title, an image, an aim, and key words on mine. Then design a 'main body' slide with a title, text font, and background which are easy on the eye. Then save this design as a template – select <File> from the top menu bar, then <Save as…> from the drop down menu. In the <Save as type:> drop down box select <Design template>. When you open this design template you will find that all your design features remain, and you can just amend the text, titles, etc., for that lesson. It is also impossible to save over the template, meaning it can never be lost. I have a design template for each topic (i.e., social, developmental, etc.) and have also created a similar worksheet template in Word so that there is consistency across topics for my students. Using templates ensures you only put the hard design work in once, but are still able to make your presentations a little less dull! You could even ask your students to design the templates for you.

Bluetooth mouse – This idea requires a little investment but is extremely effective if you do not have an interactive whiteboard. Consider purchasing a Bluetooth mouse (search in Amazon, you can get them for around £30 at time of writing). They are essentially a wireless mouse but the signal is much more powerful. This means they can be used at the back of the classroom by your students! You can set up matching games, etc., in Publisher, Word, or other software – and your students can play them from their seats! I like to call it the 'Lazy man's interactive whiteboard'. If your laptop or computer is slightly older, you may also need to purchase a 'Bluetooth dongle', perhaps ask your IT technicians about these.

Vdownloader – Is YouTube blocked at your school? Want to download a YouTube video and save to your laptop for future use? Vdownloader is a piece of free software that downloads YouTube videos and converts them into a format that can be played using Windows Media Player. All you need to do is simply search for 'vdownloader' on Google, and download the file from any number of websites. For example, www.vdownloader.es. Once downloaded and installed onto your computer, all you have to do is copy and paste the address of the video into the software, and the rest is done for you!

Zamzar – The website www.zamzar.com does exactly the same job as vdownloader but it is a completely online process and very easy to follow. On the website you are asked to insert a URL (e.g., from YouTube) and then select the type of file you wish it to be converted to – make sure you choose either avi or wmv if you want to play the video on Windows Media Player. The website then sends the video file to your email address.

Windows Movie Maker – This is a free program which is installed on every Windows machine (unless the over zealous IT technicians at your school have removed it!). It is an extremely easy program to use and allows you to edit videos and insert text on top. This is useful to edit videos you have downloaded (e.g., using vdownloader) or videos you have recorded on a digital camera (e.g., a re-enacted student version of Milgram!). There are plenty of tutorials for using this program on the Internet, simply search for 'Windows Movie Maker tutorial' on the Internet. Alternatively, I wrote a beginners guide for a staff INSET last year which can be found at www.folensblogs.com/psychcompanion/blog/.

MonkeyJam – This free software is also relatively easy to use and allows students to make animations, with either drawings, themselves or plasticine. The process takes a while but is ideal for extended projects or after-school clubs. Searching for monkeyjam in Google should be enough to find this software. Again, there are many tutorials available on the Internet. A video camera or good webcam is required.

Making cartoons – There are some fantastic websites that allow students to make professional-looking cartoons with images they want to use. For example, they could recreate a discussion between Milgram and his critics by finding images of the relevant psychologists. Here are some easy-to-use websites you might consider: www.toondoo.com and www.stripcreator.com.

2.5 GREAT WEBSITES

Here is a list of fantastic psychology-related websites that are invaluable to any teacher! I am sure there are more out there waiting to be found, but these are the ones I have come across:

Resources

www.psycholotron.co.uk *A site packed full of ready-to-use worksheets, information sheets, video clips and interactive whiteboard files. Brilliantly organised and updated every week. A fantastic site!*

www.psychexchange.co.uk *This is a teacher sharing site contains worksheets, PowerPoints, past exam papers, video clips, ideas, a forum… everything a psychology teacher dreams about!*

www.holah.karoo.net *Although this site is primarily for teachers of the OCR spec, there is invaluable information on this site relevant to AQA A content.*

www.psychade.net *A revision site complete with well-organised notes, past papers, resources and advice.*

www.psyonline.org.uk *A site dedicated to AQA A. It has a forum, teachers resources section as well as a section for your students to use. A particularly useful element is the media area, where psychology-related TV shows and films are highlighted.*

www.davesaid.net *More video clips, resources, links, etc.*

www.coolpsychologystuff.co.uk *A great site which specialises in psychology-related products for teachers and students. Includes equipment, gifts, DVDs and posters.*

www.univiewworldwide.co.uk *A similar site to that above with products available for your classroom.*

www.clickpsych.co.uk *A collection of links to further sites, organised by topic.*

Blog sites

The following sites contain thousands of articles related to AQA A topics. They are extremely useful for using as extension tasks (see page 11). Many of the sites allow you to subscribe to their RSS feeds. This means you do not have to search each of the sites every week or so to find related articles – the articles come to you! Information on RSS feeds can be found here www.google.com/reader.

www.psychblog.com
www.alevelpsychology.co.uk
www.bps-research-digest.blogspot.com
www.folensblogs.com/psychcompanion/blog *The official blog of the Complete Companion.*

www.psychnews.co.uk
www.mindhacks.com
www.spring.org.uk
www.thepsychfiles.com
www.thesituationist.wordpress.com
www.in-mind.org
www.psychcentral.com

3 APPROACHING THE NEW AQA A SPECIFICATION

3.1 HOW WE APPROACHED SCHEMES OF WORK

Beginning teaching a unit for the first time can be a daunting prospect, well I (RCG) found it so. The following tips are by no means the definitive answer to planning a new scheme of work. However, they are pointers I have found useful to bear in mind when I sit down with a blank sheet of paper, textbook, specification and a worried crease across my brow.

Break down the specification

The *Complete Companion* textbook is very helpful, giving a guide to the different topics found in each unit. From this I produce a list of all the various topics that need to be covered to address the specification.

Unit 1 (pages in *Complete Companion* textbook)
page 2 – Cognitive psychology
page 32 – Developmental psychology
page 66 – Research methods

Unit 2 (pages in *Complete Companion* textbook)
page 116 – Biological psychology
page 146 – Social psychology
page 176 – Individual differences

Work out how many lessons you have

Diary and timetable in hand I then work out:

- How many lessons I have till the January and May exam.
- How many lessons I wish to devote to revision.
- Obviously this varies depending on institutions and staffing levels. I have included the planning used at our (RCG, MWG) school as an example.

Students receive 10 lessons a fortnight. Following a two-week timetable means students see each member of staff five times in two weeks. The specification is split so each teacher is responsible for a whole section from each unit (see later point on allocating staff).

Keep a few 'just in case' classes

Once I have identified the number of lessons available I keep one or two as 'spare' lessons. I call these 'just in case' classes as who knows what tomorrow may bring - in the event of school/college closures for snow, strikes, other unforeseen events, or a group simply needing another lesson to feel confident with the work, I like to have an extra lesson to slot in rather than planning for every teaching hour only to find I run out of time.

Make key decisions: unit order and allocating staff

Allocating staff

Within our department, topics are split based on personal interest, obviously some topics may need a little negotiation but generally we teach our preferred areas. As well as enthusiastic teaching we find it cuts out a lot of hassle chasing each other to find out what has been taught previously.

RCG – Unit 1: Cognitive psychology and Research methods, Unit 2: Biological psychology and Individual differences (defining abnormality and one or two of the approaches and their related treatments).

MWG – Unit 1: Developmental psychology and Research methods, Unit 2: Social psychology and Individual differences (approaches and their related treatments).

Teaching time	*Teacher 1*	*Teacher 2*
Autumn term September to October half term October to December break	*15 lessons* *15 lessons* *Cognitive psychology and research methods*	*15 lessons* *15 lessons* *Developmental psychology and research methods*
Spring term January to February half term February to Easter break	*15 lessons* *Biological psychology* *15 lessons* *Biological psychology and part of Individual differences*	*15 lessons* *Social psychology* *15 lessons* *Social psychology and part of Individual differences*
Summer term April to May half term May to July	*12 lessons* *Revision till exam* *20 lessons* *see post-exam activities*	*12 lessons* *Revision till exam* *20 lessons* *see post-exam activities*

When to teach research methods

Research methods is split based on suitability to the topic under study. For example, Cognitive psychology provides a lot of opportunities to cover the experimental method, while Developmental psychology allows students to consider the usefulness of observations and methods of self report.

Students may find it helpful to start the year with a two-week Introduction to Psychology, where investigations are planned and carried out. This aims to highlight Psychology's status as a science and begin to develop their understanding of research methods. See **Handout 71** for experimental planning sheets, **Handouts 92** and **93** for observation planning and **Handout 104** for content analysis guidance.

The order of units

We decided to begin with Unit 1 as we felt research methods was a key part of students' grasp of Psychology and would be helpful for developing evaluative comments across Units 1 and 2. By studying Unit 1 first, the Cognitive psychology section on mnemonics provides a useful lead into revision techniques that can be applied to their first AS exam in Psychology and other subjects, while swiftly following their exams with Unit 2's stress topics is particularly relevant to some.

However, others could argue the research methods topic is easier to teach towards the end of the AS year, as students have a greater exposure to the various research methods from their study of Unit 2 followed by Unit 1. Unit 2 may contain the topics that drew students to the subject initially (such as Individual differences) and could be the basis for choosing to study this unit first.

Be guided by the specification

After making a list of topics to be covered, I assign each topic one lesson. I then use the specification and mark scheme as a guide to allocate the remaining lessons. I try to keep in mind the maximum AO1 content a student needs is enough for 6 marks (ensuring the lesson allows them to produce accurate and reasonably detailed descriptions). In AO2, even the most detailed evaluations can only be awarded a total of 6 marks, so spending two lessons on evaluation will waste teaching time as that much information cannot be used in the exam.

Gaining extra time

Teaching all the content as well as spending time on revision is a tight squeeze. Therefore, any opportunity to gain extra time is invaluable.

- A Psychology cinema club where films relevant to the topics are shown after school or during lunch times. This saves time in lessons and raises the profile of Psychology around the school or college.
- Reading homework can be set so students come to lessons armed with an understanding of the basic principles, ideas or issues. Asking the class for a simple statement based on the information read provides a simple starter to a lesson built around the reading.
- Trying to spend less time in lessons writing notes and more time processing notes. A lot of the handouts require students to use the information in the textbooks, applying research to a new context or format rather than simply copying out text. This aims to improve recall as a deeper level of processing is needed to complete each activity.

3.2 WHAT TO DO AFTER SUMMER AS EXAMS

Traditionally, in the month or so following the May examinations, our students have carried out independent investigations for their Unit 6 coursework assignment. With the new specification removing the coursework element we were left considering what to do in the run up (or wind down if you ask some students!) to the summer holidays.

Option 1: Begin teaching A2 content

You could decide to get a head start on the A2, leaving more time for revision nearer exam time. With the new topics it may feel safer to spend a little longer than usual covering Units 4 and 5.

Option 2: Get students to help you out

Classes after the May exams tend to be split between students who definitely do not want to continue into A2, those who are certain they want to study Psychology further and a few who are waiting for their results before deciding. Different activities could be organised to cater for the different groups:

a) Those who definitely do not wish to carry on to A2 could be set the task of producing a revision booklet or bank of revision activities for the new Year 12. If your institution has the technology, students could be challenged to produce a podcast or documentary style film. In producing such resources students are reminding themselves of that AS work, should they need to re-sit a unit later on, as well as providing valuable experiences that can be mentioned in their UCAS personal statement or other letters of application.

b) Those who are certain they wish to continue into A2 could be asked to devise a lesson on one aspect of the A2 specification. Students could be given a specific section to deliver, for example the social learning theory of aggression, and asked to produce a lesson plan, resources, homework and mark scheme for that lesson. When you reach this section during the A2 teaching, students can deliver the lesson for you. This should deepen their understanding of the topic as well as help the rest of the class recall the information, as their peers have delivered the content. Once again students have the opportunity to mention their exploits on their UCAS form.

Students who are awaiting their results before making a decision could choose either activity. Those who are less than confident they did well in the AS exams may wish to produce revision materials to help them should a re-sit be required. Both these activities allow students to demonstrate independent learning; planning their own time schedules, deciding what needs to be done and creating their own resources. The added advantage is that you are left with a bank of material to use with your Psychology groups.

Option 3: The extended project

http://www.qca.org.uk/libraryAssets/media/Extended_Project_Factsheet-_October_2007.pdf

The extended project may be a further option, giving the opportunity to deepen students' understanding of the research process. The QCA website (the link shown above) provides a good outline of the aims of the project. A number of exam boards have downloadable specifications and mark schemes available. Allowing students to complete an extended project before they begin A2 may have the following advantages:

- The previous Psychology coursework framework could be used as a basis to produce an original investigation. Students gather, analyse and interpret data, add a literature review of background research and conclude with an evaluation (following a similar style to the old coursework discussion).
- Unlike the old coursework unit, their chosen topic could be from any area of Psychology that they are interested in. Students who are unsure they will continue to A2 could look to the AS units for inspiration. Those who wish to continue could consider a topic from the A2 specification that will be covered in class at a later date. Of course, students may wish to move away from specification topics. This would give a greater test of research skills and could be tailored to students' individual interests and possible post-A-level career plans.

Websites such as the BPS' research digest (http://bps-research-digest.blogspot.com/) or Scientific Mind (http://www.sciam.com/sciammind/) contain a vast number of articles from wide-ranging areas of Psychology. These may help spark an original line of enquiry for more able students. Although care should be taken to ensure topics do not raise any ethical issues and the student is able to resource further associated research to compile an adequate literature review.

The extended project is not restricted to a research investigation; meaning cross-curricular links could be forged. Students could produce an artefact (sculpture, art work) or a performance piece (dance or drama), for example, using an aspect of psychology as a starting point, as long as students can show it is a new project or significant extension and not a piece of work submitted as an assessed piece in another subject.

Students may find the additional UCAS points earned (up to 70 points for an A* grade project) and the chance to add to their personal statement a huge incentive. Linking their topic to an aspect of their chosen degree subject or career pathway will enable students to demonstrate their interest in that subject area as well as demonstrating a wide range of useful skills.

4 IMPROVING STUDENT SKILLS

4.1 GETTING YOUR STUDENTS TO ELABORATE

Elaboration ladders

Hands up who has read and been upset by this comment on their students essays: 'The ecological validity of the study is low because it is not like real life'! Aaaaggghhh!

Of course, our job as teachers is to help students to elaborate their evaluative comments – something they seem to find really hard – but undoubtedly has a significant impact on their grades if they can develop the skill.

Having read the above statement in an Asch essay for the thirtieth time last year, I (MWG) decided to try and devise a memorable teaching technique to help students with this skill. And so, the 'elaboration ladders' were born (see **Handout 4**).

The central idea behind the elaboration ladders is that students start with an introductory evaluation comment at the bottom of the ladder and then gradually elaborate this comment further and further until they reach the smiley face at the top! The box on the right-hand side is designed to prompt students into thinking of ways they could elaborate their evaluations, for example 'have I got evidence?'.

To give you an example of how this might work, consider Ainsworth's Strange Situation paradigm.

1 Students could start off by making a generic statement such as: *'It could be argued that Ainsworth's studies lacked ecological validity.'*
2 Students would then need to consider how they could elaborate this. Using the prompts on the right they may decide to include evidence: *'Indeed, Lamb* et al. *(1985) feel that the Strange Situation is highly artificial (novel and stressful) and makes attachments look stronger than they would at home.'*
3 Again, students should consider the prompts on the right such as – 'Why does this matter?' For example: *'This is a problem because it means the results of the study may not be generalisable outside of the Strange Situation and that her results may have overestimated the amount of secure attachments.'*
4 Once again, students should consider how they might elaborate this response. This time, it could come in the form of a counter argument: *'On the other hand, it may be relatively common that infants would face novel and stressful situations and Ainsworth's study is able to take that into account.'*

By going through this process, the hope is that the student is able to discuss their evaluation and its implications in more depth. This visual technique, used in conjunction with the prompts on the right, seems to have been very successful in developing elaboration skills in the students at our school.

Burger evaluation skills

This technique can be used with your students to develop their ability to evaluate *theories* with studies. I often find that students struggle with the structure of using research evidence to evaluate a theory. What students forget to do is illustrate that they understand how and why the evidence undermines or supports a theory. Instead, they simply describe a relevant study and expect the reader to draw their own conclusions!

The burger technique asks students to 'sandwich' their study descriptions with evaluative commentary (AO2). You will see from **Handout 5** that students are first encouraged to outline whether the evidence 'supports' or 'undermines' the theory at the top of the burger. Then, in the middle of the burger they outline that evidence – ensuring that they only outline the relevant information of that study, and not every detail. Lastly, and most importantly, at the bottom of the burger they must explain how that study undermines or supports the theory.

Blank burger templates are given on **Handout 6** where students can attempt the technique.

Reference

Lamb, M. E., Thompson, R. A., Gardner, W. R. and Charnov, E. L. (1985). *Infant-mother attachment: The origins and developmental significance of individual differences in Strange Situation behaviour.* Hillsdale, N.J: Lawrence Erlbaum Associates.

4.2 THINKING HATS

Edward de Bono (1985)

I (RCG) really like this technique as a way of getting students to take a different approach to thinking about a topic. It can also be adapted to encourage collaborative learning and peer teaching.

The six thinking hats

Each hat demands a different perspective to be taken when considering the information presented. Often the perspectives are alien to students and they need help to develop their thinking. However, it is a valuable tool in encouraging students to consider the wider picture and encompasses AO1 and AO2 skills. One hat is not seen as better than another hat; just a different way of looking at an issue.

The benefits

Assigning students different hats means assigning them a specific role. This allows them to explore the issue while removing their own personal view. For students who normally lack confidence it enables them to express ideas from the safety of their 'hat'. By adopting one perspective it allows students to focus their thinking on one particular area at a time to produce developed ideas. Working in small groups on one hat, and later sharing ideas with other hats, improves communication and understanding of the material.

How to use the six hats

I tend to assign students to small groups with each group taking one hat. After spending time developing their ideas for that perspective, they form new 'mixed hat' groups and share their ideas. This develops understanding of their own perspective as they teach others, improves listening skills and questioning as they are taught the approaches taken by the other hats.

What the hats stand for

The colour of each hat represents the perspective the thinker is required to adopt.

White hat - This hat takes a neutral approach, focusing on the facts and figures related to the topic or research. It requires thinkers to assess what data they have or need to find out.

Red hat - This takes a warm, emotional approach to thinking. The thinker is required to introspect: What do they feel about the information? What hunches do they have about the research? Do they like it? Do they feel it makes sense?

Black hat - The stern, serious hat. Wearing this hat, thinkers need to consider the points of caution and disadvantages of the research. Can the data be trusted? Does the theory have any vague areas or research findings it cannot explain? What criticisms can be made?

Yellow hat - The sunny hat: always looking on the bright side of life. What are the strengths of the research? Is the theory supported by research evidence?

Green hat - This creative hat allows thinking to grow in new directions. Can the theory/methodology be improved? Is there a way to overcome any negative points that exist? In what new directions could the research take us?

Blue hat - These thinkers provide a cool overview of the issue. Traditionally this hat looks at the thinking that has taken place and provides suggestions of where to go and what thinking to do next. I tend to change this to 'How does this topic fit into the overall specification? How can we use this information in the exam?' For example, if looking at the multi-store model students can identify other models of memory such as working memory or levels of processing.

Reference

De Bono, E. (1985). *Six Thinking Hats*. Little, Brown and Company.

4.3 USING ARTICLES TO STRETCH YOUR G & T

A simple extension task to give your gifted and talented students is to give them an extra article to read which is related to the lesson content. However, even the gifted and talented students can find it difficult to structure their reading and draw relevant links.

We use a standard extension proforma (**Handout 7**) which students can use with any extra reading you give them which asks them to deconstruct the article, assess the relevance to the lesson's learning objectives, and attempt to use a higher order thinking skill.

There are some fantastic blog sites out there on the Internet which frequently have articles relevant to A-level topics and give students a better overview of psychology as a whole. Some of these blog sites and how to subscribe to them are described on page 6.

4.4 OTHER STUFF YOU MIGHT FIND USEFUL

Teacher feedback form – We have included a feedback proforma for teacher essay feedback you might like to use (**Handout 8**). It is tightly based on the AQA A mark scheme. We highlight the statements we feel most closely reflect their work and justify this with brief notes, and ideas for improvement.

Essay planning form – We have also included an essay planning sheet (**Handout 9**) you could use with your students. The form asks students to consider how they will show knowledge and understanding (AO1), and what evaluation points they will include (AO2), as well as how they will elaborate those points. These forms could be used for homework, class work or even group work.

SECTION 2

Lesson notes

YOUR LESSON NOTES SECTION

This section has been written with some specific objectives in mind:

1) To provide teachers with plenty of ideas for teaching the AQA A AS psychology specification.
2) To provide teachers of psychology with a 'toolkit' that helps to alleviate workload, specifically in the planning and creation of resources.
3) To assist teachers in identifying opportunities for differentiation in their lessons and catering for different 'learning styles'.

'PLENTY OF IDEAS'

Within this section we hope you will find plenty of ideas which you might consider using when delivering the AQA A AS psychology specification.

We have tried to structure this section in a way that mirrors the AQA A course so that you can easily identify how the ideas and resources fit in with your delivery of the specification. Those of you who have purchased *The Complete Companion* will find that our structure is borrowed from the chapter breakdown used in the textbook.

The lesson notes include ideas for starters, plenaries, main activities and study replications. We have decided not to include detailed lesson plans, as there is rarely a one-size-fits-all approach to teaching – it is often more effective for teachers to adapt ideas to suit their own teaching techniques.

'CREATION OF RESOURCES'

For many of the ideas and activities included in this section, there are accompanying photocopiable handouts which can be used in lessons.

We hope that these handouts will ease some of your workload and bring you closer to that elusive work–life balance!

They are described in the lesson notes and numbered so you can find the handout easily.

DIFFERENTIATION

Undoubtedly one of the most challenging responsibilities for a teacher is planning opportunities for differentiation in lessons. In our own experience of the classroom, we have taught students predicted A's, alongside other students who are predicted U's (yes I know, hard to believe isn't it?).

Much of the time we are differentiating without even thinking about it. However, if you are anything like us, you may start to panic when asked to identify 'strategies for differentiation' on lesson plans! To a certain extent, the skill is in identifying what we are already doing, as opposed to reinventing the wheel.

Consequently, we have tried to identify how the lesson ideas in this section may provide opportunities to stretch the gifted and talented, while supporting the weaker students, so that you can highlight these on your lesson plans and schemes of work.

The lesson notes section will use the following key:

H **Higher order thinking skills**
In the previous section (page 4) RCG outlined Bloom's taxonomy. One of the best ways to stretch gifted and talented students is to provide opportunities to use the higher order thinking skills. We often provide these opportunities without specific thought for differentiation. Indeed, the new AS AQA A specification requires us to consider higher skills such as evaluation, analysis, application and hypothesising.

O **Outcome**
This is where students undertake the same activity but the outcome is different according to their ability. The task is designed in such a way that students can complete that task at their own level of understanding.

R **Resource**
Worksheets and resources can be designed to give weaker students writing frames to help them structure their work, without stifling the outcome from more gifted students.

G **Grouping**
Many tasks outlined in this pack lend themselves to mixed ability group work and the use of collaborative learning techniques (see page 3). Using mixed ability groups in a collaborative fashion allows gifted students to consolidate and 'teach' their understanding, while weaker students learn topics in a more student-friendly way from their peers.

T **Task**
This is when students are set specific tasks according to their ability. The difficulty, level of guidance, or structure can all be manipulated to achieve differentiated materials. This might also include the creation of extension tasks/worksheets to stretch the most gifted students.

S **Support**
Lengthier activities give teachers the time to target students identified as needing extra support. This could be because the task involves extended writing, or the use of mathematical concepts. These individuals can be highlighted on lesson plans alongside information from IEPs, e.g. which may provide strategies for supporting a student with dyslexia.

'LEARNING STYLES'

One thing I (MWG) have noticed about education is how training providers often present ideas which have been 'scientifically proven'. Of course in reality, they rarely present that 'evidence', but the majority of people seem to be convinced by the mere mention of these words.

Did you know, for example, that if students cover their left nostril and then inhale through the other, they are sending oxygen to right side of their brain, thereby increasing their creativity? This was an idea presented to me at one training meeting. I thought it prudent to point out that the oxygen was far more likely to travel to the lungs!

My brother (also a teacher) was once told that his students should not write in yellow on their mindmaps and must write above the branches, otherwise the information would 'fall out of their brains'! I must confess I am not aware of this dubious 'scientific' research!

As psychologists, you may have your own opinion on the reliability and validity of 'learning styles', or perhaps you haven't given them much thought.

The research evidence I have read is not complimentary. Kavale and Forness's (1987) meta-analysis of studies matching teaching to learning styles found absolutely no effect on student achievement. Snider's (1992) review highlighted the unreliability of classifying individuals to learning styles. Indeed, there is little empirical evidence that learning styles even exist. Coffield *et al.*'s (2004) review concluded that the matching of teaching and learning styles was 'highly questionable'.

The popularity of learning styles might be likened to the Forer effect (1949); aka the Barnum effect. People tend to accept vague personality descriptions as unique to themselves when they are in fact general enough to apply to anyone.

That said, the popularity of learning styles and the way in which teachers now cater for them, has almost undoubtedly improved the variety of teaching within lessons, and the quality of teaching overall. Teaching now rarely includes the monotonous reading of textbooks, followed by comprehension questions. Although that isn't to say that this is not a good learning strategy for students in moderation. However, by including different ways to teach topics, be they visual, auditory or kinaesthetic, we are surely giving our students different opportunities to understand and access the topics we teach them.

As such, while 'learning styles' may be psychologically dubious, it is still incredibly useful for teachers to consider the different ways in which our students might be able to access psychology, and the ways in which we might be able to help them to understand it. Crucially, though, we should **not** be 'matching' teaching styles to individual 'learning styles'.

In addition, the undeniable truth is that educational leaders, OFSTED and your line managers will all be looking for evidence that you are catering for 'learning styles' in your lesson plans, so we have tried to identify where our lesson ideas might fit in with this.

During the lesson notes section we will use the following key. Ironically perhaps, we have used a tick box approach!

V ✓

Visual – Resources or activities that have a written or visually descriptive format.

A ✓

Auditory – Activities that entail hearing and/or discussing information, ideas and arguments.

K ✓

Kinaesthetic – Resources or activities that involve movement and/or arrangement of ideas, concepts, or arguments.

References

Coffield, F., Mosely, D., Hall, E. and Ecclestone, K. (2004). *Should we be using learning styles?* London: Learning and Skills Development Agency. Retrieved from http://www.lsda.org.uk/files/PDF/1540.pdf

Forer, B. R. (1949). The fallacy of personal validation: A classroom demonstration of gullibility. *Journal of Abnormal and Social Psychology*, 44, 118–23.

Kavale, K. A. and Forness, S. R. (1987). Substance over style: Assessing the efficacy of modality testing and teaching. *Exceptional Children*, 54, 228–39.

Snider, V. E. (1992). Learning styles and learning to read. *Remedial and Special Education*, 13, 6–18.

V A ✓ K ★ G HANDOUT 10

TOPIC: The nature of memory: STM, LTM and duration

THE DURATION OF STM

This activity encourages students to read data and look for clues in a piece of information. By asking students to suggest what may have occurred in the study, higher order thinking skills are being developed as the students try to determine the research methodology from the graph shown. Students then check their predictions using the textbook, which encourages reading for information. The final column, in which students rate the accuracy of their predictions, allows them to reflect on their work and assess their understanding of the actual research study.

1 Students consider the graph in the centre of the sheet. This could be placed on a PowerPoint and the whole class identify information such as 'retention interval', seconds (x axis), participants were asked to recall letters and the percentage was recorded (y axis). Differentiation is possible here in terms of individual, mixed ability groups or whole class questioning: targeting more challenging questions at more able students.
2 After students have completed the left-hand 'guess' column by suggesting what may have occurred for each section, you should then direct them to the textbook to complete the right 'actual' column. Weaker students may find working in a pair to make their predictions and later colour coding each section as they read the information in the textbook may help before filling in the right-hand column.
3 The final 'accuracy' column requires students to score their predictions out of 10 for accuracy. 1 = no correct features, 10 = guess made matches actual events in the study. A variation of this could entail students swapping sheets with each other to rate their peers' accuracy.
4 A plenary activity or simple Q and A session could be used to complete the session to assess understanding of the research study.

Plenary idea 1

Nominate a student (or ask for a volunteer) to read out their comments for one section either guess or actual column. Class have to decide which column the comments belonged to. Students take it in turns to read different sections.

Plenary idea 2

Nominated student or volunteer reads out their comments from both columns for one section (e.g. aims); class then rate the student's accuracy by holding the relevant number of fingers in the air or writing score on mini whiteboards.

Reference

Peterson, L. R. and Peterson, M. J. (1959). Short-term retention of individual verbal items. *Journal of Experimental Psychology*, 58, 193–8.

V A K ✓ ★ S R HANDOUT 11

TOPIC: The nature of memory: Capacity and encoding

ENCODING IN STM AND LTM

This activity will help students develop insight into Baddeley's procedure and provide opportunities to question the class about IV, DV and research design. Instructions for the procedure can be found in textbooks (page 76 in *Complete Companion*).

Students need to read the information on the handout carefully before they begin this task. It may be beneficial if the class actually experience the procedure (for STM) before they begin this activity.

Students are required to cut the strips out then stick them under each heading (aims, procedure, findings and conclusion) in their notes. The activity requires students to read for meaning and organise their thoughts. The use of headings further reinforces the research stages of the research process.

Plenary idea

Students can swap their cut and stick notes with each other and mark their work. Any inaccuracies need to be corrected by writing the correct section next to the strip. This cuts down on your marking and acts as a check of each student's understanding. Weaker students may benefit from having a correct version of the cut and stick activity to help them complete the marking. They can then keep this with their notes.

Homework ideas

'Write a 100-word summary of Baddeley's study into encoding in to STM and LTM.' Placing a word limit on the homework encourages a concise writing style.

More able students may find the following question more challenging: 'How does Baddeley's study into encoding support the suggestion that there are two separate stores in memory as suggested by the multi-store model?'

References

Baddeley, A.D. (1966a). The influence of acoustic and semantic similarity on long-term memory for word sequences. *Quarterly Journal of Experimental Psychology*, 18, 302–9.
Baddeley, A.D. (1966b). Short-term memory for word sequences as a function of acoustic, semantic and formal similarity. *Quarterly Journal of Experimental Psychology*, 18, 362–5.

V A K✓ ★ O HANDOUT 12

TOPIC: The nature of memory: Capacity and encoding

CAPACITY OF STM

The activity introduces students to the digit span technique and serial recall. I (RCG) found this useful at the start of a lesson to introduce the notion of capacity of STM. The question 'What did you learn about the capacity of STM?' encourages students to reflect on the activity that has just taken place and the findings they have recorded. This can then be related to serial recall: digits = 9.3, letter = 7.3. If the class results differ, students can hypothesise why this might be.

The second question requires students to further their understanding by using their textbook. More able students could be directed to the Internet for academic research (a number of journal articles are freely available). Students' reading can then be used to form the main activity of the lesson by asking them to complete the statement 'the capacity of STM is ______'. This allows a wide variety of responses to be given; from the basic digit span, through to 7±2 and chunking with further elaboration from more recent research.

Reference

Jacobs, J. (1887). Experiments in prehension. *Mind*, 12, 75–9.

V✓ A✓ K ★ O HANDOUT 13

TOPIC: The multi-store model of memory

DESCRIBING THE MULTI-STORE MODEL

These two tasks aim to build upon students' memory from previous lessons on the multi-store model, organise their understanding and formulate an exam answer.

1 The first task is a simple labelling activity where students are expected to rely on their memory of the model from the previous lesson or from reading the passage in the textbook (page 8 in *Complete Companion*) then closing the book. I (RCG) try to include tasks in lessons that rely on retention of knowledge to give students the opportunity to develop their memory of psychological research and to scare them into revising! An easy way to feedback answers uses a PowerPoint display of the model with custom animation allowing labels to fly in after students have made their suggestions. Breaking this down, taking one store at a time will help all students follow the feedback and give time for corrections to be made.

2 The second task provides an opportunity for students to organise the information recalled in task 1and develops a basic writing frame to assist their writing in task 3.

3 Students now write a description of the multi-store model. I emphasise the final instruction 'try not to write more than half a page' to encourage students to write concisely. In the exam the maximum marks available for an outline of a model of memory is 6 marks with the exam paper providing roughly half a page for the answer to be written. Should students be asked to 'outline and evaluate', 12 marks are available (6 for AO1 outline, 6 for AO2 evaluate). A whole page is provided for the answer, meaning students need to give equal attention to the two skills: half a page on each.

Students can request more paper in the exam but it is expected their entire answer will fit into the space provided. Those who need more room may run the risk of waffling and wasting valuable exam time.

Marking

Peer marking can be used to assess task 3. Students use their writing frame (task 2) to check the task 3 response they are marking includes all the points needed to give an accurate and detailed answer. The AQA website provides a generic AO1 mark scheme that can be given to students to guide their peer assessment. I encourage my students to provide a brief (3 to 4 sentences) explanation of why they awarded a certain mark, one target and their name. This highlights, to me, the marker's understanding of the mark scheme and gives the author of the answer useful feedback.

Reference

Atkinson, R.C. and Shiffrin, R.M. (1968). Human memory: A proposed system and its control processes. In K.W. Spence and J.T. Spence (Eds.) *The Psychology of Learning and Motivation*. Vol. 2. London: Academic Press.

V A✓K SOR HANDOUT 14

TOPIC: The multi-store model of memory

CASE STUDIES AND THE MSM

Many students emerge from the world of GCSE study to find the expectations of A-level difficult, which can quickly dent their confidence. After being given the information in digestible form at GCSE, the prospect of extracting relevant information from a text can be daunting. The can do and can't do boxes aim to focus students' reading when faced with the case studies in your textbook (pages 100–1 of *Complete Companion*). Once the information has been broken down to a more manageable form it can be used to consider each case study as a tool for evaluating the multi-store model.

The number of case studies each student attempts can be used as a form of differentiation with more able students being encouraged to consider all three cases while weaker students should focus on just one.

A further activity for these case studies can be found within the research methods section entitled 'Case study critique' (see page 49) and addresses the AO3 element of the specification.

References

Baddeley, A.D. (1990). *Human Memory. Theory and Practice*. Boston, MA: Allyn and Bacon.
Scoville, W.B. and Milner, B. (1957). Loss of recent memory after bilateral hippocampus lesions. *Journal of Neurology, Neurosurgery, and Psychiatry*, 20, 11–21.

V✓A✓K OG HANDOUT 15

TOPIC: Evaluating the multi-store model

WHERE DO YOU STAND?

AS students (well, those I've (RCG) come across) love stickers. This continuum activity requires students to consider the usefulness of Glanzer and Cunitz's study as supporting evidence for the multi-store model. Glanzer and Cunitz's study can be found on page 9 in *Complete Companion*. An alternative study could be used if you prefer.

Before completing this task, I find it helpful to recreate the study in class. Students are shown a list of words (one word at a time) using PowerPoint, then asked to recall the words they have just seen in any order (free recall). Depending on the seating plan of your room nominate one student per table or row to act as the data collector gathering the number of words recalled. These can be quickly fed to the student nominated to enter data into Excel to create a graph for the whole class to see. This can then be compared to Glanzer and Cunitz's graph and explanations for the findings developed.

Students are given five stickers but you could use ink stamps, bingo stamp pens or coloured dots. On each continuum they place a sticker depending on how far along the line their opinion falls, using the end labels as a guide. Below each continuum, students are asked to give an explanation for their choice. This provides another opportunity for students to reflect on their thinking.

From using this activity with a number of classes I found students benefited from working in mixed ability groups. More able students were provided with the opportunity to develop their psychological vocabulary as they explained terminology to less able students. Students' responses to this task give a good insight into their understanding of key terms such as ecological validity, variables and reliability. Sometimes students can become confused over terms such as validity thinking lacking ecological validity is good as it is like real life. The continuum task acts as a good check of their understanding.

Reference

Glanzer, M. and Cunitz, A.R. (1966). Two storage mechanisms in free recall. *Journal of Verbal Learning and Verbal Behaviour*, 5, 351–60.

V✓ A✓ K ★ R HANDOUT 16

TOPIC: Evaluating the multi-store model

CHOCOLATE BEAN EVIDENCE

Students can quickly produce a page of evaluations by working with each other to further their knowledge. This activity is enjoyable as students have the chance to move around the room talking to others, gather information from their peers rather than listening to the teacher or reading a block of text and also get to eat a chocolate bean.

1 Move round the class giving each student a coloured chocolate bean. Differentiation can occur here giving easier colours to less able students; more scientific minded students can be allocated colours that relate to PET scan evidence, etc.
2 Students then use their textbook (page 10–11 of *Complete Companion*) to record information for their colour on the handout. Students could be given a guideline of three sentences for their topic.
3 Set students a time limit of 15 minutes, ask them to move around the class sharing their evidence and gathering other evidence. I find it helpful to remind students they are to teach each other not just copy from each others' sheets.

Homework activity

The exam requires students to be able to produce a 6-mark evaluation of the multi-store model. Using the sheet, ask students to produce a half page evaluation of the model. They will not have enough room to use all the information gathered, so instruct students to consider which information they wish to use.

Providing students with an AQA mark scheme (available from AQA website, alternatively a general mark scheme can be found on page vii of *Complete Companion*) will help them understand what is required for full marks.

V A✓ K ★ O HANDOUT 17

TOPIC: Evaluating the multi-store model

EVALUATING THE EVIDENCE

This extended writing activity aims to develop the length at which students consider a topic and addresses issues with the use of case studies and experiments in psychology. This is a challenging essay and students should be encouraged to follow the writing scheme closely to help structure their writing. Some students may find it difficult to identify relevant information from their notes, so it may help to go over the topics in class, but research study names have been included in the writing frame. Research such as those named on the handout can be found in textbooks (page 10–11, 100–101 in *Complete Companion*). You may wish to challenge more able students by simply blanking out these references to encourage a more independent approach.

The instructions at the bottom of the page recommend students read over their answer and tick each section to check all aspects have been included. I (RCG) ask my students to hand in this check list with their answer. This acts as another check of their understanding (have they accurately identified aspects?) and speeds up marking, as I can highlight the sections they have missed or which are underdeveloped. Giving students a choice of questions to answer is a little sneaky, as it makes essay writing seem less of a scary and horrid task, so homework hand-in rate improves.

V A K✓ ★ S R HANDOUT 18

TOPIC: Evaluating the multi-store model

PLENARY STATEMENTS

This acts as a revision topic for the multi-store model to refresh students' memory of the first model learnt and helps highlight the differences between the two models. At times students can become a little muddled between the two models and which evaluation points belong to which model. By sorting the different statements, students are organising the information and producing a revision table which hopefully leads to better, more accurate recall. Students work can be marked quickly by asking students to swap sheets and tick each correct statement. One point per correct statement can be awarded. To ensure accurate marking, answers could be projected onto your whiteboard, or photocopies of correct versions made available.

Students may find it helpful to have a PowerPoint projection of the two models side by side as they complete this activity. Whether you decide to do this depends on the ability of your students.

V ✓ A K ✓ ★ O HANDOUT 19

TOPIC: Evaluating the multi-store model

REVIEWING TOPICS

As you move through the topics it helps to stop and reflect at certain points before moving on to the next section. I (RCG) have found these reviews not only make students think about their understanding but also act as an evaluation of my teaching. For example, if a lot of students place their frog, welly boot or snail at the first box, I know I need to revisit this section with the whole class. Student responses can also be used for grouping when organising revision sessions. Either group all those who found one section difficult to work together to develop their understanding or place an expert on a certain topic with others who found it confusing. As well as providing at a quick glance a visual guide to your students' learning, it is a good example of formative assessment which will hopefully make any Ofsted inspector smile.

V ✓ A ✓ K ★ G S HANDOUT 20

TOPIC: Evaluating the multi-store model

EXAM PRACTICE ACTIVITY

Students are often daunted by the 12-mark question so taking time to develop their understanding of exam requirements and modelling responses can boost their confidence. I (RCG) find a detailed approach the first time they meet this kind of question saves time later as they are able to apply their new found understanding to 12-mark questions in other topics.

1 Explain AOs to the students (left-hand side grey box on worksheet). This helps them understand the mark schemes and any annotation you add to their written work.
2 Working in mixed ability pairs, students complete the table shown in the right-hand grey box to highlight the distinction between AO1, AO2 and AO3.

For example:

I know... (AO1)	The evaluations .... (AO2)	The scientific... (AO3)
The model has three separate stores	Beardsley (1997) and Squire *et al.*, (1992) provide evidence for STM and LTM being separate.	One way to investigate memory is to use modern brain imagery techniques in a laboratory.

3 To assess students' understanding of the distinction between AO1 and AO2 ask them to highlight the different sections of the extended answer extract.

4 Students should then be directed to the mark scheme shown below the extract in the grey box 'What do A/B graders need to show' and the table for them to record signpost words in, in the second grey box 'Signposts'. These words indicate when evaluations are being made in a piece of writing. Although this isn't as vital in the 6-mark AO2 component of the 12-mark question, it does lay a good foundation for essay writing at A2.

For example:

Strengths	Weaknesses	Comparisons
An advantage is... Is supported by....	One criticism is... A problem with	On the other hand... Is different to....

The worksheet then forms the basis of a writing guide for students' AO2 section of the question. The mark scheme's AO1 details should be used as a guide for the AO1 section.

References

Beardsley, T. (1997). The Machinery of Thought. *Scientific American*, Vol. 277, 78–83.
Squire, L.R., Ojemann, J.G., Miezin, F.M., Petersen, S.E., Videen, T.O. and Raichle, M.E. (1992). Activation of the hippocampus in normal humans: A functional anatomical study of memory. *Proceedings of the National Academy of Sciences of the United States of America*, 89(5), 1837–41.

V✓ A✓ K ★ S O HANDOUT 21

TOPIC: The working memory model

PSYCHOLOGY STORY TIME

The idea for this activity harks back to the days of primary school where the class has a 'smoothing' time listening to a story read by the teacher. When reading my students this story I (RCG) accompanied each paragraph with images from a well-known TV show in which business men and women were frequently told 'you're fired'.

Once students have listened to the story they need to complete the basic model. I drew the following images on the board for students to copy then annotate in their notes:

Brief case
Head phones
Sketchpad

Less able students may find it helpful to be given a list of the bold words from the story to help them recall the important aspects of the model.

A feedback session follows where students label the diagram on the board and the actual model is revealed. I then asked students to produce a correct diagram of the model beneath which they write six bullet points explaining the model. Pages 12–13 of the *Complete Companion* were used for this part of the activity. Description of the working memory model can be found in many textbooks.

V A✓ K✓ ★ S HANDOUTS 22 and 23

TOPIC: The working memory model

RESEARCH ACTIVITY: BADDELEY 1975a; 1975b

1975a

Often taking part in a study helps students understand the procedure and it remains in memory for longer. A further benefit is that it provides further experience of laboratory experiments. This study can be used as support for the working memory model (the existence of the phonological loop) as well as an alternative way of considering the capacity of STM (the amount articulated in 2 seconds).

1975b

This handout aims to break down the study into smaller sections to help students understand the different components of the procedure. Again this study can be used to evaluate the working memory model and develop understanding of laboratory experiments.

Students should be encouraged to consider the strength of these studies in supporting working memory in terms of validity of laboratory experiments.

Plenary idea

Can students think of real-life examples of dual tasks. For example: Fill in the blanks strips

Without my working memory I would not be able to listen to music while I painted a picture.

Similar sentences could be given to students on paper, or displayed on the board, with space available for them to add two task (see underlined phrase in example above) that use different slave systems.

References

Baddeley, A.D., Thomson, N. and Buchanan, M. (1975a). Word length and the structure of short term memory. *Journal of Verbal Learning and Verbal Behaviour,* 14, 575–89.

Baddeley, A.D., Grant, S., Wright, E. and Thomson, N. (1975b). Imagery and visual working memory. In P.M.A. Rabbitt and S. Dornic (Eds). *Attention and Performance,* Vol V. London: Academic Press.

V A✓ K ★ G HANDOUTS 24 and 25

TOPIC: Evaluating the working memory model

WORKING MEMORY AO2 AND CHEQUES

This activity helps students formulate ideas to produce an evaluation of the working memory model. Using the cheques in task 4 encourages students to peer assess each others' work.

Task 1

Arrange students into mixed ability pairs. Using the information from their textbook (page 14–15 in *Complete Companion*) students should identify either two strengths or two weaknesses and transfer them to their handout. In order for task 2 to work, half the class need to tackle strengths, with the other half covering weaknesses. Either split the class in half using your seating plan or place tickets in a bag labelled S or W and each pair draws the area they will cover. Students are instructed to summarise the points in their own words to develop their understanding of the information covered. Mixed ability grouping is helpful as more able students can guide their partner with careful explanations while furthering their own retention of information through their teaching.

Task 2

Students then snowball into a group of four: one pair having covered strengths, the other weaknesses. In these groups students teach each other the points made in task 1. As with previous activities, students need to be encouraged to actually teach rather than simply letting others copy their sheet. This does take a couple of activities to develop this method but students do adopt the approach eventually.

Task 3

Using the four points as a writing frame students now work alone to produce their own 6-mark evaluation. More able students may wish to move beyond the four points identified in their group and further their knowledge through using the textbook or their own opinions.

Task 4 (cheques)

Students move round the class reading each others' evaluations, keeping a record of evaluations they thought were particularly impressive. They then take their cheque and make it out to the student whose evaluation they liked the most. They can pay up to £100. On the back of the cheque they explain why they chose that particular evaluation. Students I have taught needed a quick explanation of how to complete a cheque (good old chip and pin!).

Plenary idea

At the end of the session students add up how much money their evaluation earned. Those who received a lot of money can read their evaluations aloud. You can then ask others in the class (who didn't receive cheques) what aspects of the evaluation they found impressive.

V✓ A K ★ S R HANDOUT 26

TOPIC: Evaluating the working memory model

EVALUATION TRAINS

This specific activity focuses on the use of dual task techniques (Baddeley 1975a,b) as support for the working memory model. However, the handout can be used to encourage students to expand other evaluations.

For example:

The first carriage could state 'so participants would have little interest or motivation in the task'.

Second carriage development 'they may not try as hard as they would in important, real-life situations'.

Third carriage 'performance may be better in real life, so experiment lacks ecological validity'.

It may help to model the first train with students or provide less able students with a range of slips, each showing one comment and students stick these onto each carriage; deciding which train they belonged to and the order they should be placed in.

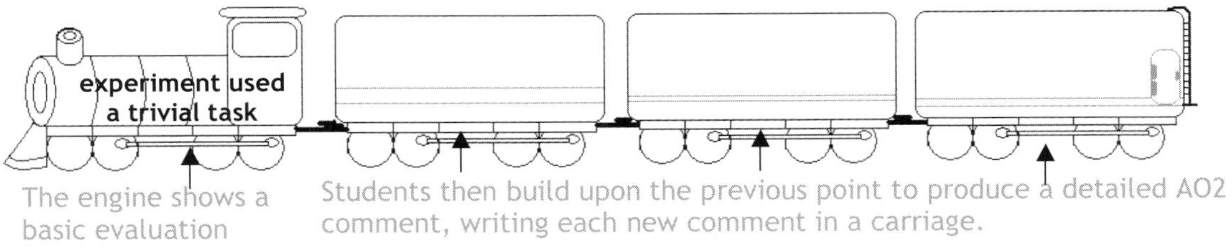
experiment used a trivial task
The engine shows a basic evaluation
Students then build upon the previous point to produce a detailed AO2 comment, writing each new comment in a carriage.

V ✓ A ✓ K O HANDOUT 27

TOPIC: Evaluating the working memory model

CONSIDERING EVALUATIONS

This task is challenging and involves higher order thinking, with students evaluating the strength of each argument. It can be used as an extension activity for more able students.

For each evaluative comment students are required to decide if it is making a positive statement about the working memory model (a strength) or a negative statement (a weakness). They then decide how convincing they find each statement. The stronger the statement, the longer the line. Positive statements have lines that originate upwards from the centre line. Negative statements show lines moving downwards from the centre line. Students could consider issues of validity, cause and effect, implications for real life in the judgements they make for each statement box. The first box has been completed as an example.

V ✓ A K ✓ O HANDOUT 28

TOPIC: Evaluating the working memory model

PUDDLE SPLASH REVIEW

After completing activities on the working memory model, both AO1 outline and AO2 evaluation points, students can use this handout to reflect on their own understanding of the model.

See 'Reviewing Topics' lesson notes (page 19) for more detailed explanation.

V ✓ A ✓ K S HANDOUT 29

TOPIC: Eyewitness testimony (EWT)

LOFTUS AND PALMER 1974

As a precursor to completing this handout I (RCG) carried out a variation of the study with the class.

1 Show students a car crash (either from a film or website clip).
2 Give students a general questionnaire about the clip they have just seen. Questions could include 'What colour were the two cars?', 'Was the driver of the first car male of female'. Included in the questionnaire will be the critical question 'How fast, in mph, was the car going when it ________ into the other car?' the blanks space is replaced by one of the following verbs: smashed, collided, bumped, hit, contacted. Ensure a good number of students experience each of the verbs.
3 Reveal to students the true aim of the study and gather their estimates from the critical question. The average for each verb can be displayed and compared to Loftus' findings. If differences are found between your study and that of Loftus and Palmer, ask the class to suggest reasons for this.

Students then complete the handout which encourages them to consider the procedure and findings (AO1), specific aspects of the study such as IV, DV, design (AO3), as well as criticisms and implications for society (AO2).

Reference

Loftus, E.F. and Palmer, J.C. (1974). Reconstruction of automobile destruction: An example of the interaction between language and memory. *Journal of Verbal Learning and Verbal Behaviour,* 13, 585–9.

V A✓K ★ S G HANDOUT 30

TOPIC: Eyewitness testimony (EWT)

POST-EVENT INFORMATION

This task concerns the following studies: Loftus and Palmer's (1974) broken glass study and Loftus, Miller and Burns (1978) Yield/stop sign study. Students use the template to produce an outline of one study into post-event information (pages 16–17 in *Complete Companion*).

This can be developed by asking students to swap their completed worksheet with a friend who researched the other study. Using this new handout they develop a 50 or 100 word outline of that study. Students then return the handout and the summary they have just written to the original owner of the worksheet. The worksheet owner uses their sheet to mark the summary they receive; correcting any mistakes or adding important missed details. The summary is then returned to the owner.

References

Loftus, E.F. and Palmer, J.C. (1974). Reconstruction of automobile destruction: An example of the interaction between language and memory. *Journal of Verbal Learning and Verbal Behaviour*, 13, 585–9.

Loftus, E.F., Miller, D.G. and Burns, H.J. (1978). Semantic integration of verbal information into visual memory. *Journal of Experimental Psychology,* 4(1), 19–31.

V A✓K ★ O HANDOUT 31

TOPIC: Factors that influence the accuracy of EWT: anxiety and age

ANXIETY AND EWT

I (RCG) introduce this topic as a practice psychologists use before giving a media interview to ensure they are clear about the message they wish to deliver, the points they want to make and that any research they discuss is accurate.

After reading information in their textbook (page 18 in *Complete Companion*) students are asked to consider the usefulness of the information and make judgements on what to include in their radio interview. The worksheet is structured into a 'must' section (which all students must complete), a 'should' section (which the majority of the class should attempt), and a 'could' section which demands higher order thinking, as they are asked to make evaluations (more able students could address this area). Once completed, the worksheet can be used in a planning session for a podcast, if you have the resources, of even a role play chat show or documentary performed live in class.

V✓A✓K ★ O S HANDOUT 32

TOPIC: Factors that influence the accuracy of EWT: anxiety and age

AGE AND EWT

This activity aims to encourage students to apply research into EWT to a real-life setting.

1. Explain the situation to students: Burglar Betty is on trial, accused of stealing a banana. The prosecution's case rests on Billy, an eyewitness to the crime. The prosecution needs to convince the jury Billy's EWT can be relied upon, while the defence has to cast doubt on the reliability of Billy's memory. I (RCG) allow students to decide how old Billy is.
2. Students use the information in their textbook (page 19 in *Complete Companion*) to complete each speech bubble. More able students may be able to construct an argument between the prosecution and defence. Other students may simply fill each speech bubble with standalone comments. For example, 'the own-age bias' suggests we find it harder to remember faces from a different age group than ourselves. Comments may take the form of research evidence and methodological evaluations as a way of undermining research findings.
3. The jury's conclusion allows students to consider all the research evidence and form their own conclusion. Can age have a significant influence on the reliability of EWT? Students can either consider their own court scene or swap sheets and after reading another work decide who is more convincing; the prosecution or defence.

Less able students do find this task challenging and may benefit from a help sheet stating researchers' name and a brief description of the conclusion.

As with 'Anxiety and EWT' this handout could be used as a basis for a drama activity.

V ✓ A ✓ K ✓ ★ S G HANDOUTS 33 and 34

TOPIC: The cognitive interview

INTERVIEWING WITNESSES

These worksheets form one overall activity. This may take longer than one lesson.

Task 1: Traditional interview

1. Students are placed into mixed ability pairs and decide amongst themselves who will be the witness and who will be the police officer. The police officers then leave the room.
2. When away from the classroom explain to the police officers they will shortly be interviewing their witnesses about a crime. It may be helpful to give a very general outline of the event their witnesses have seen. For example, 'two men are walking down a street, they meet a couple and a car is stolen'. Police officers are then left to develop five questions to elicit information from their witnesses.
3. While police officers are away from the classroom developing their questions, the witnesses are shown a film clip of an incident such as a car crash, robbery or mugging.
4. Police officers then return and interview their witness using the questions they have developed.
5. Students then watch the film together and then discuss the accuracy of this standard interview technique and predict how useful it would be in a real-life setting.

Task 2: Cognitive interview

1. Students then switch roles: police become witnesses and witnesses become police.
2. While outside the classroom police recap the four components of the cognitive interview and practise asking questions to ensure they are not leading the witnesses and clearly instruct witnesses for each component.
3. Witnesses watch a different incident along a similar theme. For both film clips I (RCG) chose a 15-rated film to avoid any ethical issues.
4. Police officers return and the interview is conducted.
5. As with task 1 students watch the clip together and evaluate the usefulness of the cognitive interview.

Plenary idea

Students are given a blank piece of paper also known as a 'voting slip'. Students record which interview technique they feel is more useful and write one sentence explaining their choice. Once all have voted, slips are collected and counted and the winning interview style is announced. The teacher, or student volunteers, can read out explanations, asking the class for their additional comments.

V A ✓ K ✓ ★ S HANDOUT 35

TOPIC: The cognitive interview

EVALUATION ACTIVITY: COGNITIVE INTERVIEW

Another opportunity to cut and stick!

This task encourages students to read for meaning and organise that information into a coherent form. The overall aim is to further develop students' understanding of how to expand evaluations.

This activity is based on a commonly used method of teaching paragraphing – the PEE method. (P) Make your point, (E) give evidence for that point, (E) then explain how the evidence relates to the point.

When teaching less able groups I (RCG) tend to ask students to identify whether each box contains a 'point', a piece of 'evidence' or is an 'explanation' of evidence. Once students have circled point, evidence or evaluation and these have been checked, they then cut out the boxes and begin organising them into PEE groups. The evidence relating to the point and explanation concerning Stein and Memon's (2006) study is not clear (as Brazil is not mentioned in the evidence section). Students should be able to work this out by a process of elimination as the other PEE groups have clear clues in the wording. However, textbooks (page 21 in *Complete Companion*) could be made available for students to check their groupings.

References

Kebbell, M.R. and Wagstaff, G.F. (1996). Enhancing the practicality of the cognitive interview in forensic situations. Psycholoquy [on-line serial], 7(6), Available FTP:Hostname: Princeton.edu Directory: pub/harnard/Psycholoquy/1996. volume.7 File: psyc.96.7.16.witness-memory.3.kebbell

Stein, L. and Memon, A. (2006). Testing the efficacy of the Cognitive Interview in a developing country. *Applied Cognitive Psychology*, 20, 597–605.

V A✓ K✓ ★ RG HANDOUT 36

TOPIC: Strategies for memory improvement

TEACHING TOWERS

Students I (RCG) have taught tend to easily remember the various mnemonics that can be employed to improve memory and are confident in describing them. However, they struggle when asked HOW these techniques improve chances of recalling information. Teaching towers aims to give students a page of structured notes that clearly set out the different explanations for why mnemonics prove effective.

1 In groups of three, students use information in their textbooks (page 23 in *Complete Companion*) to complete one tower. Differentiation is possible here. The role of elaborative rehearsal is a shorter explanation and may relate to work previously covered (page 11 for Hyde and Jenkins (1973) in *Complete Companion*) so may suit slower readers.
2 One student now stays with the group's tower to teach other people about that topic.
3 The others from the group need to split up and visit other towers to learn one topic each.
4 Students then regroup and teach each other the two new tower topics.

The bottom of the handout displays a list of rules that need to be followed to ensure the activity is successful. For a large class, two (or more) groups can cover each tower, or group size could be increased to four students per group.

Plenary idea
Once all have completed their handout, students can attempt an exam question relating to mnemonics (the sample exam paper on the AQA website has a suitable question). Although each student completes the activity individually, their end score is determined by the overall performance of their group (in steps 1 and 4). This is done by adding each student's score together and calculating the mean score for the group. Groups who score highly are congratulated on teaching each other well.

V✓ A✓ K✓ ★ SG HANDOUTS 37 and 38

TOPIC: Strategies for memory improvement

ASSESSING MNEMONICS AND METHOD OF LOCI

Teaching mnemonics at the end of the cognitive topic is helpful as the mnemonic techniques can be experienced using previously learnt material, thus providing a revision opportunity for earlier topics.

Task 1: Students decide on two topics they wish to revise.
For example, multi-store model and working memory model. The topics could be set by the teacher based on areas the class seem to struggle with.

For one of the topics students produce a mind map, for the other they complete the method of loci sheet.

Method of loci sheet – students draw objects in each room of their house and link them to aspects of the topic to be revised. For example, in the living room Peterson and Peterson are sitting together on a sofa, a big clock showing 30 is on the wall. The carpet is patterned with trigrams, while on the television, a timer is counting down from 100. The more imaginative the better for this task.

Task 2: Testing recall of the topics
One week later give the class a test on the two topics. This could simply be asking students to list as many points as they are able to recall about the two topics. Did one technique lead to better recall? Students then complete the worksheet reflecting on the two techniques, how they improve recall and evaluate the usefulness of each technique.

V✓ A K✓ ★ O HANDOUT 39

TOPIC: Strategies for memory improvement

SLUG TO SNAIL REVIEW

After completing activities on eyewitness testimony, the cognitive interview and strategies for memory improvement, students can use this handout to reflect on their own understanding of the model.

See 'Reviewing Topics' lesson notes (page 19) for more detailed explanation.

V ✓ A K ✓ ★ G HANDOUTS 40 and 41

TOPIC: Explanations of attachment

MATCHING RACE! CLASSICAL CONDITIONING

Classical conditioning is one of the most daunting explanations for students to learn. Perhaps not because of its difficulty, but because of the intimidating amount of new key terms students must be aware of.

A nice way to help your students review these key terms, as well as some of the key principles, is in the form of a matching game.

On **Handouts 40 and 41** there are 20 cards which can be cut out. The 10 cards on the left refer to key terms and questions relating to classical conditioning, and the 10 cards on the right are the definitions and answers they can be paired with.

You could devise this game in any number of ways, but here is a particularly 'kinaesthetic' suggestion.

Divide the class into two teams, or more if necessary. Place the key terms and questions face down on the table where each team is sitting.

Place the answers and definitions face up on a separate table, perhaps on the other side of the classroom.

The race starts when one member of each team turns one key term/question face up, then runs to the other table to find the correct definition/answer.

When that team member has successfully 'paired' a key term or question with its definition or answer, a new team member takes over.

The winning team is that which pairs all the cards correctly in the quickest time!

Answers

Unconditioned Stimulus – A stimulus which caused an unlearnt response. For example, hunger leads to salivation.

Unconditioned Response – An unlearnt behaviour/action which is caused by a stimulus. For example, pain leads to screaming.

Neutral Stimulus – This becomes the conditioned stimulus once conditioning has occurred (i.e., it has been paired with an unconditioned stimulus). For example, the bell with Pavlov's dogs.

Conditioned Stimulus – A new stimulus that had been paired with an unconditioned stimulus so that an animal/ human associates the two together. Before conditioning it was the neutral stimulus.

Conditioned Response – A learnt response to a previously neutral stimulus.

Why are infants happy around their mothers? According to learning theory, it is because they have learnt to associate them with food via classical conditioning.

Who proposed classical conditioning? Pavlov, after observing the behaviour of dogs.

According to learning theory, all behaviour is the result of…? Classical and operant conditioning.

In attachment, the conditioned stimulus is…? The mother/ caregiver.

An explanation is..? Like a theory. It attempts to account for behaviour which has been observed by psychologists, e.g. why dogs salivate at the sound of a bell.

V ✓ A K ✓ ★ HORTS HANDOUT 42

TOPIC: Explanations of attachment

BURGER EVALUATION SKILLS

The 'burger' evaluation technique specifically aims to help students to use studies when evaluating theories/ explanations – an area where many students appear to lack confidence.

The principles of this technique are outlined earlier, 'Burger Evaluation Skills' on page 10.

Handout 42 provides students with an example of how this technique could be used with Harlow (1959) in order to evaluate the learning theory explanation of attachment.

Deconstruct this technique with your students, and then ask them to evaluate the learning theory explanation of attachment using Fox (1997) and Schaffer and Emerson (1964).

Encourage your gifted and talented students to provide extra commentary at the end to indicate a greater depth of analysis and understanding.

References

Fox, N. (1997). Attachment of Kibbutz infants to mother and metapelet. *Child Development,* 48, 1228–39.
Harlow, H.F. (1959). Love in infant monkeys. *Scientific American,* 200(6), 68–74.
Schaffer, H.R. and Emerson, P.E. (1964). The development of social attachments in infancy. *Monographs of the Society for Research in Child Development,* 29(3) Serial No. 94.

V✓ A✓ K ★ H G

TOPIC: Evolutionary perspective – Bowlby's attachment theory

BABY FACE!

To introduce Bowlby's idea that attachment is innate and evolutionarily adaptive, show students images of young mammals and ask them if they notice similarities.

This is related to the *baby face hypothesis* and the idea that young mammals have the same distinctive features (big eyes, large forehead, squashed up nose).

You can find some excellent images for this at www.thingsthatmakeyougoaahh.com

Your students will almost certainly 'aaawww' at the sight of these cute images (although some of the lads tend to play it cool!). Drawing on this, ask them why these characteristics in young mammals might have evolved. You could also use a collaborative learning structure (see page 3) in which to do this.

Bowlby suggested that these features acted as 'triggers' for parenting behaviour, which is necessary for a young animal's survival. They elicit our desire to look after and care for babies.

V✓ A K✓ ★ H O R S HANDOUT 43

TOPIC: Evolutionary perspective – Bowlby's attachment theory

BOWLBY – 'CONNECT 5'

Bowlby's theory of attachment contains many different elements, principles and terms which students have to be aware of.

However, even if they understand and are aware of all these different elements, they can often still lack an overall understanding of the theory as a whole – how it fits together.

Handout 43 is an activity which aims to encourage students to link different elements of the theory together.

In the boxed areas, students should articulate their understanding of the principles, i.e. social releasers, adaptive/innate, sensitive period, monotropy, and secure base. They could do this using their textbooks (in the *Complete Companion* the relevant pages are 36 and 37).

In between the box areas, students should try and explain how the elements of the theory link together. For example, social releasers are adaptive because they elicit parenting behaviour which helps them to survive, they are innate because social releasers are inborn characteristics which all human infants possess.

If you and your students are feeling especially creative, you could even run this activity with different coloured strips of paper in order to make a Bowlby-themed paper chain!

The end result is hopefully that students have a more holistic understanding of Bowlby's theory, and they are encouraged to use higher order thinking skills.

V A✓ K ★ H G S HANDOUT 44

TOPIC: Evolutionary perspective – Bowlby's attachment theory

PSYCHOLOGY JACKANORY – INTERNAL WORKING MODEL

As we have already noted, something strange but endearing happens to sixth formers, they seem to regress to an earlier stage of development! For example, sixth formers at our school (female and male) will badger, cheat, and sell their souls for the chance of being rewarded one of our department's custom-made psychology stickers! So much so that this year we have decided to award psychology t-shirts to those students who achieve a collection of 10 stickers in a year! Now try this technique with year 10 and 11 and you get an altogether more different reaction…!

Now try this, why not transport your students back to primary school circle time, turn the lights out, and read them a story… *'when you are sitting comfortably, I will begin…!'*

On **Handout 44** is a story you can read, or ask your students to read. It is a silly story but may help students start to think about the concepts of the internal working model.

Set some time in the future, the story describes a girl who receives an 'Edward Bear' for her birthday. This is a futuristic toy (hopefully your students will have the necessary imagination) where children can essentially create a teddy bear which behaves just like a 'living being'. However, the girl does not like what she has created…

Disappointed with the fruit of her labour, Katie stuffed Edward into a dark cupboard, leaving him to contemplate his bleak future.

Stop the story at this point and ask your students to consider the following questions (your students will need to stretch their imagination somewhat!):

1. The bear's first experience of the world is being rejected by its creator and stuffed in a dark cupboard. Based on this first experience, what do you think the bear thinks about himself?
2. What do you think the bear thinks about other 'living beings'?
3. Based on your answers, how do you think the bear will behave in the future? Think about its social and emotional development.

Then finish reading the story. Ask your students why they think you read them the story, and what relevance it might have to attachment and developmental psychology. You could then introduce the concepts of the internal working model and the continuity hypothesis.

V A ✓ K ★ HOTS

TOPIC: Evolutionary perspective – Bowlby's attachment theory

PLENARY QUESTIONS - EASY/MEDIUM/HARD/MEGA HARD

Here are some plenary questions you could use to test your students on their knowledge and understanding of both learning theory and Bowlby's evolutionary perspective. The slight twist being that students can select whether they wish to answer an easy, medium, hard or mega hard question.

Sort your class into teams and explain the rules. You will go round each team in turn and select one individual from that team. They must decide which level of difficulty question they would like to answer. The more difficult they choose, the more points available!

Easy questions – 1 point

- According to learning theory, all behaviour is learnt through ____________ and ____________ conditioning.

Classical and Operant

- Name one study (name(s) sufficient) which undermines the learning theory explanation of attachment.

e.g. *Harlow, Fox, Schaffer and Emerson*

- Name two elements/principles/key terms relevant to Bowlby's theory of attachment.

Innate, adaptive, evolutionary, social releasers, sensitive period, monotropy, secure base, etc.

Medium questions – 2 points

- Briefly explain what Bowlby meant by the sensitive period.

There is a limited window for the development of attachment. It becomes more difficult to develop an attachment after this window has passed.

- Briefly explain what Bowlby meant by the term monotropy.

Infants develop one attachment of special importance, this bias towards one special attachment is called monotropy.

- Mother and happiness. Which is the conditioned stimulus, and which is the conditioned response?

Mother = Conditioned stimulus
Happiness = Conditioned response

Hard questions – 3 points

- Explain why Harlow's study undermines the learning theory explanation of attachment.

The learning theory account assumes that attachment is formed due to the fact that an infant associates the mother with food. However, Harlow's study showed that infant rhesus monkeys choose to attach themselves for 'contact comfort' rather than a caregiver that provides food.

- Name four key terms related to Bowlby's theory of attachment and explain one of them.

Students may choose to define the following key words: adaptive, innate, social releasers, evolutionary, monotropy, internal working model, continuity hypothesis, critical period, sensitive period, imprinting.

- Fully explain the role of evolution in developing cute 'baby faces' in young mammals?

It helps them to elicit parenting behaviour from adults and therefore helps them form an attachment with an adult caregiver. This is related to evolution because without an adult caregiver, infants would find it difficult to survive – from adults they gain food and protection.

Mega hard questions – 4 points

- The Czech twins were found when they were 7 years of age. The had been locked up by their stepmother and completely isolated from human beings. When they were found, they could not even talk. They were discovered and looked after by two loving adoptive sisters, and by age 14 had normal intellectual and social functioning. Which element of Bowlby's theory does this undermine and why?

Sensitive period – the window for development would have passed, meaning they should not be able to form meaningful attachments. Answers relating to internal working model and continuity hypothesis may also be used.

- Harlow's study undermines the idea that food is the basis for attachment and therefore is evidence against the learning theory explanation of attachment. Provide a counter argument to this.

e.g. *Harlow's study was conducted with rhesus monkeys and so the results may not generalise to the behaviour of human infants.*

- Identify one difference between the learning theory account of attachment and Bowlby's attachment theory.

Learning theory suggests that attachment is learnt behaviour whereas Bowlby's theory states that attachment behaviour is innate.

V A K S HANDOUT 45

TOPIC: Evaluating Bowlby's theory of attachment

RESEARCH ACTIVITY: HAZAN AND SHAVER (1987) LOVE QUIZ

This research activity links nicely to the evaluation of Bowlby's theory, since Hazan and Shaver's (1987) study can be said to have provided evidence in support of Bowlby's internal working model and continuity hypothesis.

Bowlby's theory of attachment suggests that the infant's relationships with their caregiver forms the basis of the child's internal working model of relationships. This will affect the child's expectations about what relationships (including romantic ones) will be like. Therefore, we would expect a link between early attachments, attitudes about romantic relationships and actual romantic relationships. This is called the *continuity hypothesis*.

Hazan and Shaver's study

Hazan and Shaver (1987) tested Bowlby's hypothesis with their 'love quiz'. The quiz, which contained nearly 100 questions, was published in the *Rocky Mountain News*. They received 620 replies to their questionnaire and drew the following conclusions:

Securely attached adults:

- had certain beliefs about relationships (love is enduring)
- reported certain experiences in relationships (e.g., mutual trust)
- were less likely to have been divorced.

Insecurely attached adults:

- felt true love was rare, and fell in and out of love easily
- found relationships less easy
- were more likely to be divorced.

(See table below)

	Secure adults	**Resistant (anxious) adults**	**Avoidant adults**
Different love experiences	Relationships are positive	Preoccupied by love	Fearful of closeness
Adults' views of relationships	Trust others and believe in enduring love	Fall in love easily but have trouble finding *true* love	Love is not durable nor necessary for happiness
Memories of the mother–child relationship	Positive image of mother as dependable and caring	Conflicting memories of mother being positive *and* rejecting	Remember mothers as cold and rejecting

Analysis of the data revealed that infant attachment style predicted attitudes towards love (internal working model) and experience of love (continuity hypothesis).

In the short version of the quiz on **Handout 45** the questions make assessments as follows:

- Q 1, 2 and 3 assess attachment history.
- Q 4, 5 and 6 assess adult attachment type.
- Q 7, 8 and 9 assess mental models of relationships.

Ethics briefing

This study involves questions that may be related to sensitive information about an individual's early life experience and which may suggest problematic adult relationships. When replicating this study, always seek informed consent beforehand, where possible, or offer a thorough debriefing, including the right to withhold individual data.

It should also be emphasised that the suggested association between early experience and later relationships is not 100% – there are many individuals who overcome early unfavourable circumstances. In addition this correlation is not proven.

A further point to make is that the original survey involved nearly 100 questions, whereas this shorter version involves just nine. Therefore, the reliability and validity of this exercise will be low, so little can be read into the results.

That said, it is a useful exercise to undertake to understand how Hazan and Shaver collected the evidence which is often used to support Bowlby's hypothesis.
To work out scores use the table below.

Question	a	b	c
1	secure	insecure avoidant	insecure resistant
2	secure	insecure resistant	insecure avoidant
3	insecure resistant	secure	insecure avoidant
Score for part A (the dominant category chosen: secure, insecure-avoidant or insecure-resistant) =			
4	insecure resistant	insecure avoidant	secure
5	secure	insecure resistant	insecure avoidant
6	insecure avoidant	secure	insecure resistant
Score for part B (the dominant category chosen: secure, insecure-avoidant or insecure-resistant) =			
7	insecure avoidant	insecure resistant	secure
8	insecure avoidant	secure	insecure resistant
9	insecure resistant	secure	insecure avoidant
Score for part C (the dominant category chosen: secure, insecure-avoidant or insecure-resistant) =			

Reference

Hazan, C., and Shaver, P.R. (1987). Romantic love conceptualised as an attachment process. *Journal of Personality and Social Psychology*, 52, 511–24.

V A K ✓ HORS HANDOUTS 46 and 47

TOPIC: Evaluating Bowlby's theory of attachment

BOWLBY – LOOKING AT THE EVIDENCE

This activity is designed to help students to evaluate Bowlby's theory using research evidence. It also introduces the concept of 'signposts' to students – ways to introduce evaluative arguments.

Signposts
Students often get into the habit of using the same phrases over and over again. For example, 'This is supported by…', or 'This study backs up…'

Handout 46 asks students to brainstorm different 'signposts' they could use to introduce evaluations for and against Bowlby's theory of attachment.

Essay fragments
Handout 47 provides students with a series of essay fragments (mostly descriptions of studies significant to Bowlby's theory).

Following the tasks stated on the sheet, students are encouraged to use these fragments to evaluate specific elements of Bowlby's theory of attachment, as well as using some of the signposts from the previous activity.

References

Erickson, M.F., Sroufe, L.A. and Egeland, B. (1985). The relationship between quality of attachment and behaviour problems in preschool in a high-risk sample. In I. Bretherton and E. Waters (Eds.), *Monographs of the Society for Research in Child Development*, 50 (Serial No. 209, pp. 147–66).
Hazan, C. and Shaver, P.R. (1987). Romantic love conceptualised as an attachment process. *Journal of Personality and Social Psychology, 52,* 511–24.
Hodges, J. and Tizard, B. (1989). Social and family relationships of ex-institutional adolescents. *Journal of Child Psychology and Psychiatry,* 30, 77–97.
Kagan, J. (1984). *The Nature of the Child.* New York: Basic Books.
Schaffer, H.R. and Emerson, P.E. (1964). The development of social attachments in infancy. *Monographs of the Society for Research in Child Development,* 29(3), Serial No. 94.
Sroufe, L.A., Egeland, B., Carlson, E.A. and Collins, W.A. (2005). *The Development of the Person: The Minnesota study of risk and adaption from birth to adulthood.* New York: Guilford.

V A✓K ★HOG

TOPIC: Types of attachment

ARE ALL ATTACHMENTS THE SAME?

Use the 'group statements' collaborative learning structure (see page 3) and ask your students the following question:

'Are all attachments between infants and caregivers the same? Explain and justify your answer.'

Of course the obvious answer to this question is 'no', but each group may contribute different ideas as to why attachments may vary.

V✓A K✓★OS

TOPIC: Types of attachment

'PLAY DOH' CHALLENGE – MODELLING ATTACHMENT BEHAVIOURS

While this is just a fun, little activity that I (MWG) tend to use when I teach developmental psychology, it can also be used to tick the 'ICT across the curriculum' box if desired!

Give a small amount of plasticine to each of your students and instruct them to create an infant and a caregiver.

Then, either in the lesson or for homework, get them to model certain behaviours related to attachment. For example: separation anxiety, pleasure when reunited, stranger anxiety, and using a caregiver as a secure base (a particularly challenging one).

I ask my students to take pictures of these models using either their own digital cameras, digital cameras at school, or cameras on their mobile phones.

They then have to insert these images into Microsoft Word or PowerPoint and clearly label their images and what they intend to show. They are also asked to email these files to me as an attachment (no pun intended!).

I never fail to be amazed by the standard of work they produce. One boy even created a series of *Wallace* and *Gromit*-style movies!

V✓A K✓★OS

TOPIC: Types of attachment

ROLE PLAYING AINSWORTH

I have to confess that the idea of using role play fills me with absolute horror! Myself (MWG) and Ros both work at a performing arts school where the students take their drama very seriously. Combine that with the fact that I am extremely uncomfortable with performance myself, and you'll understand why role play does not find its way into my lesson plans!

However, I am well aware that role play can be an excellent tool for helping students remember and understand psychological studies. So, for those of you who are confident and willing, Ainsworth's Strange Situation does seem to lend itself particularly well to this kind of activity.

In Ainsworth's original research, observers recorded infant behaviour under five categories:

1. Proximity and contact-seeking behaviours.
2. Contact-maintaining behaviours.
3. Proximity and interaction-avoiding behaviours.
4. Contact and interaction-avoiding behaviours.
5. Search behaviours.

Every 15 seconds the observers made a note of which of the above behaviours were being displayed, also scoring the behaviour for intensity on a scale of 1 to 7.

To role play with students, ask for three groups of volunteers. In each group there should be a caregiver, stranger and infant. In Group 1 the infant should act as securely attached. In Group 2 the infant should act insecure-avoidant, and in Group 3 insecure-resistant.

Using information from their textbooks, each group should act out the episodes of the Strange Situation. This provides the rest of the class (those who do not act as stranger, caregiver, or infant) with the opportunity to practise making observations (and find out just how hard this is). Observers should record behaviours over the eight episodes of the Strange Situation (it might be prudent for them to design a grid on which to do this).

Afterwards class members can compare their results using descriptive statistics (e.g., measures of central tendency, graphs, etc.) and consider their conclusions (which infant was which attachment type).

V✓ A K ★ R S HANDOUT 48

TOPIC: Types of attachment

SPOT THE DIFFERENCE!

Many students understandably get confused between the two major insecure attachment types: avoidant and resistant.

Using **Handout 48**, students could complete a 'spot the difference' exercise to help them remember and understand the differences between the two attachment types.

Students should construct simple drawings that illustrate the differences in the willingness to explore, stranger anxiety, separation anxiety, and reunion behaviour of infants who have insecure-avoidant and insecure-resistant attachment types.

These drawings can be really simple. I often tell my students to use little stickmen-style infants and caregivers, and to use thought and speech bubbles to present their understanding, because like me, many of them are not confident in their artistic expression!

V A K✓ ★ O

TOPIC: Types of attachment

WHAT HAPPENED NEXT?

You can play a simple plenary game to assess your students' knowledge of the Strange Situation and the characteristics of the attachment types.

To do this, simply present the students with the following events, and ask them 'What happens next?'

1 The mother of a securely attached child leaves the room.
2 The mother of a child with an insecure-avoidant attachment type leaves the room.
3 The mother of a child with an insecure-resistant attachment type re-enters the room.
4 The mother of a securely attached child attempts to soothe their distressed child.
5 A stranger attempts to comfort a distressed child with an insecure-avoidant attachment type.

Showdown

To make this game a little more competitive, consider putting your students into small teams and playing 'showdown'.

Present event 1 to the students and ask them to consider 'What happens next'? Each team member must *individually* write down their answer. When the teacher gives the signal, all team members reveal their answers at the same time. If all the answers in the team are correct and match each other, that team gets 5 points.

And so on, until all events have been presented.

V✓A K ★HTS HANDOUT 49

TOPIC: Evaluating types of attachment

CAREGIVER VS TEMPERAMENT HYPOTHESIS

One way of evaluating Ainsworth and her research into types of attachment is by undermining her conclusions.

Ainsworth and Bell (1970) concluded that the mother's behaviour was the determining factor in the infant's attachment type. This was known as the *caregiver hypothesis*. For example, they suggested that mothers of securely attached children are more effective at soothing their children, whereas mothers of insecurely attached children are less sensitive to the child's needs.

However, Kagan (1984) and Thompson and Lamb (1984) proposed an alternative *temperament hypothesis*. They suggest that the inborn temperament of the child affects the behaviour of the infant in the Strange Situation. For example, a 'difficult' child will show more extreme separation anxiety when the mother leaves the room.

These competing hypotheses contribute to the never-ending nature versus nurture debate in psychology.

Handout 49 provides students with an opportunity to identify evidence both for and against the competing hypotheses.

Students should shade in the key using three different colours, and then shade in the evidence as they see appropriate.

An extension task for gifted and talented students could be to use the 'burger technique' (see page 10) with those studies to evaluate Ainsworth's caregiver hypothesis.

References

Ainsworth, M.D.S. and Bell, S.M. (1970). Attachment, exploration and separation: Illustrated by two-year-olds in a Strange Situation. *Child Development*, 41, 49–65.

Belsky, J. (1984). The determinates of parenting: A process model. *Child Development*, 55, 83–96.

Grossmann, K., Grossmann, K.E., Spangler, G., Suess, G. and Unzer, L. (1985). Maternal sensitivity and newborns' orientation responses as related to quality of attachment in northern Germany. In I. Bretherton and E. Walters (Eds.), Growing points in attachment theory and research. *Monographs of the Society for Research in Child Development*, 50, 233–56.

Kagan, J. (1984). *The Nature of the Child*. New York: Basic Books.

Main, M. and Weston, D.R. (1981). The quality of the toddler's relationship to mother and father: Related conflict behaviour and the readiness to establish new relationships. *Child Development*, 52, 932–40.

Spangler, G. (1990). Mother, child, and situational correlates of toddlers' social competence. *Infant Behaviour and Development*, 13, 405–19.

Thomas, A. and Chess, S. (1986). The New York Longitudinal Study: From infancy to early life. In R. Plomin and J. Dunn (Eds.), *The Study of Temperament: Changes, continuities and challenges*. Hillsdale, N.J.: Erlbaum.

Thompson, R.A. and Lamb, W.E. (1984). Assessing qualitative dimensions of emotional responsiveness infants: Separation reactions to the Strange Situation. *Infant Behaviour and Development*, 7, 423–45.

V✓A K ★HORS HANDOUTS 50–52

TOPIC: Cultural variations in attachment

UNDERSTANDING CULTURAL VARIATIONS IN ATTACHMENT

I (MWG) think this has to be one of the most difficult topics to teach in the developmental psychology section of the specification. The students that I have taught always seem to find it very difficult to remove themselves from Sutton Coldfield in order to understand cultural variations in child-rearing values and how they influence attachment types. But having a full and deep understanding of these concepts is crucial for being able to explain and evaluate cultural variations in attachment.

Ask your students to read **Handout 50**. This sheet outlines the child-rearing values of three different cultures: Israel, Japan and Germany. Of course, these values are somewhat simplistic and not generalisable to the whole of those cultures, but are useful for the purpose of this activity. You could perhaps discuss how these values are different to what we are familiar with in the UK.

Next, get your students to attempt **Handout 51**. Using the information they have read, students are asked to make predictions about how infants from each culture would behave if placed in the Strange Situation, and the percentages of attachment types that would be found.

The students should also justify their predictions with reference to the information outlined in **Handout 50**. By asking the students to do this, the aim is that they will be able to understand the link between cultural variations in child-rearing values, and the behaviour of infants from different cultures in the Strange Situation.

Following this activity, students will hopefully be in a position to study Van Ijzendoorn and Kroonenberg's (1988) research, and be able to explain some of the results. They can also compare their predictions from **Handout 51** with the results of Van Ijzendoorn and Kroonenberg's meta-analysis. A study outline is given on **Handout 52** which you may like to give to your students for their folders.

Reference

Van Ijzendoorn, M.H. and Kroonenberg, P.M. (1988). Cross-cultural patterns of attachment: A meta-analysis of the Strange Situation. *Child Development*, 59, 147–56.

V ✓A K HORS HANDOUTS 53 and 54

TOPIC: Evaluating cultural variations in attachment

WORLD RESTAURANT CUP!

One of the most compelling evaluations of studies like Van Ijzendoorn and Kroonenberg (1988) is that the use of the Strange Situation is not a valid way of measuring cultural variations in attachment – it is culturally biased. The Strange Situation was created in the USA and reflects the norms and values of American culture, but assumes behaviour has the same meaning in all cultures.

In Japan, for example, infants are rarely separated from their mothers. As a result, the Strange Situation poses more of a threat to these infants than infants in the USA. This means infants from Japan are more likely to be classed as insecurely attached and a negative judgement made on Japanese mothers. As such, the Strange Situation could be said to be ethnocentrically biased.

However, this is a very difficult evaluation to teach to AS students, particularly the weaker ones.

World Restaurant Cup

While tearing my (MWG) hair out last year trying to help my students understand this evaluation, I had the inspired idea of relating these concepts to something they know and are enthusiastic about – eating and food!

Using **Handout 54**, present your students with the 'World Restaurant Cup' competition, telling them it has just been launched by the USA and giving them the criteria for judging the restaurants which have also just been announced.

Students should read the information on **Handout 53** which details cultural values regarding food and restaurants in France, USA, and China.

Students should then use this information to evaluate the fairness (validity) of the criteria for judging restaurants in France, USA, and China, as well as drawing overall conclusions at the end.

I found that when using the activity this year, students had a far better understanding when we related their evaluations to the use of the Strange Situation to measure attachments across cultures. The following activity **'World Attachment Competition'** (**Handout 55**) is designed to follow on naturally from this activity.

Reference

Van Ijzendoorn, M.H. and Kroonenberg, P.M. (1988). Cross-cultural patterns of attachment: A meta-analysis of the Strange Situation. *Child Development*, 59, 147–56.

V ✓A K HORS HANDOUT 55

TOPIC: Evaluating cultural variations in attachment

WORLD ATTACHMENT COMPETITION!

This activity is a continuation from the previous **'World Restaurant Cup'** task. Students will find it much easier to complete if they attempted and understood the previous task.

In essence the task outlined on **Handout 55** is the same but with a slight difference. This time the students are asked to consider the validity of the Strange Situation criteria as a measure of attachments across cultures.

In order to complete this they may wish to read the information provided on **Handout 50**.

Ideally, the students will conclude something similar to the evaluation of Van Ijzendoorn and Kroonenberg (1998) outlined on the previous page.

'One of the most compelling evaluations of studies such as Van Ijzendoorn and Kroonenberg (1988) is that the use of the Strange Situation is not a valid way of measuring cultural variations in attachment – it is culturally biased.'

V ✓A K HTS HANDOUTS 56 and 57

TOPIC: Evaluating cultural variations in attachment

EXTENSIONS: VAN IJZENDOORN AND KROONENBERG EVALUATION

It is often necessary to have extra tasks up your sleeve for the strongest students who race through your activities. **Handouts 56** and **57** may help in this respect, providing a challenge for even your most gifted students.

The extensions consist of flawed arguments on the left-hand side relating to food across cultures, as well as explanations as to why those arguments are flawed.

For example, 'All Germans eat sausages, and sausages are their favourite foods'. This is flawed because, while the German culture is well known for enjoying different varieties of sausages, it is too simplified to suggest that *all* Germans eat and enjoy sausages.

The task for students is to relate these flawed arguments to the implicit but flawed assumptions made by Van Ijzendoorn and Kroonenberg's research.

V A✓ K✓ OG

TOPIC: Disruption of attachment

SNOWBALLING – REASONS FOR SEPARATION

Disruption of attachment refers to a situation where the attachment between an infant and their caregiver has been damaged or lost.

This disruption is sometimes caused by a physical separation from the caregiver that results in a loss of emotional care. There can be many causes of this lack of emotional care, which students should be aware of.

Use the collaborative learning structure **'snowballing'** (see page 3) with your students to brainstorm the possible different causes of physical separation between infant and caregiver.

Some of the reasons students could suggest are: day care, hospitalisation, death, divorce, mental illness, school, holiday, postnatal depression, etc.

V✓ A K✓ HORS HANDOUTS 58 and 59

TOPIC: Disruption of attachment

DECONSTRUCTING ROBERTSON AND ROBERTSON (1967–1973)

The work of James Robertson and his wife Joyce has increased our understanding of the effects of lack of emotional care and, in particular, how the negative effects might be avoided. The Robertsons (1967–1973) made a landmark series of films featuring young children in situations where they were separated from their primary attachment figure and had no alternative good emotional care.

Handout 58 contains an extract from *The Complete Companion* which outlines the details of these case studies and their findings. A series of highlighting tasks at the bottom of the page are designed to help students deconstruct the information and make sense of it.

Once students have completed this worksheet, it may be useful for them to transfer this information into **Handout 59**. The format of this sheet will hopefully enable students to spot patterns in the results and ultimately, support the two conclusions at the bottom:

1. The absence of substitute emotional care can disrupt the long-term attachment between infant and caregiver.
2. The negative effects of lack of emotional care between infant and caregiver can be reversed.

Reference

Robertson, J. and Robertson, J. (1967–1973). *Young children in brief separation*. A film study. Concord Video and Film Council. New York University Film Library.

V✓A K✓ HORS HANDOUT 60

TOPIC: Disruption of attachment

APPLYING KNOWLEDGE

Undoubtedly the scariest thing about the AQA AS examinations is the emphasis that is placed on the application of knowledge (AO2). Students can no longer rely on regurgitating model answers that we have beautifully prepared for them! This is clearly a positive move by AQA, but will mean that we must give our students every opportunity to practise applying what we have already helped them to understand.

Drawing on their knowledge of disruption of attachment research (e.g., Robertson and Robertson, 1967–1973), **Handout 60** requires students to read the stimulus material and then answer an exam question.

It is important to explain to students that in order to get all 3 marks available, they need to elaborate their responses accordingly.

For example, if a question asks students to outline a strategy to minimise the negative effects of separation from a caregiver, students could do 3 distinct things to earn those marks:

1. Briefly introduce the strategy.
2. Explain (psychologically) why this strategy would work.
3. Briefly provide evidence (i.e. from a study or theory) that this strategy would work.

This is one way in which students might approach this question, but there are certainly other ways.

Model answers are provided below:

Strategy 1: One strategy Alana's parents could use is to visit her regularly throughout her stay.

Explanation: This would ensure emotional links between Alana and her parents are maintained whilst she is in hospital.

Evidence: Indeed, the Robertson's studies indicated that when emotional links were maintained throughout a physical separation from the caregiver (e.g., Jane, Lucy, etc.), there were no long-term effects on attachment.

Strategy 2: One strategy Alana's parents could use it to ensure that she has a consistent caregiver(s) whilst in hospital (i.e., one or two nurses).

Explanation: This would ensure that Alana has substitute emotional care to counter the fact she will be losing the emotional care from her main caregiver.

Evidence: The Robertsons' studies showed that when substitute emotional care was provided (e.g., loving foster care for Jane, Lucy, etc.), there were no long-term effects on attachment. When there was no substitute emotional care (e.g., John), the negative effects lasted for some time.

Reference

Robertson, J. and Robertson, J. (1967–1973). *Young children in brief separation*. A film study. Concord Video and Film Council. New York University Film Library.

V✓A K HOS

TOPIC: Failure to form attachment

PIES – EFFECTS OF FAILURE TO FORM ATTACHMENT

This is an activity borrowed from GCSE Health and Social Care.

Ask students to brainstorm what they think are the possible effects of the failure to form attachment (as distinct from disruption of attachment).

To give them some structure for doing this, ask them to consider the effects on **P**hysical development, **I**ntellectual development, **E**motional development, and **S**ocial development – **PIES**!

They could even draw a pie to brainstorm their ideas within.

Consider having a class feedback session afterwards.

V ✓ A ✓ K ORS HANDOUTS 61 and 62

TOPIC: Failure to form attachment

CASE STUDY – GENIE

One of the most famous case studies of failure to form attachment is Genie. Genie was locked in a room by her father until she was 13½ (because she was thought to be retarded). When she was 'found' she could not stand erect and could not speak. She never fully recovered socially. She apparently showed a *disinterest* in other people. Her lack of recovery might have been due to her extreme emotional privation. The late age at which she was 'discovered' (past Bowlby's sensitive age for effective attachment) could also have been responsible for the fact that recovery was not possible (Curtiss, 1977).

Students never fail to be interested in this extreme case study and it is definitely worth reviewing her story in more detail. **Handouts 61 and 62** contain a series of questions for students to answer.

The best way for students to find the answers is to watch either the documentary *'NOVA: Secret of the Wild Child'*, or the moving film *'Mockingbird Don't Sing'*, both of which are solely based on this case study.

At the time of writing, both DVDs were available and reasonably priced on www.amazon.co.uk. Simply search for the titles on the homepage.

There was also a BBC Horizon documentary on the case. This programme (at time of writing) was available at www.psychexchange.co.uk

The alternative is to set this as an independent study activity, with students seeking information from a variety of sources: the Internet, textbooks, the library, YouTube, etc.

Reference

Curtiss, S. (1977). *Genie: A psycholinguistic study of a modern day 'wild child'*. London: Academic Press.

V ✓ A K ✓ HRS HANDOUT 63

TOPIC: Failure to form attachment

ASSESSMENT EXERCISE

Training students to self- and peer-assess essays is a difficult task. An easy mistake to make is to show students an essay, give them the AQA mark scheme and then expect them to be able to mark accurately. As you may be aware from marking essays yourself, mark schemes can be vague, abstract and difficult to understand – and that's for the teachers!

A good way to build up students' knowledge, confidence and understanding of the mark schemes is to break it down into simple tasks. For example, **Handout 63** provides two example essay answers (taken from *The Complete Companion,* page 63). It asks students to complete simple tasks designed to help them deconstruct those essays into smaller markable chunks, and encourages them to consider the content of those essays.

Once your students have finished this task, you can discuss the essays as a class and what might be learned from them.

The following are the 'Examiner's comments' supplied with the answers in *The Complete Companion*:

Alice has taken a no-nonsense approach to this essay and written four paragraphs which are clear in their intent. The first two paragraphs are clearly AO1 (knowledge and description), accurate and detailed. Thus Alice gets ***4 out of 4 marks for AO1****.*

The final two paragraphs are all AO2, each one matching a descriptive paragraph. The evaluation of Hodges and Tizard's research is not well developed – why is this a weakness of the research? It is an explanation of the findings but not an evaluation. The second evaluative point is more of a conclusion than a criticism and contains unsubstantiated claims – what evidence is there to support the claim that they functioned adequately? Remember the three point rule – always present evidence to support your claim. Alice gets ***3 out of 4 marks for AO2****.*

Tom's answer is less effective than Alice's in many ways. Most importantly Tom has failed to focus on the question and included evidence about disruption of attachment rather than focussing solely on privation, as required. Tom would receive only ***2 out of 4 for AO1****.*

There is rather little AO2 material – the statement about being a case study and the conclusion drawn from the Czech Twin study are both potential AO2 points but have not been made effectively. For example just stating 'this was another case study' lacks that all important AO2 vocabulary to make it clear that this is a critical point (e.g. as 'however'). So ***0 out of 4 for AO2****.*

Alice's total for this question is ***7 out of 8*** *and Tom's is* ***2 out of 8****.*

TOPIC: Failure to form attachment

ROLLING SHOW – EFFECTS OF INSTITUTIONALISATION

'Rolling shows' are essentially slideshows of images that automatically change after a set period of time – 5 seconds, for example. Details on how to setup Rolling Shows using PowerPoint are outlined on page 5.

These slideshows make an excellent start to the lesson. I usually have one running with some appropriate music before the students arrive, so that from the moment they turn up, the topic and tone of the lesson are clear.

The effects of institutionalisation is a pertinent topic to try this technique with as there are some very moving images available on the Internet illustrating the conditions of the Romanian Orphanages in the 1980s–1990s. Simply searching on Google images will provide you with many possible images to use.

For those unsure of the history, Romania's orphan problem began under the Communist rule of Nicolae Ceausescu who banned abortion and denied access to contraception at a time of severe food and energy shortages. Many Romanians abandoned their newborn children, leaving thousands to suffer at under-funded, state-run orphanages.

TOPIC: Failure to form attachment

POST-IT NOTE ON A PICTURE

An idea for a plenary when teaching the effects of institutionalisation is to display an image of a child living in one of Romania's under-funded, state-run institutions (see last activity).

Give each student a post-it note and ask them to write the following information on it:

- Explain one way in which this child's situation might affect them later in life.
- Justify this with evidence.
- Extension: Give a counter argument or determining factor.

This plenary activity encourages students to summarise the research they have studied in class. This particular task works best after teaching Rutter *et al.*'s (2007) longitudinal study of Romanian orphans, but might be equally adaptable to other studies of institutionalisation, e.g. Hodges and Tizard (1989).

When I (MWG) taught the topic this year, I bought a large and cheap (I love Ikea!) frame to display the post-it notes, putting the image in the middle. That frame is now up in my room and provides quite a thought-provoking display for other students to read.

References

Hodges, J. and Tizard, B. (1989). Social and family relationships of ex-institutional adolescents. *Journal of Child Psychology and Psychiatry*, 30, 77–97.

Rutter, M., Colvert, E., Kreppner, J., Beckett, C., Castle, J., Groothues, C., Hawkins, A., Stevens, S.E. and Souga-Barke, E.J.S. (2007). Early adolescent outcomes for institutionally-deprived and non-deprived adoptees. I: Disinhibited attachment. *Journal of Child Psychology and Psychiatry*, 48(1), 17–30.

TOPIC: The impact of day care

THINKING ABOUT DAY CARE

A good way to start the day care topic is to simply mindmap or brainstorm some of the variables involved, and the potential arguments for and against day care.

One of the evaluation points students may later come back to is the idea that it is difficult to see clear patterns in the research on day care because of the different factors involved: type of day care, quality of day care, time spent in day care, etc. As such, it is important that students consider these factors before they begin to look at the impact of day care.

Why not start the branches of the mindmap off for students (see my example) and ask them to complete it using their own ideas. You can then have a class feedback session.

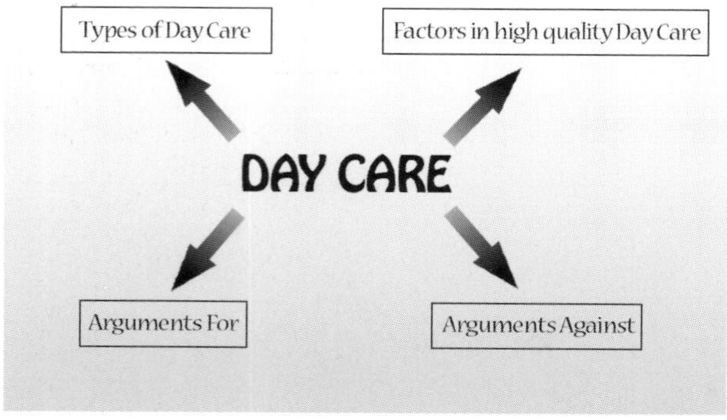

V A✓K ★HOG

TOPIC: The impact of day care

WHY IS THE DAY CARE DEBATE SO DIFFICULT TO CONCLUDE?

Once students have completed the previous activity 'Thinking about day care', use the collaborative learning structure 'group statements' (see page 3) and ask them the following question:

Why is it difficult to find definitive evidence and answers to the question 'Is day care harmful'?

Students will hopefully draw on the problem of so many factors being involved, making it almost impossible to draw definitive conclusions.

V✓A K✓ ★HOS

TOPIC: The impact of day care

ATTACHMENT AND DAY CARE – MAKING LINKS

The day care topic is usually the last section that we teach in developmental psychology. As a result, students should (we hope!) have a wealth of knowledge on attachment to draw on.

At the beginning of this topic it is important to emphasise to students that debating the merits of day care is not an opportunity for them to include unsubstantiated opinion and anecdotal evidence – 'Day care never did me any harm!'

One activity to discourage this is to get all students to write down any two key terms, studies, theories or explanations that they have studied so far in the topic: e.g., 'disruption of attachment', and 'secure base'.

Once all of your students have done this, ask them to explain how what they have written might be relevant to day care. This is usually possible with around 95% of the terms, studies, theories and explanations that students come up with, and they tend to have some really good ideas. More importantly, they are being encouraged to link their knowledge of attachment to a real-life application.

You could even make a display showing how the different topics you have covered can be linked to the day care debate.

V✓A K✓ ★HORS HANDOUT 64

TOPIC: The impact of day care

RESEARCH ACTIVITY: DAY CARE CORRELATIONAL STUDY

This activity is taken from *The Complete Companion*, page 54.

In the new specification, a far larger emphasis has been placed on students understanding research methods and 'How Science Works'. When students conduct their own research it enables them to find out more about the process of research design and gives them an opportunity to think more deeply about day care issues.

Much of the research relating to day care and its impact on social development has been correlational in nature.

As such, why not ask your students to conduct correlational research between day care and sociability (the tendency to be friendly towards and get on with others).

If day care has a positive effect on sociability, we would expect people who have spent more time in day care to be more sociable (a positive correlation).

Instructions for students are given on **Handout 64**.

Ethics

You may find this activity presents an opportunity for highlighting some potential ethical issues, such as protecting participants from psychological harm.

Measuring a person's sociability and relating this to past experiences may create anxiety. Therefore, this research should not be conducted with children under the age of 16, and data should be kept confidential.

V ✓ A K ✓ HORS HANDOUTS 65 and 66

TOPIC: Evaluating research on day care

EVALUATION REVISION CARDS

One of the most successful lesson structures I have used is a very simple one:

1 Starter
2 Introduce revision technique to students
3 Students use that revision technique to learn and remember a topic
4 Plenary – test the students at the end of the lesson with either a quiz or exam-style question.

These lessons seem to work particularly well because students are motivated to learn the material you give them (because they know they will be tested!), but also because they get to evaluate different revision techniques.

This activity, with **Handouts 65 and 66** is designed with this in mind.

Handout 65 provides an extract from *The Complete Companion*, page 54, which outlines some of the evaluation issues surrounding the NICHD (2003) study and correlational research generally.

Handout 66 provides five revision cards featuring questions relating to the evaluation of day care research. Students can cut these cards out and write their answers on the back.

When they have finished, they can test themselves and each other (e.g., by picking a card, answering it aloud, and then checking the answer written on the back).

At the end of the lesson, provide some kind of test, quiz, or exam-style question that will assess how well the revision technique worked for each student.

References

Belsky, J., Vandell, D.L., Burchinal, M., Clarke-Stewart, K.A., McCartney, K. and Owen, M.T. (The NICHD Early Child Care Research Network) (2007). Are there long-term effects of early child care? *Child Development*, 78(2), 681–701.
Dingfelder, S. (2004). Shortcomings of the 2003 NICHD day care study. *APA Monitor*, 35(9). www.apa.org/monitor/oct04/nichd.html
Lang, H. (2006). The trouble with day care. *Psychology Today*, http://psychologytoday.com/rss/pto-20050504-000004.html
NICHD Early Child Care Research Network (2003). Social functioning in first grade: Associations with earlier home and childcare predictors and with current classroom experiences. *Child Development*, 74, 1639–63.

V ✓ A K ✓ HORS HANDOUTS 67 and 68

TOPIC: Evaluating research on day care

REVIEWING DAY CARE EVIDENCE

Handouts 67 and **68** provide students with an opportunity to assemble research evidence related to day care and its impact on social development.

It also encourages students to explore the kind of evidence they could use in an essay. This highlights the fact that they could be specifically asked about the effects of day care on peer relations or aggression.

References

Belsky, J. and Rovine, M. (1988). Non-maternal care in the first year of life and the security of parent-infant attachment. *Child Development*, 59, 157–67.
Clarke-Stewart, K.A., Gruber, C.P. and Fitzgerald, L.M. (1994). *Children at Home and in Day Care*. Hillsdale NJ, Erlbaum.
Egeland, B. and Hiester, M. (1995). The long-term consequences of infant day-care and mother-infant attachment. *Child Development*, 66, 474–85.
Field, T. (1991). Quality infant day-care and grade school behavior and performance. *Child Development*, 62, 863–70.
Gregg, P., Washbrook, E., Propper, C. and Burgess, S. (2005), 'The Effects of a Mother's Return to Work Decision on Child Development in the UK', *Economic Journal*, 115 (501): 48–80.
Melhuish, E. C. (2004). *A Literature review of the impact of early years provision on young children, with emphasis given to children from disadvantaged backgrounds.* Institute for the Study of Children, prepared for the National Audit Office, Families and Social Issues. Birbeck: University of London.
NICHD Early Child Care Research Network (1997). The effects of infant child care on infant-mother attachment security: Results of the NICHD study of early child care. *Child Development*, 68(5), 860–79.
Pennebaker, J.W., Hendler, C.S., Durrett, M.E. and Richards, P. (1981). Social factors influencing absenteeism due to illness in nursery school children. *Child Development*, 52, 692–700.
Robertson, J., and Robertson, J. (1967–1973) *Young children in brief separation*. A film study. Concord Video and Film Council. New York University Film Library.
Sroufe, L.A., Egeland, B., Carlson, E.A. and Collins, W.A. (2005). *The Development of the Person: The Minnesota study of risk and adaption from birth to adulthood*. New York: Guilford.

V✓ A✓ K✓ ★ HORG

TOPIC: Evaluating research on day care

STUDENT DIMENSION LINE

Use the collaborative learning structure **'student dimension line'** outlined on page 3 to ask your students the following question:

'Overall, do you think day care has a positive or negative impact on children's social development?'

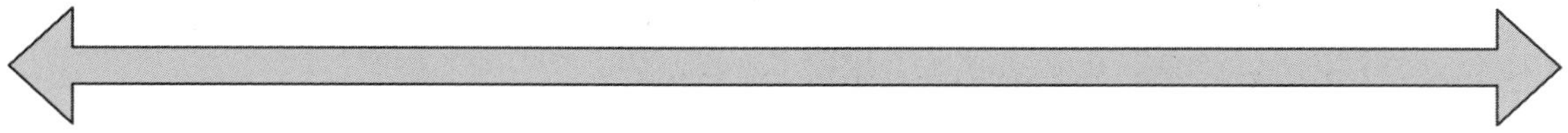
Day care has negative effects on social development
Day care has positive effects on social development

V✓ A✓ K✓ ★ OGS HANDOUTS 69 and 70

TOPIC: Implications of research into attachment and day care

TEACH EACH OTHER THE IMPLICATIONS OF RESEARCH!

This is another opportunity to increase your students' collaborative learning skills while delivering some of the developmental psychology content.

Split the class into mixed-ability groups of three and give each group **one** copy of **Handouts 69** or **70** (depending on which of the topics you wish them to learn about). The groups should then cut these handouts along the dotted lines.

Every member of each group should be given responsibility for teaching one of the sections from each sheet to the rest of their group.

The most important rule is that students may not read or copy out the information relating to their group members' sections. This encourages students to teach and learn content in different ways, such as using mnemonics, pictures, poems, stories, etc. Usually they are very creative in this respect.

Before they start the activity, also make it clear to students that they will tested (e.g., quiz, or exam question) afterwards, so the quality of their teaching will have a direct impact on their team members' performance. The aim of this is to ensure that the students do work collaboratively, because it is in their best interests to do so.

You could then repeat the activity with the other handout – i.e. either **Handout 69** or **70** depending which you gave to groups the first time round.

To test students after the task, I would set the following question:

'Outline two implications of research into attachment and/or day care for child care practices *(3 + 3 marks).'*

References

NICHD Early Child Care Research Network (1999). Child care and mother-child interactions in the first three years of life. *Developmental Psychology*, 35, 1399–1413.

Schaffer, H. R. (1998). *Making Decisions about Children.* Oxford: Blackwell.

Sylva, K., Melhuish, E., Sammons, P., Siraj-Blatchford, I., Taggert, B. and Elliot, K. (2003). The Effective Provision of Pre-School Education (EPPE) Project: Findings from the pre-school Period. Summary of findings. http://www.ioe.ac.uk/cdl/eppe/pdfs/eppe_brief2503.pdf London: Institute of Education.

V A K ✓ SHGO HANDOUTS 71 and 72

TOPIC: Introduction

EXPERIMENT PLANNING AND ANALYSIS

These two handouts can be used alongside other activities from this section to develop students' understanding of the research process. Early into the teaching of Unit 1 students can devise their own piece of research into an aspect of memory and use these sheets to help plan and later analyse findings as well as evaluate their work. It may be helpful to devote one lesson a week to research methods specifically, making links to aspects of memory and attachment research covered in recent lessons. Each research lesson deals with one aspect of the experiment planning or analysis sheet, using other activities to develop understanding. Towards the end of the lesson students could fill in the relevant section of their experiment planning or analysis handout. This acts as a good plenary, assessing their understanding of the lesson's content.

Working in small mixed ability groups will give more able students the opportunity to lead sessions.

V A ✓ K S HANDOUT 73

TOPIC: Validity

THREATS TO INTERNAL VALIDITY

You do not have to distinguish between internal and external validity at AS but you do at A2. In this activity students simply match each box to either participant reactivity or investigator effects. The first section requires students to identify three boxes as relating to participant reactivity, leaving three outlining investigator effects. In the second part of the handout students' understanding can be checked by asking them to identify which of the examples demonstrate reactivity and which highlight the impact of the investigator.

References

Greenspoon, J. (1955). The reinforcing effect of two spoken sounds on the frequency of two responses. *American Journal of Psychology*, 68, 409–16. http://garfield.library.upenn.edu/classics1982/A1982NP20300001.pdf

Orne, M.T. (1962). On the social psychology of the psychology experiment: With particular reference to demand characteristics and their implications. *American Psychologist*, 17, 776–83.

Roethlisberger, F.J. and Dickson, W.J. (1939). *Management and the Worker: an account of a research program conducted by the Western Electric Company, Chicago.* Cambridge, MA: Harvard University Press.

V ✓ A ✓ K S O HANDOUT 74

TOPIC: Validity

WORD WALL

Students seem to be able to understand reliability and validity when responding verbally to questions in class but use the terms interchangeably in their written work. This task aims to produce a glossary of the four terms for students to refer to when completing written tasks.

1 Students assign a colour to each of the terms shown in bold at the top of the wall.
2 They then colour code each brick below the terms so that it relates to the correct word displayed at the top of the wall. Each term has four related bricks.
3 Students then use all bricks of one colour to write a definition of the related key word.

This task could be differentiated by stating all students MUST produce one definition, most COULD create two definitions, a few SHOULD try to complete all four definitions. The class can then feedback their definitions by asking one student to read a definition out while the class listen and check all four bricks were referred to. This could then be done for the remaining three words. Alternatively, working in small groups students could check each other's definitions.

Follow-up starter activity

In the following lesson the word wall can be used for a quick game of taboo (see page 47). Students have to describe one form of validity or reliability without using that word's four words from the wall.

V A✓K ★G HANDOUT 75

TOPIC: Ethical issues

ETHICAL CONSIDERATIONS: PROPOSAL

Once students have planned their experiment, this activity requires them to present their proposed methodology to an ethical committee made up of their peers. This handout forms a research proposal in which students could use their textbook (pages 72–73 in *Complete Companion*) to help them identify any ethical issues in their procedure.

Students need to consider how they will overcome these issues to ensure the committee approve the study and allow it to take place.

V A✓K ★G HANDOUT 76

TOPIC: How psychologists deal with ethical issues

ETHICAL CONSIDERATIONS: COMMITTEE

After each group has completed the proposal these can be swapped among the groups so that each has the task of approving or rejecting another group's proposal based on ethical grounds.

Students could be directed to the British Psychological Society's Code of Ethics and Conduct (2006) to help them reach their decision. Visit http://www.bps.org.uk/the-society/code-of-conduct/ethical-principles-for-conducting-research-with-human-participants.cfm

Students' textbook (pages 72–73 in *Complete Companion*) will also help them consider the ethical issues the proposal has identified and the effectiveness of the proposed measures of dealing with the issues.

If a committee feels the proposal is not adequate they must suggest ways of dealing with the issues that the researchers could carry out to allow the investigation to take place.

V A✓K ★HGSO HANDOUT 77

TOPIC: How psychologists deal with ethical issues

WHAT IF?

Students work in small groups (or individually if you wish to make it a competition) to suggest 20 outcomes if ethical guidelines were not in place. The more imaginative the better.

For example, 'I would have less to revise for the Unit 1 exam', 'you could conduct experiments such as jumping out on young children in the supermarket to see if they seek their mother for comfort (attachment)'.

V✓A✓K ★S HANDOUT 78

TOPIC: Experiments and hypotheses

DIRECTIONAL OR NON-DIRECTIONAL?

A little task that aims to acts as a guide for hypothesis writing for students' own research projects. Students first highlight the IV and DV in each statement to illustrate the need for both variables to be identified. Once this has been completed they revisit each hypothesis and decide if it makes a directional or non-directional prediction.

V A✓K ★O HANDOUT 79

TOPIC: Experiments and hypotheses

WRITING HYPOTHESES

Students may need a little more support than simple examples of hypotheses (as in the directional or non-directional handout) when constructing a hypothesis for the first time. This handout provides a writing frame with step-by-step instructions and examples to help them produce a fully operationalised prediction.

V A K✓ ★S HANDOUT 80

TOPIC: Experimental design

DESIGN STRENGTHS AND WEAKNESSES

Students can take a small short cut with their revision if they realise the strengths of the independent measures design are the weaknesses of the repeated measures design and vice versa. By completing the lower boxes relating to counterbalancing and matched pairs, this handout forms a revision sheet for experimental design.

V A✓K ★G HANDOUT 81

TOPIC: Experimental design

DEFENDING THE DESIGN

To develop students' appreciation for the strengths and weaknesses of different experimental designs, students are required to work in small groups to defend different research designs in the three situations shown. This task mimics the 'research methods in context questions' that may appear in the exam, which expects students to refer to the stimulus material in their responses. Placing students in groups encourages discussion of each situation.

This may help students consider their own choice of design when conducting their own investigation.

V A✓K✓ ★HR HANDOUT 82

TOPIC: Extraneous variables

SORT IT OUT!

This activity requires students to access higher order thinking skills as they make judgements about the word shown on each card. The second part of the handout involves students using their understanding from the sorting task.

1 Students cut out the cards, making sure they keep the instructions safe.
2 They then arrange the cards based on one of the categories suggested on the handout (or any other you think of).
3 The class can feedback ideas or share their ideas with a partner.

The cards could be produced on a large scale with one student being given a note card each. Different corners of the classroom can represent categories with students moving to the corner they feel they belong to. By having more than one student with the same note card students can see whether they agree with each other. In this activity certain students can be given certain note cards based on their level of understanding.

Extension task

Students who complete their note card sort quickly and feel confident in their understanding can complete the 'dealing with extraneous variables' table found below the note cards.

V A✓K ★O HANDOUT 83

TOPIC: Extraneous variables

TEACHER TIME

This handout introduces students to the fun that teachers have marking students work! Students read the passage and mark the work using the symbols shown to the right of the page. Students could award themselves one mark for each error they spotted and labelled correctly. The development tasks ask students to provide the author with suggestions for ways to improve their work.

V A K✓ ★GS HANDOUTS 84–86

TOPIC: Quantitative data analysis

CALCULATING DATA

After reading about Rich's study at the beginning of **Handout 84**, students calculate the different measures of central tendency. Students can use their textbook (page 80 in *Complete Companion*) if needed, to help them calculate each measure of central tendency and consider their usefulness in the 'reviewing measures of central tendency' at the bottom of **Handout 85**.

Most calculators should have a standard deviation button students can use to understand the spread of the data around the mean in Rich's data (shown on **Handout 84**). If any students did well at GCSE Maths or are studying the subject at A-level, they could be the experts of the class and work with their peers who find maths daunting.

V A✓K ★GS HANDOUT 87

TOPIC: Laboratory and field experiments

BLENDING BRAINS

This activity involves collaborative learning; encouraging students to listen to others' ideas and combine them with their own to produce fully developed answers. As well as furthering their understanding of research methods, students are revising a key study relating to the duration of STM.

Students complete the first box of each row individually. If they are unsure of the answer it doesn't matter but they do need to attempt an answer. Reassure them it does not matter if they are wrong. Once each question has been answered students form pairs to share ideas. Any additional ideas gained (or corrections made) from this discussion should be added in the second box. Finally students use the third box to produce a detailed and accurate answer to each question. Students could either be placed in mixed ability pairs providing more able students an opportunity to reinforce their understanding as they help their peers or pair students of similar ability, leaving you time to work with students more likely to struggle with the work.

Reference

Peterson, L.R. and Peterson, M.J. (1959). Short-term retention of individual verbal items. *Journal of Experimental Psychology*, 58, 193–8.

V A✓K ★O HANDOUT 88

TOPIC: Natural experiments

WHICH WORD?

The first task provides a revision opportunity for an important study in EWT and anxiety. Students read through the passage and on meeting the bold text, circle the correct word or phrase.

Answers – independent variable, dependent variable, natural experiment, does not, IV, DV, unethical, privation, causal relationships, validity.

Task 2 requires students to identify whether the study outlined is a laboratory, field or natural experiment and then to give one advantage or disadvantage of that method, making sure their answer is in context.

For example, the study into primary school reading schemes is a natural experiment. One disadvantage of this may be that the teacher of the children from one of the primary schools may have been a better teacher or the children in the class are better behaved, meaning these children will do better at reading anyway regardless of the scheme they follow.

Reference

Christianson, S.A. and Hubinette, B. (1993). Hands up! A study of witness' emotional reactions and memories associated with bank robberies. *Applied Cognitive Psychology*, 7, 365–79.

V✓A✓K ★HO HANDOUT 89

TOPIC: Natural experiments

PSYCHOBABBLE

The handout enables students to clearly represent the various views relating to the use of experiments in psychology. The simplest way to use the activity is to imagine a group of psychologists talking, with each speech bubble belonging to a different speaker. More able students may be able to create a conversation between two speakers, turning the conversation into a debate, with each point building upon or stemming from the previous comment.

For example: 'Have you considered the benefits of field experiments they… *…have more ecological validity than lab experiments as they take place in a real life situation such as a town centre instead of in a classroom.'*

'It seems to be you are forgetting… *…that conducting a study in a natural environment can mean a reduction in your ability to control extraneous variables which could affect the validity of your findings.'*

'I see your point but… *…what is the point of carrying out a study that tells us nothing about real life? Steps can be taken to limit the impact of some extraneous variables.'*

V ✓ A ✓ K OS HANDOUT 90

TOPIC: Observational methods and techniques

SAY WHAT YOU SEE

Split the class into two groups. Half need to summarise the information on naturalistic observation using drawings and a maximum of three words. It may help students to work in a group first to decide on how to visually represent the passage. The other half of the class do the same with the information relating to controlled observations.

Students then find a partner who was given a different passage to them. After explaining their pictures to each other, they each write a summary of their friend's drawings in the right-hand box. Should students complete this task quickly, they can consider any information that was not represented in the picture and add these details to the left-hand box.

References

Ainsworth, M.D.S. (1967). *Infancy in Uganda: Child care and the growth of love*. Baltimore: Johns Hopkins University Press.

Ainsworth, M.D.S. and Wittig, B.A. (1969). Attachment and exploratory behaviour of one-year-olds in a strange situation. In B.A. Foss (Ed.), *Determinants of Infant Behaviour* (Vol. 4). London: Methuen.

V ✓ A ✓ K OS HANDOUT 91

TOPIC: Observational methods and techniques

LEVELS OF THINKING

Bloom's taxonomy demonstrates the wide range of thinking skills that can be employed when considering information. These range from the simple, lower order thinking skills through to challenging higher order thinking skills. In this activity each question is more challenging than the one before as they progress along Bloom's taxonomy of thinking skills. The question types can be used as a form of differentiation with all students completing the lower order thinking questions, most of the class attempting both lower and middle order thinking questions and a few students tackling all three sections.

As with other tasks in this topic area, the handout can be used as a revision tool for other sections found in Unit 1 of the AQA A Specification. This activity encourages students to apply their knowledge of observations as a research method to a specific area of psychology.

References

Ainsworth, M.D.S. (1967). *Infancy in Uganda: Child care and the growth of love*. Baltimore: Johns Hopkins University Press.

Ainsworth, M.D.S. and Wittig, B.A. (1969). Attachment and exploratory behaviour of one-year-olds in a strange situation. In B.A. Foss (Ed.), *Determinants of Infant Behaviour* (Vol. 4). London: Methuen.

V A ✓ K GS HANDOUTS 92 and 93

TOPIC: Designing observational research

ORGANISING A NATURALISTIC OBSERVATION

The class can carry out a naturalistic observation either in small groups or as a teacher-led activity. Students could carry out an observation around their school or college, investigating topics such as:

Gender and size of social group – students could investigate whether differences can be seen in the groups their fellow students spend lunch time with. Sitting in the canteen or lunch hall, students identify single sex groups and count the number of members in them.

The 'organising an observation' handout can be used in conjunction with the 'naturalistic observation' handout. **Handout 92** acts as a prompt sheet to help students develop an idea for their observation and suggests issues that need to be considered before the observation is carried out. Once the plan has been completed at the bottom of **Handout 92** students can use **Handout 93** 'naturalistic observation' to record their investigation.

V A✓K ★G HANDOUT 94

TOPIC: Evaluating observational research

ROLL WITH IT

Working in groups, students take it in turns to role two dice. Taking either one face of one dice or adding the two faces together students answer the question related to that number. For example, if two dice thrown show 2 and 5, students can chose from question 2, 5 or (2+5=) 7. Students have space below each question to write the answer given.

Homework activity

Once all questions have been answered, students check each answer is correct using their notes and/or the textbook, making corrections or adding any missed details if needed.

Students could even score their group's performance. Starting with 24 marks, every correction needed or additional detail that needed to be added results in the deduction of one mark.

V A✓K✓ ★O HANDOUT 95

TOPIC: Selection of participants

SELECTING PARTICIPANTS

This is a quick revision activity once students have gained an understanding of sampling techniques.

Main activity

Using stickers, sweets or any other 'goodie', demonstrate the different sampling techniques to the class.

1. Random sampling: before the lesson place all students' names in a plastic wallet. After introducing the terms sampling and target population, ask one student to pick five names from the wallet. These five students receive a goodie. Ask students to suggest the strengths and weaknesses of this method to create a sample.
2. Opportunity sampling: give a goodie to the five students nearest to you, explaining that you took the opportunity to give out goodies to the first people you meet. Again ask students for their views of this form of sampling.
3. Volunteer sampling: ask students 'who wants a goodie?' (make sure there are enough to go around!). As with the previous two methods, ask students to give advantages and disadvantages of the technique.

Students should then complete the handout based on their experience of the techniques and class suggestions.

V A✓K ★O HANDOUT 96

TOPIC: Selection of participants

SAMPLING TECHNIQUES

This homework activity can be used following the 'selecting participants' handout. After reading the different situations, students identify the sampling technique used, recording this in the box below each stimulus, then suggest possible strengths and weaknesses of the technique for the specific situation.

This task aims to reinforce the need to refer to context in their responses in exam questions.

V A✓K ★O S HANDOUT 97

TOPIC: Self-report techniques

TABOO

The taboo activity requires students to focus on issues that need to be considered when constructing a questionnaire. Each statement on the handout describes an issue without actually mentioning the issue by name (the taboo word).

After reading each taboo statement students decide which taboo word (shown on the right-hand side of the handout) they are describing. Students then rewrite the definition using the related words.

An extension activity follows in which students create their own taboo statement for the words 'structured interview' and 'unstructured interview'. Their taboo statements should not include the term or the related words shown. Once completed, these could be shared with the rest of the class who can try to identify the taboo words.

O H HANDOUT 98

TOPIC: Evaluating self-report techn…

SELF-REPORT VENN…

Venn diagrams visually represent the re… between two concepts. The top half of … requires students to identify the similarities … differences between interviews and questio… For example, one similarity is that both can c… closed or open questions. One difference cou… how they are delivered; questionnaires do not … a researcher to be present (postal), interviews r… a researcher (or employee of researcher) to be p…

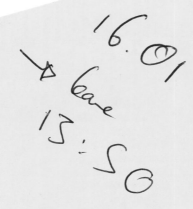

…ts to do the same …ch method. For …y would suffer if …ifference would …tor effects, …tor effects. … examples as a

V A✓K ✓S HANDOUT 99

TOPIC: Evaluating self-report techniques

EVALUATING SELF-REPORT TECHNIQUES

This handout provides students with an opportunity to consider the issues surrounding self-report procedures (and volunteer sampling) as well as revising Hazan and Shaver's research into adult attachments. Students simply read the outline of the love styles study using their textbook (pages 96–97 in *Complete Companion*) and complete the questions surrounding the passage.

Extension or homework activity

Students could be challenged to create their handout using this format for another Unit 1 (or 2) study. Questions could be about a range of aspects from the research method topic.

References

Hazan, C. and Shaver, P.R. (1987). Romantic love conceptualised as an attachment process. *Journal of Personality and Social Psychology*, 52, 511–24.
Bowlby, J. (1969). *Attachment and Love, Volume 1: Attachment*. London: Hogarth.

V✓A K✓ S G HANDOUTS 100 and 101

TOPIC: Studies using a correlational analysis

CONDUCTING CORRELATIONS

A mini research project to illustrate the negative correlation, this activity works well if students have access to computers within the lesson to calculate scores and produce a graph. Use of ICT in lessons is one area of focus in Ofsted inspections.

1 Before collecting data, students write a hypothesis, typing up their hypothesis in a word processor. Opening sentences for the hypothesis can be found on **Handout 100**.

   There is a positive correlation between…
   There is a negative correlation between…
   There is no correlation between…

2 Students use the questionnaire shown on **Handout 101** to ask 10 participants to complete the questions on exam stress and exam confidence. This handout has a number of question slips to reduce the amount of A4 photocopies needed for a class set.

3 When data has been collected, students input scores into Excel and carry out a correlation coefficient analysis (Insert/function/correl).

4 Students can also visually represent their findings by producing a scattergraph. (Highlight data. Select <insert> <chart> <XY scatter> and press <next> and <next> again.) Add a suitable title, and axis titles, then select <finish>.)

5 Once the graph has formed between students write a conclusion stating what the findings were (including the correlation coefficient) and if there is a relationship between the variables exam stress and exam confidence.

   Is it positive, negative or is there no correlation? Can the hypothesis be accepted (was the prediction right)?

Students use the information sheet to check whether their results are significant (if they are/are not, explain what this means).

This activity can also be used when considering workplace stress and hardy personalities in Unit 2 Biological Psychology. Students could produce a literature review of research into this area and explain their findings in relation to previous research.

V ✓ A ✓ K ★ S O HANDOUT 102

TOPIC: Case studies

USING CASE STUDIES

A visual breakdown of the various aspects of case studies into memory (pages 100-101 in *Complete Companion*). Focusing on memory research will help students revise for Unit 1's Cognitive Psychology topic at the same time as considering the use of case studies as a research tool. Once students have identified the illness or injury suffered, the effect on memory, and evaluated the methodology, this information can be used to complete the second task.

'Having considered the use of case studies to research memory and the strengths and weakness of the method I feel that…'

This task is differentiated:

All students **must** explain one strength and one weakness of using case studies to research memory then make their own conclusion relating to their usefulness in researching memory.

Most students **should** explain two strengths and two weaknesses of using case studies to research memory then make their own conclusion relating to their usefulness in researching memory.

Some students **could** explain two strengths and two weaknesses of using case studies to research memory and consider their validity before reaching their own conclusion about the usefulness of case studies when researching memory.

V A ✓ K ★ H HANDOUT 103

TOPIC: Case studies

CASE STUDY CRITIQUE

The task requires students to form their own opinion about case studies as a method of investigation. After reading each statement students decide whether they (strongly) agree or (strongly) disagree and give reasons for their point of view. Higher order thinking is needed as students are forced to develop an opinion of their own rather than rote learn a list of strengths and weaknesses.

V A K ✓ ★ H G HANDOUT 104

TOPIC: Content analysis

CONTENT ANALYSIS: TV TODAY

By carrying out their own mini-content analysis students will gain an understanding of the decisions that need to be made when planning the procedure and analysing their findings.

Working in mixed ability groups, students plan their own investigation to identify the television available to viewers in society today. A little background on the notion of media's influence on pro and anti-social behaviour may add context to activity.

Students decide on the channels to be included in the analysis and the time frame the procedure will follow, e.g. 7:00pm to 11:00pm for one day. Justifications for choices are asked for to encourage reflection on the decision-making process. Once students have thought of programme types and how these will be operationalised, the group can either watch television in their free time as dictated by their time frame or analyse a television guide. Students record the amount of times the different types of programmes occur on their chosen channels within their time frame. Once the analysis has taken place students should analyse their findings using descriptive statistics and give graphical representations to strengthen their understanding of this aspect of research methods. Finally students reflect on their investigation by answering the questions found in the 'evaluation of findings' box.

V A✓K ★HO HANDOUT 105

TOPIC: Content analysis

ONE WORD REVIEW

1 Students read the passage outlining qualitative and quantitative data. They then spend time considering which words are most important to the meaning of the passage and highlight these.
2 Using one of these words or a new word not from the passage, students choose one word to represent the passage and explain why they have chosen this word. This task is difficult as two forms of data are contained in the passage. A simple option may be to choose the word 'data' from which the two different types of data, qualitative and quantitative, can be explained. More able students may develop their own words such as 'amount' which can be used to represent amount of data gathered in terms of large sample (quantitative data) or amount referring to the depth for each participant (qualitative data).

Students have the opportunity to record their peers' ideas to further develop their appreciation of the different data types.

V A✓K ★S HANDOUTS 106–108

TOPIC: Other research methods and techniques

WORK IT OUT WORD SEARCH

Students work alone or in pairs to answer the questions relating to the work it out word search. Once questions have been answered students hunt for these words in the grid (answers are provided on **Handout 108**). If students cannot find an answer to a question, they could work in reverse by identifying words in the grid and matching them to the relevant question. A reflection section is provided below the word search grid to help students consider their level of understanding and strategies they can carry out to improve.

References

Ainsworth, M.D.S. (1967). *Infancy in Uganda: Child care and the growth of love*. Baltimore: Johns Hopkins University Press.
Ainsworth, M.D.S. and Wittig, B.A. (1969). Attachment and exploratory behaviour of one-year-olds in a strange situation. In B.A. Foss (Ed.), *Determinants of Infant Behaviour* (Vol. 4). London: Methuen.
Deffenbacher, K.A., Bornstein, B.H., Penrod, S.D. and McGorty, E.K. (2004). A meta-analytic review of the effects of high stress on eyewitness testimony. *Law and Human Behaviour*, 28, 687–706.
Haney, C., Banks, W.C. and Zimbardo, P.G. (1973). Study of prisoners and guards in a simulated prison. *Naval Research Reviews*, 9, 1–17. Washington, DC: Office of Naval Research.
Hodges, J. and Tizard, B. (1989). Social and family relationships of ex-institutional adolescents. *Journal of Child Psychology and Psychiatry*, 30, 77–9.
Schaffer, H.R. and Emerson, P.E. (1964). The development of social attachments in infancy. *Monographs of the Society for Research into Child Development*, 29(3) Serial No. 94.
Van Ijzendoorn, M.H. and Kroonenberg, P.M. (1988). Cross-cultural patterns of attachment: A meta-analysis of the Strange Situation. *Child Development*, 59, 147–56.

V A✓K ★O HANDOUT 109

TOPIC: Other research methods and techniques

TRUE OR FALSE?

Students use *Complete Companion* pages 104–105 to decide whether each statement is true or false. If true, students can expand the statement by adding further details in the box below the statement. If false, the space is used to write an accurate version of the statement.

Homework

1 Students could produce their own true or false activity for another section of the research methods topic. These can then be swapped with another student.
2 For the second homework, students complete the true or false activity they have received.
3 The final homework requires students to return the completed true or false sheet to the author who marks it, checking corrects are accurate and expansions make sense.

References

Köhnken, G., Milne, R., Memon, A. and Bull, R. (1999). The cognitive interview: a meta-analysis. *Psychology, Crime and Law*, 5, 1–35.
Schaffer, H.R. and Emerson, P.E. (1964). The development of social attachments in infancy. *Monographs of the Society for Research into Child Development*, 29(3) Serial No. 94.

V A✓K ★HS HANDOUT 110

TOPIC: The body's response to stress

LET ME TELL YOU

At the start of the lesson the class could discuss what stress feels like. If they have just sat an AS exam or seen a scary movie, they could think back to how they felt physically and emotionally. If students have already covered Unit 1, you can remind them of the Yerkes-Dodson law and ask them why stress may have been useful to our survival in the past (energy = fight or flight, 'scared stiff' = keep still so less obvious to predators). I (RCG) begin the lesson talking students through a flowchart of the SAM pathway and the HPA system. More able students may benefit from being given a range of images (such as hypothalamus, adrenal gland, adrenaline, etc.) and trying to order them in a chain of events.

Working in pairs, students use the information boxes at the top of the handout to write two explanations of the stress reaction: one for a year 7 student, one for an AS student. Students should be advised they need to think carefully about how much detail to include and the terminology they would use. Year 7s may even benefit from an analogy or a picture/diagram to help their understanding. If the pairs are of mixed ability, they tackle both explanations, pairs of weaker ability may wish to just tackle one, allowing longer to be spent on the task.

Extension idea

Students could swap explanations with another pair and score the work out of ten for the following criteria:

Suitability for age range
Clarity of explanation
Use of terminology
Accuracy of explanation.

V A✓K ★S HANDOUT 111

TOPIC: The body's response to stress

DEFINITION DOCTOR

The body's response to stress involves a lot of biological terminology. The handout forms a mini glossary to help students understand the information in their textbook (pages 118–19 in *Complete Companion*). The words to be defined are followed by 'tips' to help students remember the bodily response, e.g. medulla is in the middle on the adrenal gland so think 'M for middle and medulla'.

Following the activities on **Handouts 110 and 111** students could be encouraged to produce visual diagrams of the sympathomedullary pathway and the pituitary-adrenal system. This can be displayed around the classroom as constant reminders of the stress response. You could even hold a 'biological art' exhibition: the more imaginative, colourful, detailed diagrams the better.

V A✓K ★O HANDOUT 112

TOPIC: Stress-related illness: The immune system

IMMUNE ISSUES

Students complete the four boxes, each relating to a piece of research into the effects of stress on the immune system. Headings 'Research into…' are provided should studies investigate similar stressors. The right-hand 'measure' column of each box provides space to record the biological measure used. For example, Kiecolt-Glaser *et al.* (1984) assessed NK cell activity in blood samples taken before and after exam period. Students will find research into stress and the immune system in their textbooks. Should your class be using the *Complete Companion*, page 120 provides two studies into examination stress while page 121 outlines two studies into relationship stress. The three boxes at the bottom of the handout require students to consider the usefulness of such studies, which can act as a writing frame for an evaluation of research into stress and immune function.

Reference

Kiecolt-Glaser, J.K., Garner, W., Speicher, C.E., Penn, G.M., Holliday, J. and Glaser, R. (1984). Psychosocial modifiers of immunocompetence in medical students. *Psychosomatic Medicine*, 46, 7–14.

V A✓K ★HR HANDOUT 113

TOPIC: Stress-related illness: The immune system

HEALTH SCARE

After reading the news article, students are asked to consider how different groups in society would react to the story. Students could work in small teams, each focused on one of the groups mentioned. Differentiation can be used here to stretch more able or biologically minded students, asking them to predict the reaction of doctors or psychologists, while less able students could write from less scientific stances. If using this as a homework task, students could be given free choice group(s).

Should you have access to a video recorder, students could use their responses to this activity to produce a news section or health documentary where different concerned groups share their views or knowledge. Once recorded, the film can be viewed again nearer exam time as part of a revision session.

V A✓K ★HSO HANDOUT 114

TOPIC: Stress-related illness: Cardiovascular and psychiatric disorders

STRESS AND THE HEART

Students read the answer to the question: 'Explain the link between stress, the cardiovascular system and cardiovascular disorders', then highlight five words they deem most important from the passage. Ask the class to call out their choices and write them on the board. The class then agree on the five words and write them in the boxes below the passage. Students then write their own answer to the question ensuring that the five words chosen by the class are included in their response. Asking them to highlight each word in their own (or another's) writing acts as a good check and encourages them to read over written work.

V A✓K ★SOG HANDOUT 115

TOPIC: Stress-related illness: Cardiovascular and psychiatric disorders

MATCH MAKING

This summary exercise requires students to use page 122 of the *Complete Companion* to match each word to the correct study by writing that word in the relevant box. Those who finish quickly can become experts. These experts move round the class offering help to others. They are not allowed to tell their peers the answer but can give clues to help the student work out which bit the word belongs to. For example, a clue for the word fatal could be 'this study used participants with reduced blood flow to their heart'.

If your students are not using this textbook, you could challenge the class to produce a similar handout for the studies covered in their textbook. These can then be exchanged among each other and completed.

References

Orth-Gomér, K., Wamala, S.P., Horsten, M., Schenck-Gustafsson, K., Schneiderman, N. and Mittleman, M.A. (2000). Marital stress worsens prognosis in women with coronary heart disease: The Stockholm Female Coronary Risk Study. *Journal of American Medical Association*, 284, 3008–14.

Russek, H. (1962). Emotional stress and coronary heart disease in American physicians, dentists and lawyers. *American Journal of Medical Science*, 243, 716–25.

Sheps, D.S., McMahon, R.P., Becker, L., Carney, R.M., Freedland, K.E., Cohen, J.D., Sheffield, D., Goldberg, A.D., Ketterer, M.W., Pepine, C.J., Raczynski, J.M., Light, K., Krantz, D.S., Stone, P.H., Knatterud, G.L. and Kaufmann, P.G. (2002). Mental stress-induced ischemia and all-cause mortality in patients with coronary artery disease: results from the Psychophysiological Investigations of myocardial Ischemia study. *Circulation*, 105, 1780–4.

Williams, J.E., Paton, C.C., Siegler, I.C., Eigenbrodt, M.L., Nieto, F.J. and Tyroler, H.A. (2000). Anger proneness predicts coronary heart disease risk: Prospective analysis from the atherosclerosis risk in communities (AIRC) study. *Circulation,* 101 (17), 2034–9.

V A ✓ K O HANDOUT 116

TOPIC: Stress-related illness: Cardiovascular and psychiatric disorders

TRIPLETS

The words shown at the start of the handout all relate to research into stress-related illness. For each set, students choose three words that link together in some way. The lines to the right of the set give students the opportunity to explain the connection between the words.

There is no right or wrong answer as long as a connection can be made. Differentiation can take the form of must, should, could: all students must do one set, most could do two sets, some should try to aim for three or more.

For example: women – marital conflict – heart. Explanation: Orth-Gomér *et al.* (2000) showed that among married or co-habiting women, marital conflict was associated with a 2.9 fold increase in recurrent events, e.g. heart attacks, if they had existing coronary heart disease.

Reference

Orth-Gomér, K., Wamala, S.P., Horsten, M., Schenck-Gustafsson, K., Schneiderman, N. and Mittleman, M.A. (2000). Marital stress worsens prognosis in women with coronary heart disease: The Stockholm Female Coronary Risk Study. *Journal of American Medical Association*, 284, 3008–14.

V ✓ A K H O HANDOUT 117

TOPIC: Stress-related illness: Cardiovascular and psychiatric disorders

SMILEY SCALE

A simple activity asking students to reflect on their understanding of the more biological aspects of this topic: the bodily response, immune system and cardiovascular disorders. Once students decide where they fall on the smiley scale, they need to set themselves targets to either move towards the right of the scale or remain at the top spot. Students tend to find target setting difficult, tending to make broad, immeasurable targets such as 'revise more'. Encourage students to make specific, measurable targets. For example, 'I will write a 50-word summary of one study into stress and the immune system by ______(date) and ask my teacher to mark it'. Their targets could form part of their homework for that week.

V A ✓ K S O HANDOUT 118

TOPIC: Life changes

TRUE OR FALSE?

This is a simple activity that provides space for students to develop their judgments. Students first decide whether the statement is true or false. If a statement is true, they can use the space below to develop the statement by adding more details. If false, the space below offers an opportunity to correct the statement.

Homework idea

Students use their worksheet as a guide to produce a half page outline of Holmes and Rahe's SRRS.

References

Holmes, T.H. and Rahe, R.H. (1967). The social readjustment rating scale. *Journal of Psychosomatic Research*, 11, 213–18.

Rahe, R.H., Mahan, J. and Arthur, R. (1970). Prediction of near-future health-change from subjects' preceding life changes. *Journal of Psychosomatic Research*, 14, 401–6.

V A✓ K✓ ★ O R HANDOUT 119

TOPIC: Life changes

CHAT ABOUT CHANGES

Students move round the classroom asking their peers for information to complete each speech bubble. Students can use their textbook (page 124 in *Complete Companion*) to identify points they can explain to their peers.

Each bubble first provides a line for the speaker's name to be recorded. This helps assessment and also deters any silly comments. Speech bubbles cover a range of abilities from simple identification of key words to higher order thinking such as identifying importance. These can be taken in to assess learning of the whole class. For example, if one student appears on a number of sheets saying the same comment, it may suggest they need more help to broaden the scope of their understanding. You could even offer a reward for the student who appears on the most sheets making the widest range of comments.

V A✓ K✓ ★ G S R H HANDOUT 120

TOPIC: Daily hassles

THE SIX HATS

After students have developed an understanding of daily hassles and life changes, this activity can be used to consider the usefulness of daily hassles as an explanation of stress. Assign students to a hat. Students sit with students of the same hat and work together to complete their section. The red and white hats should be accessible to most students, whereas green hat and blue hat require higher order thinking. Once students have finished their section they then form new groups (three students of different hats for two sessions seems to work better than a single session with a group of six) to share their ideas.

See page 11 for an explanation of the meaning of the six hats.

References

Bouteyre, E., Maurel, M. and Bernard, J-L. (2007). Daily hassles and depressive symptoms among first year psychology students in France: The role of coping and social support. *Stress and Health*, 23 (2), 93.

DeLongis, A., Coyne, J.C., Dakof, G., Folkman, S. and Lazarus, R.S. (1982). The impact of daily hassles, uplifts and major life events to health status. *Health Psychology*, 1, 119–36.

Gervais, R. (2005). *Daily hassles beaten back by uplifting experiences*. Poster presented at British Psychological Society Annual Conference, University of Manchester.

V A✓ K ★ S O R HANDOUT 121

TOPIC: Daily hassles

OPINIONATED OCTOPUS

Challenge students to fill the placards held by the opinionated octopus with evaluation points. Students can either fill each placard with separate unconnected points, or identify two points and expand these. The second variation may be more suited to more able students. For this version the top two placards held above the octopus' head contain the two initial evaluation points. The point on the left is then developed by moving anticlockwise to the next space and developing the initial point, further commentary is then written in the two boxes below. The same procedure is applied to the top right placard, moving clockwise to the bottom.

References

Bouteyre, E., Maurel, M. and Bernaud, J-L. (2007). Daily hassles and depressive symptoms among first year psychology students in France: The role of coping and social support. *Stress and Health*, 23 (2), 93.

DeLongis, A., Coyne, J.C., Dakof, G., Folkman, S. and Lazarus, R.S. (1982). The impact of daily hassles, uplifts and major life events to health status. *Health Psychology*, 1, 119–36.

Gervais, R. (2005). *Daily hassles beaten back by uplifting experiences*. Poster presented at British Psychological Society Annual Conference, University of Manchester.

V A✓ K O HANDOUT 122

TOPIC: Workplace stress

STRESS AND WORK

Students complete the questionnaire themselves or interview a friend or relative. The brief questionnaire aims to give an insight into workload, control and role conflict. Students could use these simple questions to devise a much more in-depth questionnaire. Data can be compiled as a class and measures of central tendency and dispersion can be calculated for each component of workplace stress. Opportunities for investigation include gender differences and difference in stress between school students and full time workers.

To develop their AO1 notes students use their textbook (pages 128–9 in *Complete Companion*) to complete a summary of research into the three listed components of workplace stressors. Students then apply their understanding of research to the data collected to produce a report on their interviewee. This activity gives students an insight into one aspect of occupational psychology and may give them possible career ideas.

V✓ A✓ K G HANDOUT 123

TOPIC: Workplace stress

ESSAY PLAN

This planning handout provides a visual breakdown of the different sections that need to be covered to fully address the question: 'Outline and evaluate two or more factors that lead to stress in the workplace (12 marks)'. Once students have completed their plan they swap their sheet with another student. I (RCG) would use mixed ability grouping here; a more able student exchanges ideas with a less able student. This will allow the less able student to see a model of a detailed essay plan, while the more able student will cement their understanding by considering what the lesson plan they are assessing requires to improve in quality. If a section needs to be edited, students write the letter of that section in one of the boxes for the amendment required shown at the bottom of the handout.

V A✓ K O HANDOUT 124

TOPIC: Workplace stress

EXAM PRACTICE

Students initially judge the answers provided by Alice and Tom by highlighting the AO1 and AO2 comments and scoring each response to the exam question: 'Discuss how factors in the workplace may affect stress (8 marks)'. Page 143 of *Complete Companion* provides commentary on each answer and the marks they would have been awarded. Using Alice's and Tom's work as a guide, students answer the 12-mark question: 'Outline and evaluate the contribution of two or more factors to stress in the workplace'. It may help students to fold their paper in two and list on one side points to include from the handout and on the other side points to include from their own notes.

References

Johansson, G., Aronsson, G. and Lindström, B.O. (1978). Social psychological and neuro-endocrine stress reactions in highly mechanised work. *Ergonomics*, 21, 583–99.

Lazarus, R.S. (1995). Vexing research problems inherent in cognitive-mediational theories of emotion and some solutions. *Psychological Inquiry*, 6, 183–265.

Marmot, M., Bosma, H., Hemingway, H., Brunner, E. and Stansfield, S. (1997). Contribution of job control and other risk factors to social variation in health disease incidence. *The Lancet*, 350, 235–9.

V A✓K ☆O HANDOUT 125

TOPIC: Personality factors and stress

PERSONALITY

This handout presents a writing frame which students can then use to answer the following question: 'Discuss what psychological research has shown about the way personality affects a person's experience of stress (12 marks)'. Students are required to develop evaluations using research from Friedman and Rosenman, and Kobasa as well as considering the usefulness of these studies. By providing limited space and setting a specific word limit students are encouraged to be concise in their writing.

References

Friedman, M. and Rosenman, R.H. (1959). Association of specific overt behaviour pattern with blood and cardiovascular findings. *Journal of American Medical Association*, 169, 1286–96.

Kobasa, S.C. (1979). Stressful life events, personality and health: an inquiry into hardiness. *Journal of Personality and Social Psychology*, 37, 1–11.

Kobasa, S.C., Maddi, S.R. and Kahn, S. (1982). Hardiness and health: a prospective study. *Journal of Personality and Social Psychology*, 42, 168–77.

V A✓K ☆GH HANDOUT 126

TOPIC: Personality factors and stress

CRITICAL QUESTIONING

After reading the central passage, students then work in mixed ability pairs to fill in the surrounding boxes. Each box requires a different form of thinking. Some boxes are simple, for example 'Identify the facts: what happened'. Other boxes demand a higher order of thinking: 'How is the Type A personality related to increased stress?'.

An alternative to mixed pairs would be to ask students to work individually for 10 minutes on boxes of their choice then to join with another student to work on one box together for 10 minutes. Following this, students form a new pair and share ideas for the boxes completed so far. The final session could see student pairs forming groups of four to tackle any empty boxes.

Reference

Friedman, M. and Rosenman, R.H. (1959). Association of specific overt behaviour pattern with blood and cardiovascular findings. *Journal of the American Medical Association*, 169, 1286–96.

V A✓K✓ ☆G HANDOUTS 127 and 128

TOPIC: Personality factors and stress

READING RACE

This activity takes the form of a competition between students in the class. Before beginning, assign students to small mixed groups and explain the rules of the race:

a) All students need to complete the question boxes on the 'Reading race' **Handout 127**.
b) One student approaches the question master(s) with the groups' worksheets.
c) Once the accurate AND detailed boxes are ticked a new question can be given to the group.
d) Line up in an orderly fashion to approach the question master.
e) The first group to finish is the winner.
f) Play continues till all groups are finished.

Initially, the teacher can play the role of question master (questions and answers are found on **Handout 128**). As soon as one group finishes, they can take over the role of question master. As groups finish they can act as experts to other groups or add to the bank of question masters to reduce queuing time.

References

Friedman, M. and Rosenman, R.H. (1959). Association of specific overt behaviour pattern with blood and cardiovascular findings. *Journal of the American Medical Association*, 169, 1286–96.

Kobasa, S.C., Maddi, S.R. and Kahn, S. (1982). Hardiness and health: a prospective study. *Journal of Personality and Social Psychology*, 42, 168–77.

Myrtek, M. (2001). Meta-analyses of prospective studies on coronary heart disease, type A personality, and hostility. *International Journal of Cardiology*, 79, 245–51.

Ragland, D.R. and Brand, R.J. (1988). Type A behaviour and mortality from coronary heart disease. *New England Journal of Medicine*, 318 (2), 65–9.

V ✓ A ✓ K SO HANDOUT 129

TOPIC: Approaches to coping with stress

COPING CARD

This handout provides a quick way to access the information found in their textbook (page 132 in *Complete Companion*). Students simply follow the instructions on the sheet; beginning with AO1, students identify which statement relates to problem-focused coping and which refers to emotion-focused. Students are then asked to write a summary of each form of coping. Less able students could use the highlighted statements as a starting point for their summaries. This procedure is then repeated for the AO2 section for the worksheet.

References

Folkman, S. and Lazarus, R.S. (1980). An analysis of coping in a middle-aged community sample. *Journal of Health and Social Behaviour*, 21, 219–39.

Folkman, S. and Lazarus, R.S. (1985). If it changes it must be a process: Study of emotions and coping during three stages of a college examination. *Journal of Personality and Social Psychology*, 48, 150–70.

Gilbar, O. (2005). Breast cancer: How do Israeli women cope? A cross-sectional sample. *Family, Systems and Health*, 23, 161–71.

Penley, J.A., Tomaka, J. and Wiebe, J.S. (2002). The association of coping to physical and psychological health outcomes: A meta-analytic review. *Journal of Behavioural Medicine*, 6, 551–603.

Rukholm, E.E. and Viverais, G.A. (1993). A multifactorial study of test anxiety and coping responses during a challenge examination. *Nurse Education Today*, April 13(2), 91–9.

V A ✓ K SO HANDOUT 130

TOPIC: Approaches to coping with stress

DESCRIBE/DISTINGUISH

The AQA specification requires students to distinguish between problem-focused and emotion-focused coping. As well as distinguishing between the two, students need to be able to describe each way of coping. In this handout students first have to identify which passage describes the two forms of coping (right-hand speech bubble) and which passage distinguishes between the two (left-hand side). In the box below, students identify words they could use to show the examiner they are doing more than describing, such as: whereas, one difference, however). The final section asks students to answer the question 'explain the difference between problem-focused and emotion-focused approaches to coping with stress (4 marks)'.

V A ✓ K S HANDOUT 131

TOPIC: Psychological methods of stress management

CUT IT OUT

This task requires students to consider the most valuable points in the information box and use these to reduce the passage down to a 100-word summary. This can be taken further by reducing again to 50 words to form a neat revision sound bite. If daunted by writing only 100 words, students could initially work in pairs, highlighting the words and phrases they feel must be included in their answer.

Reference

Meichenbaum, D. (1985). *Stress Inoculation Training*. New York: Pergamon.

V A ✓ K S HANDOUT 132

TOPIC: Psychological methods of stress management

BUILD IT UP

If you feel students struggle with the previous 'cut it out' activity, the 'build it up' handout works in the opposite direction. Students begin with a 50 (58)-word summary and have to use their knowledge of SIT (page 134 in *Complete Companion*) to develop a more detailed outline of this psychological method of stress management.

This activity could also be used in a revision session without textbooks, maybe working in pairs to develop an accurate and detailed version of the passage.

V ✓ A K ★ G R HANDOUT 133

TOPIC: Psychological methods of stress management

IMAGE-IN IT

Divide the class into five groups. Assign groups of students to one of the bullet pointed topics shown on **Handout 133**. The first three bullet points are easier to translate into pictures.

Task 1

Students decide on four images to represent the information relating to their bullet point (pages 134–5 in *Complete Companion*). Each group needs four plain pieces of paper to draw the group's images in preparation for Task 2. Only one word per box is allowed.

Task 2

Groups then distribute their pictures among the other groups. Groups now have four new pictures (each picture must come from a different group). Students draw the donated pictures in each box on their handout and give a written explanation below each image.

The images students drew to share with other groups can be collected in and used in a classroom display of stress management techniques or as a starter activity the following lesson.

Follow-up starter idea

To begin the next lesson, display the bullet points from the handout numbering them 1–5. Hold up images from the 'Image-in it' task and ask students to hold up the relevant number of fingers to demonstrate which bullet pointed topic the image represents.

V A ✓ K ★ S G HANDOUT 134

TOPIC: Physiological methods of stress management

CRYSTAL BALL

Working in pairs or small groups, students develop their own ideas regarding the strengths and weaknesses of drug therapies. Being able to talk to others helps develop their ideas and can provide new points to consider.

Students then use their textbook (page 137 in *Complete Companion*), to identify whether their predictions were correct or incorrect. This part of the activity gives meaning to students' reading.

V A K ✓ ★ S HANDOUT 135

TOPIC: Physiological methods of stress management

SORT IT OUT

The strips relate to the action of either Benzodiazepines or Beta-blockers. Students cut out each strip and sort them into two separate groups.

Extension

Once strips have been sorted, more able students should consider arranging each strip into a coherent order to form a paragraph. Students use the strips to help them write 100 words about each type of drug.

V A ✓ K ★ S O HANDOUT 136

TOPIC: Physiological methods of stress management

DEBATING DRUGS

Students begin by giving three reasons why drug therapies are an effective form of stress management and three reasons why drug therapies are an ineffective form of management. The AO2 boxes below require students to evaluate the strength of the statements just made by providing evidence that supports the AO1 claims.

The class could be split into two with half completing the left-hand side of the handout (positives of drug therapies) and half tackling the right-hand side (negatives of drug therapies). Pairs can then be formed, with students from each half coming together to swap ideas before answering the essay 'Discuss the effectiveness of using drugs to manage stress (12 marks)'.

V A ✓ K ★ H G HANDOUT 137

TOPIC: Physiological methods of stress management

SUGGESTING SOLUTIONS

Working alone or in a small group, students choose one of the case studies and suggest a suitable programme of stress management therapies. Students may wish to focus on one therapy or combine a number of treatments. A detailed reason for each choice should be given to explain their reasoning.

If students are overwhelmed by the task, they could begin by highlighting any physical, emotional or situational details in different colours to help them identify which method of stress management may be suitable.

V A ✓ K ★ O H HANDOUT 138

TOPIC: Physiological methods of stress management

STRESS A-Z REVIEW

This activity can be used at any point in a scheme of work but I (RCG) find it useful at the end of the topic as students have a wider range of terminology to use. It also acts as a good kick start for revision. Students work alone to complete the A-Z of stress (A could stand for adrenal, B = beta-blockers and so on). At times a little lateral thinking may be needed for less obvious letters (Z could be (B)Zs for Benzodiazepines). If students struggle to finish the entire alphabet, they could form small groups to share ideas or use textbooks to hunt for the last few letters. The questions below the alphabet require students to review their recall of each letter and make judgements about their own knowledge (a higher order thinking skill). Students then rate each work with a happy face ☺(I understand the term), a neutral face 😐(I am a little unsure/have a vague memory of the term) or an unhappy face ☹ (I haven't a clue!). The unhappy faces can act as a good starting point for revision.

Follow-up starter activity

In preparation for the next lesson students can produce a class list of unhappy face words which they have to learn for the next lesson. The starter for that lesson can be a quick 5-minute test on the unhappy words.

V A✓K

TOPIC: Conformity to majority influence

STARTER – BEANS IN A JAR

Conformity is a great topic to teach, my favourite in fact, and generally the students are enthusiastic about it, too.

As we know, the key to generating intrigue and interest around a topic is through well-designed 'starter' activities.

There are several ways you could introduce conformity and social influence. 'Beans in a jar' is one way, more examples follow in this section (see 'Conformity quotes rolling show', and 'What would you wear at your wedding?').

Beans in a jar

Jenness (1932) conducted an experiment using beans in a jar to demonstrate the power of conformity.

To replicate this activity, fill a jar with beans (or smarties, pasta shells, etc.). Ask your students to estimate how many beans are in the jar.

In order to determine whether their behaviour is influenced by others, you need to ask the students to write their answers on pieces of paper where previous students have recorded theirs (I told my students I had already asked my tutor group to do it that morning, though of course, I had made up their estimates).

Some of the pieces of paper should contain high estimates (group 1), others should have lower estimates (group 2).

Participants in each condition should differ in terms of their mean estimates, as a consequence of conforming to the estimates they see.

Reference

Jenness, A. (1932). The role of discussion in changing opinion regarding the matter of fact. *Journal of Abnormal and Social Psychology*, 27, 279–96.

V✓A✓K HOG

TOPIC: Conformity to majority influence

STARTER – WHAT WOULD YOU WEAR AT YOUR WEDDING?

Introduce the topic of social influence and conformity by asking your students to draw a picture of themselves on their wedding day. Ask them to pay particular attention to what they are wearing.

After they have done this, ask the boys to raise their hands if they have drawn themselves in a suit. Ask the girls to raise their hands if they have drawn themselves in a white dress.

The chances are the majority of students will raise their hands. Here is an opportunity to set a brief discussion question:

'How did I know what you would draw? Why do most people wear the similar clothes at weddings? Why do very few people deviate from this?'

You could use one of the collaborative learning structures to do this (see page 3).

Hopefully this will stimulate a discussion whereby you can introduce the concepts of social norms, majority influence, compliance and internalisation.

V✓A✓K

TOPIC: Conformity to majority influence

STARTER – CONFORMITY QUOTES ROLLING SHOW

'Rolling shows' are essentially slideshows of images that automatically change after a set period of time – 5 seconds, for example. Details on how to setup rolling shows using PowerPoint are outlined on page 5.

These slideshows make an excellent start to the lesson. I (MWG) usually have one running with some appropriate music before the students arrive, so that from the moment they turn up, the topic and tone of the lesson are clear.

You could fill multiple slides on your PowerPoint show with quotes about conformity. There are some excellent thought-provoking conformity quotes on this website:

http://www.quotegarden.com/conformity.html

You could also include some images that illustrate conformity in action: people queuing, students with their shirts untucked, etc.

V✓ A✓ K✓ HANDOUTS 139–144

TOPIC: Conformity to majority influence

RESEARCH ACTIVITY – ASCH (1956)

There are perhaps two ways in which this study could be replicated with your class.

1 If you have a situation where one student is absent, brief the rest of the class on Asch's experiment and enlist them as confederates. In the next lesson when the absent student returns, run the experiment by showing the stimulus lines and comparison line (these are provided for you on the handouts, but need to be transferred to cards or OHTs). On 12 out of 18 trials everyone should give the wrong answer. Interview the 'absent' student(s) about what they felt and debrief.

2 Prepare instructions for each member of the class detailing their role in the experiment. Every member of the class should receive 'confederate' instructions apart from one, who receives the 'participant' instructions. In this case, it would be important to emphasise to students the importance of not sharing what is written with the people around them, and to not show reactions (e.g., giggling!), which would give away their role as confederates.

This activity should help to embed the procedures of the study and also give some insight into both why people conform and associated ethical issues.

Reference

Asch, S.E. (1956). Studies of independence and conformity: A minority of one against a unanimous majority. *Psychological Monographs*, 70 (Whole no. 416).

The correct answers are:

1C, **2**C, **3**B, **4**A, **5**B, **6**C, **7**A, **8**B, **9**C, **10**A, **11**A, **12**B, **13**C, **14**B, **15**B, **16**C, **17**A, **18**A.

The confederates should give right answers on 6 critical trials, e.g. 1, 3, 7, 8, 11, 15.

Therefore their answers would be:

1C, **2**B, **3**B, **4**C, **5**A, **6**B, **7**A, **8**B, **9**A, **10**C, **11**A, **12**A, **13**B, **14**A, **15**B, **16**B, **17**C, **18**C.

V✓ A K ★ OS

TOPIC: Conformity to majority influence

BUILDING UP A PICTURE

This is an excellent way to review and consolidate learning of Asch's (1956) study.

At the start of the next lesson, ask individual students to come up to the whiteboard and draw something they can remember about Asch's study. This could be an actual drawing (e.g., the stimulus lines and comparison line cards) or a symbol to represent part of the procedure (e.g., last year one of my students drew a sheep with the word 'findings' underneath to highlight the fact that many participants had conformed to the confederates).

Once the first student has drawn something, a second student should add to it, and so on. Then all students can copy down the finished picture for their notes, to help them remember the study.

V A✓ K ★ OS HANDOUT 145

TOPIC: Conformity to majority influence

PSYCHOLOGY JACKANORY

You could use this as a starter or plenary. **Handout 145** contains two short stories of conformity.

A nice idea is to read these stories to your students, taking them back to their primary school days! If you had time, you could even illustrate them and place the images on a PowerPoint slideshow, moving through the images as you read the story. Alternatively, ask some of your students to read the stories.

The first of the short stories relates to compliance and normative social influence.

The second of the short stories relates to internalisation and informational social influence.

They could be used for the basis of discussion, an exam question, worksheet or even display work of some kind.

V A ✓ K HORTS HANDOUTS 146 and 147

TOPIC: Evaluating research into conformity

ELABORATION LADDERS

The idea behind and the technique for using elaboration ladders are outlined on page 10.

It is basically a way to encourage students to write about their evaluative points in more depth and to avoid basic and superficial comments such as 'Asch's study has low ecological validity because it is not like real life'.

Students start with an introductory evaluation comment at the bottom of the ladder and then gradually elaborate this comment further and further until they reach the smiley face at the top! The box on the right-hand side is designed to prompt students into thinking of ways they could elaborate their evaluations (see page 10 for examples).

Asch (1956) is a good study to use this technique with because, although the evaluations are relatively simple, students rarely elaborate them effectively.

Handouts 146 and **147** provide the framework and some starting points. **Handout 146** is aimed at brighter students who should be encouraged to think for themselves, whereas **Handout 147** is designed to give weaker students more support. As such, you can differentiate this activity by task (see page 13).

V ✓ A ✓ K ✓ HOG

TOPIC: Evaluating research into conformity

MUSICAL EXAM ANSWERS

Once students have evaluated conformity research (e.g., Asch), they are then in a position to tackle essay questions such as:

Outline and evaluate research into types of conformity. (12 marks)

'Musical exam answers' is an activity that requires students to work collaboratively in order to write material relevant to a particular essay question.

Arrange your students into groups of three or four. Ask each of them to write down on a post-it note one fact/evaluation point/term relevant to the essay question set.

Pick a music track that not will not interfere too much with their concentration (chill out albums are usually good for this) and explain that they have until the end of the track to write as much on the essay question as they can. They should start off by writing the part of the essay that is relevant to what they have written on their post-it note (so that not all students in the group are writing the same information).

At the end of the music track, students should pass their work to the person on their left. They should then be given the length of another music track to continue answering the essay question from where the last person left off. Explain to them they must read what the previous person wrote and correct mistakes if necessary, but then continue with the answer as best they can. Carry on until each member of the group has contributed to each answer.

An alternative to this is using three or four different essay questions within the same group.

There will be good opportunities for self- and peer assessment here.

The activity also gives students the chance to experience other students' writing styles and essay techniques – good and bad.

V ✓ A ✓ K ✓ HOG

TOPIC: Conformity to minority influence

WHERE WOULD WE BE WITHOUT MINORITY INFLUENCE?

Display a definition of minority influence on your whiteboard:

'A form of social influence where people reject the established norm of the majority of the group members and move to the position of the minority.'

Then, using a collaborative learning structure such as **'group statements'** or **'random numbers'** (see page 3), set the following discussion question, asking students to fully elaborate and justify their responses:

'Where would we be without minority influence?'

V✓A K ★HOS HANDOUTS 148 and 149

TOPIC: Conformity to minority influence

DECONSTRUCTING MOSCOVICI *ET AL.* (1969)

Now that psychology is officially a science (it seems the old debate from PYA5 has now been settled!), the new specifications require students to have a much better understanding of the principles underpinning scientific psychological research.

One way to encourage this is to ask your students to deconstruct psychological studies into their constituent parts. **Handouts 148** and **149** give students a framework and guidance for doing this.

Selected answers

Research method – Experimental

Investigation design – Independent measures

Independent variable (IV) – Consistency with which minority states their beliefs.

IV operationalised – Consistency with which minority of confederates stated the slides were green (Consistent = 36 out of 36 slides; Inconsistent = 24 out of 36 slides).

Dependent variable (DV) – Rate at which majority conforms to the beliefs of the minority.

DV operationalised – Amount of time participants agreed with confederates the 'blue' slides were green.

Ethical issues – Deception, protection from harm (participants may be embarrassed about their responses).

Reference

Moscovici, S., Lage, E. and Naffrenchoux, M. (1969). Influence of a consistent minority on the responses of a majority in a colour perception task. *Sociometry*, 32, 365–80.

V✓A K✓★OS

TOPIC: Explanations of why people conform

STICKMAN THEORIES

I've used this activity quite often with my students. They tend to remember theories better as a result, as they have to understand the theories in order to illustrate them.

Display one of the explanations of why people conform on your whiteboard (e.g., normative social influence). It is best to break this down for students with simple bullet points so students are not overwhelmed with complex language.

Then give them an allotted amount of time, say 7 minutes, to illustrate how those explanations work in a visual way. Tell students to use simple stick-people.

I usually add the rule that they must include the words that I display on the board in bold. They should not use any other words in order to explain their drawings, that is unless they are contained within thought or speech bubbles.

This ensures students do not simply copy out the explanations on the board and then add 'token' images to appease you!

After they have completed the first explanation of why people conform (e.g., informational social influence), give them another amount of allotted time to complete the second.

Suggested bullet-point forms of the explanations to display on the whiteboard are given below:

Normative social influence

- As people we have a **need to be accepted** by others and make a favourable impression on them.
- To gain acceptance from others and make a favourable impression on them we are inclined to **conform**.
- This results in **compliance**, because we might change our behaviour or articulate views **publicly** in order to be accepted or liked, but **privately** we do not.

Informational social influence

- People have a basic need to **evaluate their ideas and attitudes** in order to check they are accurate or correct.
- Therefore, in **ambiguous situations**, where the right course of action or opinion is not clear, we might change (conform) our behaviour or views in line with others.
- This results in **internalisation**, because there is a change in both our **public** *and* **private** attitudes and behaviours.

V ✓ A K ★ O S HANDOUT 150

TOPIC: Explanations of why people conform

SPOT THE DELIBERATE MISTAKES!

Once you have taught the explanations of why people conform, you could test your students' knowledge and understanding by asking them to spot the 10 deliberate mistakes on **Handout 150**. The correct version is shown below.

Correct version: words in bold replace wrong ones on the worksheet.

Normative social influence

It is possible to behave like the majority without really accepting its point of view. Psychologists have called this type of conformity **compliance**. A majority may be able to control other group members by making it difficult for them to deviate from the majority point of view, and thus exerting pressure on them to **conform**. Going against the majority **isn't** easy, as demonstrated by Asch's study, where participants clearly felt uncomfortable deviating from the majority position. Humans are a social species and have a fundamental need for social companionship and a fear of rejection. It is this that forms the basis for normative social influence.

Informational social influence

In some cases individuals go along with others because they genuinely believe them to be right. As a result, we don't just to comply in behaviour alone, but we also *change* our point of view in line with the position of those influencing. Because this involves changing both our public *and* private attitudes and behaviours, this is an example of ***internalisation***. Informational social influence is most likely when:

- The situation is **ambiguous** – i.e. the right course of action is not clear.
- The situation is a crisis – i.e. rapid action is required.
- We believe **others** to be experts – i.e. we believe that **others** are more likely to know what to do.

Social impact theory

Latané (1981) developed a theory to explain why people conform in some situations but not in others. There are several principles included in this explanation:

- *Number* – the more people present, the more influence they will have on an individual. However, the rate of increase in impact grows less as each new individual is added. For example, Asch found that conformity rates rose dramatically up to three or four, but not much beyond that size.
- *Strength* – the more important the people are to the individual, the more influence they will have. For example in Perrin and Spencer's research, when the majority were probation officers and the individual was someone on probation, conformity rates were relatively **high**.
- *Immediacy* – each individual can influence others; but the more people are present, the less influence any one individual will have. Thus, we are more likely to listen attentively to a speaker if we are in a **small** group than if we are in a **large** group.

Reference

Latané, B. (1981). The psychology of social impact. *American Psychologist*, 36, 343–56.

V ✓ A K ★ O S HANDOUT 151

TOPIC: Explanations of why people conform

APPLYING KNOWLEDGE TO EXAMPLES OF CONFORMITY

It is important that we constantly help students to practise applying their knowledge to unseen examples, as this will happen in their exam.

Handout 151 describes a series of conformity examples. Ask your students to identify the types of conformity shown, and how that conformity might be explained. It may well be that for some of the examples, students feel there is more than one possible type and explanation of conformity.

References

Asch, S.E. (1956). Studies of independence and conformity: A minority of one against a unanimous majority. *Psychological Monographs*, 70 (Whole no. 416).
Moscovici, S., Lage, E. and Naffrenchoux, M. (1969). Influence of a consistent minority on the responses of a majority in a colour perception task. *Sociometry*, 32, 365–80.

V✓ A✓ K✓ ☆OS

TOPIC: Obedience to authority

DEMONSTRATING OBEDIENCE – I'M A LITTLE TEAPOT!

As the teacher, ask the class to do something, e.g. 'Can everyone please stand behind their chairs. Place your right hand on your right hip. Now place your left hand in the air, and then slant/bend your body to the left (I'm a little teapot!).'

This excellent idea was submitted by Sara Berman in the previous version of *The Teacher Companion*:

Ask the class to do strange things, e.g. get them to sit in a row according to birthdays; lots of chat relaxes them. Then ask them all to stand behind their chairs, on their desks, with some A4 paper, tear it carefully into strips, drop every fourth strip on the floor, all those with birthdays between March and June get down and pick up paper, etc. Nothing dangerous or embarrassing but keep going until someone asks 'Why?'

It's extremely interesting to see how far they will obey totally absurd requests. You can then discuss why they obey. What was it about the situation, my role, their role, socialisation process of school behaviour.

This can also lead to discussion of Orne's research on demand characteristics.

Orne (1962) observed that people behave in quite unusual ways if they think they are taking part in a psychology experiment. For example, in one experiment he asked participants to add up columns of numbers on a sheet of paper and then tear the paper up and repeat this again. If people believed this was part of a psychology experiment some were willing to continue the task for over six hours! This led Orne to develop the idea of *demand characteristics*.

People taking part in an experiment want to please an investigator and want their performance to be helpful. A demand characteristic acts as a confounding variable.

Reference

Orne, M.T. (1962). On the social psychology of the psychological experiment: With particular reference to demand characteristics and their implications. *American Psychologist*, 17, 776–83.

V✓ A✓ K ☆OGS

TOPIC: Obedience to authority

ODD ONE OUT

This is an idea for a starter, outlined on page 2.

Most of us will start teaching obedience after the conformity topic. One way of getting the obedience topic started is to get students thinking about the differences between the two terms.

Before telling students what the next topic will be, display three pictures/events which illustrate conformity (such as people queuing, school students with their shirts untucked, etc.), and one picture that illustrates obedience (such as a policeman pointing).

Then, perhaps using a collaborative learning structure such as **'random heads'** (see page 3), ask students which picture/event they feel is the odd one out and to justify why.

V ✓ A ✓ K ✓ OS

TOPIC: Obedience to authority

THE ROLF HARRIS SCHOOL OF TEACHING

What follows is an exceptionally good idea that was included by Adrian Frost in the previous version of *The Teacher Companion*, so good it seemed a shame to not include it this time round!

I (AF) do make quite a lot of use of visual learning, mainly because I like doodling on the board.

Some kind of visual approach is useful for the social influence section of the specification because it helps students to keep track of what's going on in the studies.

Research like that of Asch, Crutchfield or Moscovici can get very confusing for students over time, as they try to keep track of the varying stimulus material, majorities, minorities, confederates, dissenters and experimenters. I always find it best to draw the varying conditions on the board, even if I only use stick men. Little speech bubbles can be added and I do genuinely find that it helps the students remember the material.

If you're not big on drawing, get the students to do it for you. Some students just like to draw, and can be relied upon to produce excellent visual aids and revision material. A surprising amount of material can be crammed into one image (see the Milgram example below).

Some students really like this approach, others groan.

Ask students to produce cartoons

Get a big compilation book of cartoons. Books of newspaper cartoons like 'Peanuts' or 'Calvin and Hobbes' work best, as they contain hundreds of images of the same people, drawn at about the same size, wearing the same clothes in each frame. Photocopy lots of different figures and then cut out and stick them onto a sheet of A3 paper. This is time consuming but you only have to do it once.

Photocopy this A3 'resource sheet' and distribute to students. Ask them to cut out figures and stick on paper, and then they have to add speech bubbles of their own. This works well with two characters where they have to debate a particular issue, with each figure holding a viewpoint and the argument alternating between the two viewpoints, so that you end up with something like 'Calvin and Hobbes debate the ethics of Milgram's research', with one character presenting the criticisms and the other presenting counterpoints. This really helps the students to produce balanced argument, discussion and debate, rather than rote learn AO2 points.

One you've got the sheets, you only have to rustle up scissors and glue anytime you want to use the exercise. (In my experience groups like the exercise so long as they are only ever asked to do it once or twice.) The results look great if photocopied onto coloured card and it is guaranteed that other staff will ask to photocopy your master sheet.

For an alternative ICT approach to creating cartoons, see page 6.

V✓A K✓ ★HOS HANDOUTS 152 and 153

TOPIC: Obedience to authority

OBEDIENCE BAROMETER

In Milgram's (1963) original study of obedience, he found that 65% of participants continued to shock the learners up to 450 volts. This was the maximum voltage and far beyond what was marked 'Danger: Severe shock'.

Milgram (1974) then carried out a series of variations of the obedience experiment in order to identify some of the influencing factors.

Some of those variations are described in **Handout 152**, and the suggested activity is that students place these variations onto the 'obedience barometer' on **Handout 153** to indicate the obedience level they think was found.

This activity would also serve as a good introduction to the explanations of why people obey.

References

Milgram, S. (1963). Behavioural study of obedience. *Journal of Abnormal and Social Psychology*, 67, 371–8.
Milgram, S. (1974). *Obedience to Authority: An experimental view*. New York: Harper and Row.

V✓A K✓ ★HORTS HANDOUTS 154 and 155

TOPIC: Evaluating research into obedience to authority

PEE-ING ON MILGRAM

Many of you may have heard of, or used, the PEE technique with your students before. PEE stands for Point, Explanation, Evidence and is a structure that aims to help students with their evaluation writing skills. That is, they introduce their evaluation *point*, then *explain* its relevance, and then provide *evidence* to support their point.

It is an alternative or supplementary technique to the 'elaboration ladders' and 'burger technique' (see page 10). Perhaps a useful starting point for learning this technique is to match up ready-made points, explanations, and evidence.

Handout 154 contains a series of 'Points' relevant to the evaluation of Milgram's study: *'Population validity is low'*, for example. Students should try and match this with the relevant explanation of this evaluation point: *'Used only American and male participants, so the extent to which obedience occurs may not be representative of other cultures or the female gender'*. Lastly, students should find the evidence that supports this point: *'Using the Milgram experimental procedure, Kilham and Mann (1974) found that 40% of Australian male students would administer the maximum shock voltage, but only 16% of Australian female students would.'*

Once students have completed this activity, they could attempt **Handout 155**. This is designed to help students practise the PEE technique in writing evaluation paragraphs.

At the bottom of this handout there are also some extension activities for your gifted and talented students to attempt.

It might be worth discussing with your students the fact that their evaluation paragraphs do not have to strictly follow the *Point*, then *Explanation*, then *Evidence* ordering. At times it might be necessary to fiddle with the order, or have a larger emphasis on the explanation. However, students should be looking to use this as a basic, but flexible, template for evaluation.

References

Darley, J.M. (1992). Social organisation for the production of evil. *Psychological Enquiry*, 3(2), 199–218.
Kilham, W. and Mann, L. (1974). Level of destructive obedience as a function of transmitter and expectant roles in the Milgram obedience paradigm. *Journal of Personality and Social Psychology*, 29, 696–702.
Orne, M.T. and Holland, C.C. (1968). On the ecological validity of laboratory deceptions. *International Journal of Psychiatry*, 6(4), 282–93.
Rank, S.G. and Jacobsen, C.K. (1977). Hospital nurses' compliance with medical overdose orders: A failure to replicate. *Journal of Health and Social Behaviour*, 18, 188–93.

V A✓K ★HOGTS

TOPIC: Evaluating research into obedience to authority

DEBATES

'Debates' scare me! I (MWG) once planned a lesson with a 30-minute debate in mind. It lasted about 5 minutes, with a 25-minute black hole in my lesson ensuing!

The mistake I made was not providing sufficient structure and guidance for the students. There are many different ways you could do this – there is no one-size-fits-all approach, since every debate is different in its requirements and characteristics. However, I'll describe some of the ways my colleagues have conducted debates with some success, and hopefully you will be able to adapt some of those ideas. Milgram gives us a wonderful opportunity for this, particularly in respect of ethics.

Students could be assigned to debate teams, and given a position to defend. For example, 'The benefits of Milgram's research outweigh the ethical costs to participants', and vice versa.

Students should then be given time to prepare for the debate, perfect their arguments and prepare for rebuttals. It is often students' lack of confidence that inhibits their participation in debates, so this period of reflection is quite important.

It might also be useful to formalise the debate by having a specific order to adhere to. For example, the debate should begin with one team presenting their arguments to support their position. The opposing team is then given the opportunity to rebut those arguments. Then, depending on the time available, the original team could answer those criticisms. There may also be opportunity to open the debate to the floor, with the teacher acting as facilitator.

House of Commons

An interesting variation to this would be contextualising the debate within The House of Commons, with one group presenting a bill with some relevance to the ethics debate, and the other team opposing the bill (for example, a bill which seeks to tighten the ethical rules within which psychologists have to operate). Students must also address each other in accordance with the proper parliamentary rule: 'My Honourable Friend…'!

Court cases

Is Milgram guilty of crimes towards psychology? Crimes against ethics? The abuse of participants?

You could also frame the debate in such a way that students argue for either guilty or not-guilty positions.

You really could go to town on this by assigning students different roles according to their skills and confidence.

Possible roles that could be used include a prosecution team, a defence team, expert witnesses (e.g. the defendant, opposing psychologists, the original participants) and a jury. Those with active roles must research their parts before the trial, whereas the jury must write notes during the trial, and then present a reasoned decision afterwards based on the arguments.

V✓A K ★HORS HANDOUT 156

TOPIC: Evaluating research into obedience to authority

ECOLOGICAL VALIDITY – SPOT THE DIFFERENCE

At various intervals within the lesson notes section, I (MWG) have described my frustration at students' use of the ecological validity evaluation. Principally, the way in which they blandly and vaguely state: 'It has low ecological validity because the study is in a lab and therefore not like real life'.

This is yet another activity designed to discourage that.

Display the definition of ecological validity to your students:

The degree to which a research finding can be generalised to other settings.

For this lesson, I usually ban all talk of 'real life' and tell them that if it appears in their essays I will burn them!

The emphasis of this lesson should be on analysing the studies to ascertain why we might not be able to *generalise the findings to other settings*. So, for example, Milgram found that 65% of participants shocked another person up to 450 volts when told to by an authority figure, but does this research finding *generalise to other settings*? For example, when people are not aware they are in a psychology study?

Use **Handout 156** to help your students think about this. Ask them to draw simple stickmen cartoons to illustrate the potential differences in behaviour of people in the various studies (Asch, Moscovici, and Milgram), when compared to behaviour outside of the research setting.

It could be argued, for example, that Asch's line comparison task is insignificant. Here, it costs participants very little to conform to the incorrect answer, as compared with conformity to smoking, where the potential costs are far higher in terms of health, life expectancy, and bad breath. Therefore, Asch's study lacks ecological validity as it is questionable whether his research findings can be generalised outside of the research setting to those settings where the consequences of conformity are higher.

V✓ A✓ K✓ ★OGTS HANDOUT 157

TOPIC: Explanations of why people obey

TEACH YOURSELF – WHY DO WE OBEY?

Earlier I (MWG) suggested that students draw the explanations of conformity, because the explanations lend themselves well to the pictorial form, and this also encourages students to understand the explanations as opposed to simply rote learning them.

I think the explanations of why we obey lend themselves to a similar activity. This time though, why not get your students to teach each other the explanations using this technique.

This is another opportunity to increase your students' collaborative learning skills, and some people may already know this type of activity as the 'Jigsaw technique'.

Like the activity described on page 41, split the class into mixed-ability groups of three and give each group **one** copy of **Handout 157**. The groups should then cut these handouts along the dotted lines.

Every member of each group should then be given responsibility for teaching one of Milgram's explanations of why people obey to the rest of their group. I would be tempted to ensure that the brightest member of each group is given the responsibility of 'agentic state', as this is probably the most difficult.

Students might be encouraged to question their 'teacher' so they really understand, or the 'teacher' may ask questions themselves.

The most important rule is that students may not read or copy out the information from their group members' sections. This encourages students to teach and learn content in different ways, such as using mnemonics, pictures, poems, stories, etc. Usually they are very creative in this respect.

Before they start the activity, also make it clear to students that they will tested (e.g., by quiz or exam question) afterwards, so the quality of their teaching will have a direct impact on their team members' performance. The aim of this is to ensure that the students do work collaboratively, because it is in their best interests to do so.

I would set students the following question:

'Outline two explanations of why people obey *(3 + 3 marks).'*

Reference

Milgram, S. (1974). *Obedience to Authority: An experimental view.* Harper and Row, New York.

V A✓ K ★OS

TOPIC: Explanations of why people obey

ROLL UP! ROLL UP!

You can use this plenary activity for any topic really, as it is a good way to randomly test your students' knowledge of key terms and concepts.

Display the following on your whiteboard or a PowerPoint slide:

1 Gradual commitment
2 Evidence of gradual commitment
3 Agentic state
4 Autonomous state
5 Buffers
6 Evidence of buffers

Then, either as a small group or whole class activity, have individual students roll a dice and then explain the corresponding term/concept/evidence.

V A✓ K

TOPIC: Independent behaviour: Resisting social influence

ROLLING SHOW – RESISTING OBEDIENCE

I've (MWG) outlined the idea of a 'rolling show' a few times already. On page 5 you can find instructions for creating a rolling show and some of the reasons why they are such a great start to the lesson.

Resisting conformity and obedience is a particularly poignant topic for using the rolling show, as there are so many examples from history where resistance from social influence could have prevented terrible events.

For the rolling show you could use images from the Holocaust, the Rwandan Genocide, Jonestown, Abu Ghraib, the Suffragettes, Rosa Parkes, etc.

V A✓ K OG

TOPIC: Independent behaviour: Resisting social influence

IS IT BETTER TO BE RESISTANT OR OBEDIENT?

Another way to introduce the topic is by discussing the following question:

Is it better to be resistant or obedient?

Think about using one of the collaborative learning structures outlined on page 3, particularly **'group statements'** or **'random numbers'**.

V✓ A K HORS HANDOUT 158

TOPIC: Independent behaviour: Resisting social influence

RESIST THE INFLUENCE!

In many ways, you have already taught your students explanations of independent behaviour – they just haven't realised it yet.

All your students need to do is take the studies of conformity and obedience they have already looked at, identify the factors that *increase* conformity and obedience, and simply turn these inside out.

For example, if 'buffers' increase the likelihood that people will obey an authority figure, then the 'removal of buffers' could be one way to explain an increase in independent behaviour.

You could use **Handout 158** with your students in order to structure this.

V✓ A K HANDOUT 159

TOPIC: Individual differences in independent behaviour

ROTTER'S (1966) LOCUS OF CONTROL

One of the new topics on the AQA A AS course is *individual differences in independent behaviour.* Personality, in particular, plays a role in this, and *locus of control* is named in the specification.

The term **locus of control** (Rotter, 1966) refers to a person's perception of personal control over their own behaviour. It is measured along a dimension of 'high internal' to 'high external'. High internals perceive themselves as having a great deal of control over their behaviour, and are therefore more likely to take personal responsibility for it (e.g., 'that happened because I made it happen'). In contrast, high externals perceive their behaviour as being caused more by external forces or luck (e.g., 'that happened because I was in the wrong place at the wrong time').

Some of the research in this area has indicated that high internals are less likely to rely on the opinions of others, and better able to resist coercion from others.

Handout 159 provides you with a questionnaire to give to students so that they can work out their own locus of control. This questionnaire is Rotter's I-E scale.

You could combine this with a survey of some kind on the ability to resist coercion from others in order to undertake a correlational analysis between the two variables.

To score the scale

Score internal statements as follows (question numbers 2, 3, 5, 7, 9, 11, 12, 13, 14, 15, 16, 20):

Give each statement a score between 1 and 6, where the answer 'agree very much' = 1 and 'disagree very much' = 6.

Score external statements as follows (questions numbers 1, 4, 6, 8, 10, 17, 18, 19):

Give each statement a score between 1 and 6, where the answer 'agree very much' = 6 and 'disagree very much' = 1.

Add up total score. Scores range from 20 to 120. A low score indicates an internal locus of control.

Reference

Rotter, J.B. (1966). Generalised expectations for internal versus external control of reinforcement. *Psychological Monographs*, 30(1), 1–26.

V A✓ K ★ HGS HANDOUT 160

TOPIC: Individual differences in independent behaviour

LOCUS OF CONTROL – DISCUSSION POINTS

Handout 160 contains five discussion points relevant to locus of control. Cut out these discussion points and split your class into five mixed-ability groups.

Using a collaborative learning structure such as **'random heads'** or **'group statements'**, ask your students to consider one of the five discussion points from the handout. Each group can then feedback their question and fully elaborated answers to the rest of the class.

Reference

Twenge, J.M., Zhang, L. and Im, C. (2004). It's beyond my control: A cross-temporal meta-analysis on increasing externality in locus of control, 1960–2002. *Personality and Social Psychology Review*, 8, 308–19.

V✓ A K ★ HORST HANDOUTS 161 and 162

TOPIC: Implications for social change

ESSAY PLANNING

Handouts 161 and **162** help students plan and prepare for the following essay question:

Discuss the implications for social change of research into social influence (12 marks).

This is perhaps one of the most difficult essay questions for students to cope with. Firstly, because they cannot use the simple structure of outlining a study/theory, and then evaluating it. Secondly, because the question is so broad.

This question requires a little more thought and analysis. The activities outlined on **Handout 161** are designed to help students to do this.

Reference

Moscovici, S., Lage, E. and Naffrenchoux, M. (1969). Influence of a consistent minority on the responses of a majority in a colour perception task. *Sociometry*, 32, 365–80.

V✓ A K ★ OS

TOPIC: Implications for social change

JERRY SPRINGER – WHAT HAVE WE LEARNT?

This idea for a plenary was outlined on page 2, but is included here because it works particularly well at this stage.

At the end of his shows, Jerry Springer always does a 'summing up'. It usually starts with the phrase: 'So… what have we learnt here today? We have learnt that…'.

Now we have reached the end of the social influence topic, ask your students to write a Jerry Springer style 'summing up'.

Ask some of your students to share these with the class. In the past I have used 'Rolling shows' (see page 5) to display the students summaries on a PowerPoint as they arrive during the next lesson.

V ✓ A K HORS HANDOUTS 163 and 164

TOPIC: Review

ETHICS AND SOCIAL INFLUENCE RESEARCH

It seems likely that examiners will still want to test students' knowledge of ethical issues and how to deal with them within the social influence topic of the specification.

As such, it would be sensible to review the ethical issues contained within the social influence studies you have covered, and identify the ways they were dealt with (or could have been dealt with).

Handout 163 provides a framework which students could use, along with prompts on what the major ethical issues are, and they ways they are dealt with.

If you have taught different studies from those listed in the table, your students could simply cross them out and replace them or you can change the sheet.

On completion of this activity, you may wish to ask your students to complete **Handout 164**, which is designed to help them practise their discussion and elaboration skills.

Students can often identify ethical issues in research, but struggle to **discuss** and **elaborate** on why those ethical issues are or are not a problem.

References

Asch, S.E. (1956). Studies of independence and conformity: A minority of one against a unanimous majority. *Psychological Monographs*, 70 (Whole no. 416).

Hofling, K.C., Brontzman, E., Dalrymple, S., Graves, N. and Pierce, C.M. (1966). An experimental study on the nurse-physician relationship. *Journal of Mental and Nervous Disorders*, 43, 171–8.

Milgram, S. (1963). Behavioural study of obedience. *Journal of Abnormal and Social Psychology*, 67, 371–8.

Moscovici, S., Lage, E. and Naffrenchoux, M. (1969). Influence of a consistent minority on the responses of a majority in a colour perception task. *Sociometry*, 32, 365–80.

V ✓ A K ✓ HORS HANDOUTS 165–168

TOPIC: Review

SOCIAL INFLUENCE DOMINOES

I often think 'dominoes' is a great way to help students review key terms, concepts, studies and evaluation points. However, I rarely do this activity with my students because it is quite labour intensive to set up and construct the cards.

Handouts 165–168 are some I prepared earlier so you don't have to!

Students should match the key terms, etc., with their relevant definitions until all cards are matched.

V ✓ A ✓ K ★ HOS

TOPIC: Definitions of abnormality

THE SHIRT!

A simple way to start the abnormality topic is to begin teaching the lesson wearing an unusual item of clothing. I (MWG) tend to do this with a shirt I bought while on a cricket tour in Sri Lanka – to say it is 'colourful' and 'loud' is something of an understatement!

As the students arrived to the lesson their reactions were fantastic. I used this as the basis for an introductory discussion – what is abnormal? How can we define abnormal?

I then proceeded to teach the lesson in my favourite shirt (last year the head walked in looking rather bemused by it all!).

V ✓ A ✓ K ✓ ★ HOGS

TOPIC: Definitions of abnormality

CELEBRITY ABNORMALITIES

Another way to stimulate interest in the definitions of abnormality topic is to consider the 'normality' and 'abnormality' of certain celebrities.

Split your class into groups. Give each group pictures of around eight celebrities, asking them to rank the celebrities in order of most 'normal' to 'least' normal. Try to give them a variety of celebrities that could be classed as 'abnormal' through different definitions, i.e. deviation from social norms, failure to function adequately, deviation from ideal mental health.

Afterwards, this can stimulate a class discussion on why the groups have chosen the order they have. If celebrity X is the least normal, why?

V ✓ A ✓ K ★ HOS

TOPIC: Definitions of abnormality

HANNIBAL LECTER

Consider showing a short video clip of a film/TV character like the one above. Alternatively you could use a recent media story if you feel it can be used appropriately. The BBC news website often has videos that can be played for free.

Ask students to identify all the ways in which the behaviours they see might be considered 'abnormal'.

Brainstorm these on the whiteboard and then discuss each of the behaviours in turn, asking students *how* and *why* we would define these behaviours as abnormal.

Try to play devil's advocate during this discussion so that your students can discover how difficult it is to actually pin down a definition of abnormality.

V ✓ A ✓ K ★ S HANDOUT 169

TOPIC: Definitions of abnormality

RECOGNISING ABNORMALITY

Handout 169 is a further resource you could use to highlight the subjectivity of 'abnormality'.

V✓A✓K HORS HANDOUT 170

TOPIC: Definitions of abnormality

WHO'S CALLING ME ABNORMAL?

Once your students have studied the three methods of defining abnormality, **Handout 170** may be useful to help them review their understanding and application skills.

In the feedback session, there may also be an opportunity to apply some of the definition AO2 points to the examples.

V✓A✓K HORS HANDOUT 171

TOPIC: Definitions of abnormality

USING CULTURAL RELATIVISM

Although no longer specifically required by the exam board, cultural relativism is still a great way for students to evaluate each of the definitions.

This is helpful to students because whatever the definition they are asked to evaluate, they know that one of their points can be related to cultural relativism.

However, it is important for them to remember that cultural relativism affects each definition in different ways. With this in mind, they could use **Handout 171** to structure their notes.

V✓A K✓ OS HANDOUTS 172–174

TOPIC: Definitions of abnormality

DOMINOES

Once again, I (MWG) think 'dominoes' can be a great way for students to review terms and concepts at the end of a topic. However, the activity can be labour intensive to set up.

Handouts 172–174 are some I prepared earlier so you don't have to!

Students should match the key terms, etc., with their relevant definitions until all cards are matched.

V✓A K✓ HORS HANDOUTS 175 and 176

TOPIC: The biological approach to psychopathology

BIOLOGICAL MODEL – CONNECT 4

Handout 175 details some of the basic principles of the biological model for your students to read.

Often students are fazed by the biological model because of the 'long words'(!) and the interconnected nature of it. Therefore, it is important to help students deconstruct the model into its basic parts, and then to help them link it together. This is the aim of the accompanying **Handout 176** (the same technique was used earlier for Bowlby's theory).

In the boxes, students should articulate their understanding of the principles, i.e. genetic inheritance, biochemistry and neuroanatomy, etc.

In between the boxes, students should try and explain how the elements of the theory link together. For example, genetic inheritance is linked to biochemistry because genes tell the body how to function, and therefore determine the level of hormones and neurotransmitters in the body.

Reference

Torrey, E.F. (2001). *Surviving Schizophrenia: A manual for families, consumers, and providers* (4th edn). New York: HarperCollins.

V✓ A✓ K ★HOGS

TOPIC: The biological approach to psychopathology

SEX ON THEIR BRAIN – THINKING ABOUT DETERMINISM

I (MWG) remember watching a documentary on Channel 4 a few years ago. It told the stories of a series of people who had shown abnormal sexual behaviours, such as inappropriate touching, gesturing and propositioning. One man had even been jailed for molesting his daughter.

There were many similarities between their stories, one of which was that each of the individuals had at some point suffered some kind of head injury or brain tumour, with the inappropriate behaviour starting afterwards. Before suffering these injuries, all indications were that their behaviour was 'normal'.

One suggestion made was that the individuals had suffered injuries to the higher parts of the brain that normally function to dampen our instinctive urges.

When one man had his brain tumour removed, which was crushing his frontal lobe, the inappropriate behaviour ceased.

Webpages come and go, but at time of writing, these similar stories were available:

http://www.channel4.com/health/microsites/S/sex_on_the_brain/index.html

http://www.dailymail.co.uk/health/article-393938/The-freak-accident-left-son-obsessed-sex.html

Describe these, or similar stories to your students and consider a brief discussion on the implications. For example:

Is all behaviour determined biologically?

If abnormal behaviour has a biological cause, should those individuals be punished if they break the law? Can they be held responsible?

If we could predict deviant behaviour through genetic screening, or other relevant techniques – should we arrest people before they commit the act?

You could perhaps use a series of collaborative learning structures (see page 3) to discuss these questions.

V✓ A K✓ ★HOGS HANDOUTS 177 and 178

TOPIC: The psychodynamic approach to psychopathology

THE BIGGER PICTURE

Freud and the psychodynamic approach are really fun to teach but it can be tempting to go off on too many tangents because you know your students will want to hear about it!

Students tend to hold on the 'shocking' elements they hear about the psychodynamic approach but do not always fully engage with the psychodynamic approach in the holistic way that it requires.

Freud was the first person to put forward an integrated and comprehensive explanation of all human behaviour. It could be argued that he is the only person to have done this.

Consequently, it is important that students see Freud's approach for what it is – like a jigsaw of interrelated parts.

The following activity is designed to help students to do this.

The bigger picture

Have students cut out the boxes on **Handouts 177** and **178**. Then, using their notes or their textbook (page 186 in *The Complete Companion*), ask them to define the terms and concepts, i.e. regression, mental disorder, unconscious awareness, etc.

Then provide students with some poster paper, say A2 or A3. This could be done using mixed-ability groups. Ask the groups to stick the boxes onto their paper in a pattern which they feel reflects the links between the terms and concepts (this could literally be in any order, such is the interrelatedness of Freud, so reassure them this is a subjective activity).

Once they have arranged their shapes, they should then draw a series of arrows/lines to illustrate the links between them. On those arrows/lines they should write explanations of how/why these elements are linked.

If your students have done this properly, their poster should look like a web of messy associations between various elements of Freud's psychodynamic approach.

This hopefully will give students a better feel for the holistic nature of the psychodynamic approach, and reinforce the interrelated nature.

V✓ A K✓ HOGS

TOPIC: The psychodynamic approach to psychopathology

FREUD APPRECIATION SOCIETY

Undoubtedly the best part about teaching Freud is the opportunity to inform the lads that they have repressed the desire to sleep with their mothers (through fear of castration from their father), and the girls that they have repressed envy of their father's penis. God bless the Oedipus and Electra complexes!

However, in highlighting these 'interesting' elements of psychoanalysis, we do tend to take away from some of the genuine achievements of Freud. Students always dismiss psychoanalysis as 'that weird mother-love sexual stuff' and Freud as 'the perverted one'!

This of course is a little unbalanced! Whilst some of Freud's ideas now seem a little 'wacky', other elements still pervade the way we think of the mind and behaviour today.

Redressing the balance!

So, consider setting your students this homework. Tell them to look again at the psychodynamic approach and identify three good positive evaluations. They may wish to research this in their textbooks or on the Internet.

At the start of the next lesson, brainstorm these positive evaluations on the board.

Then inform students that their task will be to set up a 'Freud appreciation society'. This will entail devising a campaign to re-educate the nation on the brilliance of Freud. Students could create advertising slogans, posters, record radio or TV interviews (if your school has the necessary equipment) and so on.

Make sure that you set clear objectives for them to follow, and share tangible outcomes that they must show evidence of at the end of the activity.

V✓ A✓ K

TOPIC: The behavioural approach to psychopathology

INTRODUCING BEHAVIOURISM

Operant conditioning/Social learning

Start the lesson by asking students a series of questions about the previous topic. Every time a student puts their hand up to answer, give them a treat (reward). Very quickly, most of your students will start to raise their hands. You can use this as the basis to introduce the basic principles of operant conditioning and social learning theory.

Alternatively, you could show some video clips of the 'Supernanny'. Here, there are loads of examples of conditioning in action. For example the 'naughty step' punishment decreases the probability that the negative behaviour will reoccur, whereas her reward schemes have the opposite effect.

Classical conditioning

If you have access to a digital projector, play the Pavlov's dogs flash game with your students. At the time of writing it could be found at this web address:

http://nobelprize.org/educational_games/medicine/pavlov/

You will need flash software to play the game.

V✓ A K HOS HANDOUT 179

TOPIC: The behavioural approach to psychopathology

EXPLAINING ABNORMALITY WITH THE BEHAVIOURAL MODEL

With a far greater requirement for students to show evidence of applying their knowledge now embedded in the exams, it is wise to give your students as many opportunities as you can to practise this.

Handout 179 provides numerous descriptions of example abnormal behaviours.

Students should first decide which element of behaviourism could explain the behaviour, i.e. classical conditioning, operant conditioning or social learning. It may well be that the behaviour could be explained with more than one of these.

The students should then record a brief explanation of how this behaviour may have been learnt, using the principles of conditioning they have learnt in class.

V A ✓ K ★ O

TOPIC: The behavioural approach to psychopathology

BEHAVIOURISM BINGO

Ask your students to construct a 3 x 3 grid, or provide one for them. Then ask them to fill each square of the grid with a key term/concept taken from the following list:

- Classical conditioning
- Unconditioned stimulus
- Unconditioned response
- Neutral stimulus
- Conditioned stimulus
- Conditioned response
- Pavlov
- Operant conditioning
- Reward
- Punishment
- Reinforcement
- Social learning
- Watson and Rayner

... and any others you would like to insert.

Then ask your students a series of questions which have these terms/concepts as answers.

If students feel the answer is on their grid, they can mark it off (like bingo). The first student to mark off all their terms is the winner (once they have been checked and verified!).

V ✓ A K ★ S

TOPIC: The cognitive approach to psychopathology

DO MY EYES DECEIVE ME?

Start the cognitive approach to psychopathology topics by showing your students a series of optical illusions.

You can use these to demonstrate to students that the mind is an information processing unit, and it doesn't always get things right.

For example, with optical illusions, the mind receives visual information through the eyes, and then uses that to judge distances, angles, heights, etc. However, sometimes those judgements are wrong – such as in the optical illusions.

As a result, cognitive psychologists argue that abnormal behaviours are a result of faulty information processing.

See: www.eyetricks.com/illusions.htm, for examples of optical illusions.

V ✓ A K ★ HORS HANDOUT 180

TOPIC: The cognitive approach to psychopathology

FAULTY THINKING STRATEGIES

One of the principal ways the cognitive model explains abnormal behaviour and mental illness is through faulty and disordered thinking. The issue is not the problem itself, but the way that you *think* about it.

Handout 180 describes a series of faulty thinking strategies outlined by Beck *et al.* (1979) in order to explain mental illness – principally depression.

Ask your students to read the case study and complete the tasks at the bottom of the sheet. This encourages students to identify and explain faulty thinking strategies at work in a depressed patient.

References

Beck, A.T., Rush, A.J., Shaw, B.F. and Emery, G. (1979). *Cognitive Therapy of Depression*. New York: Guilford Press.

Fieve, R.R. (1975). *Moodswing*. New York: Morrow

V ✓ A K ★ HORTS HANDOUT 181

TOPIC: The cognitive approach to psychopathology

EVALUATION, ELABORATION, AND THE COGNITIVE APPROACH

Handout 181 is designed to illustrate to students the level of depth required to achieve top AO2 marks.

Students should start by reading the boxes on the far left-hand side of the page, which outline simple evaluation points. Ask them to highlight (or shade in) each of the boxes in that column with a different colour.

The students should then read the boxes in the next column. Each represents further explanation/elaboration of one of the evaluation points, but they are not in the same order. Students should highlight (or shade in) those boxes with the correct, corresponding colour.

They should repeat this until all boxes in all columns are shaded in. This will require some thought from the students.

Purpose

Explain to students that the more they can elaborate their original evaluation points (e.g., 'one problem with model is cause and effect'), the more AO2 marks they are likely to get. This is denoted at the top of the worksheet. The evaluation comments start at 'rudimentary', and then increase in marks the further they are elaborated, through 'basic', 'reasonable' and 'effective'. These are loosely based on the AQA essay mark schemes.

Answers

The correct answers are as follows:

'One problem with this model is cause and effect'

- That is, it could be that faulty thinking may be the effect of mental disorder, rather than the cause of it.
- For example, an individual with depression may develop negative thinking *because* he is depressed rather than the other way round.
- It could be that the original disorder is caused by biochemical factors such as the under-activity of neurotransmitter – with negative thinking being the *effect.*

'Another objection of the cognitive model is that it blames abnormality on the patient and assumes they are responsible'

- Often, the model overlooks situational factors. That is, events in the life of the individual that they cannot control.
- For example, it may not consider how life events or family problems may have contributed to the mental disorder.
- This is because the cognitive model assumes the disorder is simply in the mind of the patient, and that recovery lies in changing that – rather than what is in their environment.

'A positive aspect of the model is that it is supported by research studies'

- For example, Gustafson (1992) conducted a study which found that irrational thinking processes were displayed by many people with psychological disorders such as anxiety disorder and depression.
- This shows that people suffering from mental disorders *do* exhibit faulty thought patterns.
- Thus there *is* evidence to support the main underlying assumption of the cognitive model of abnormality.

'The model has also led to the development of successful therapies for treating disorders'

- These therapies concentrate on challenging and changing the faulty thought patterns of their patients.
- This focus has been shown to be much more effective than concentrating on immediate behaviours (as the behavioural model would) or deeper meaning (as the psychodynamic model would).
- As such, this lends support to the fact that abnormal behaviours are the result of faulty thought patterns, as opposed to conditioning (behavioural model) or unconscious drives (psychodynamic model).

Reference

Gustafson, J.P. (1992). *Self-delight in a Harsh World. The main stories of individual, marital and family psychotherapy*. New York: Norton.

V ✓ A K ★ HOS HANDOUT 182

TOPIC: The cognitive approach to psychopathology

COMPARING MODELS OF ABNORMALITY

There are no 'correct' answers as such, but **Handout 182** should encourage your students to review, compare and contrast the different models of abnormality.

V✓A✓K ★HOGS HANDOUT 183

TOPIC: Biological therapies: Drugs and ECT

CASE STUDY FOR A BIOLOGICAL THERAPIST

Students could work in collaborative learning structures (see page 3) to discuss the case study described on **Handout 183**.

Some possible biological causes of Adam's behaviour might be:

- *Genetic*. He has inherited the manic depression from his father.
- *Abnormal biochemistry*. The consumption of a large quantity of alcohol could affect his behaviour. In addition, an imbalance in his biochemistry may be affected by his genetic makeup.
- *Abnormal neuroanatomy*. The head injury he received playing rugby might have contributed to his mental health.

Following an analysis of this case study, students may wish to consider biological therapy options and the pros and cons involved.

Students could also look at the aspects of Adam's life that this approach would *ignore*, such as his relationship with his mother (Freud); learning to use alcohol in the same way that his father did (behaviourism); feelings of inadequacy (cognitive). This could lead to a discussion about whether biological factors are the cause or effect of mental illness, and the implications for biological therapies as a result.

V✓A K✓★OS

TOPIC: Biological therapies: Drugs and ECT

BLUE-TACK PLENARY

To truly understand the logic of biochemical therapies, students need to have at least a basic awareness of the biochemistry itself and the underlying physiological processes in the body.

Many students find that the best way to learn these processes is visually (e.g., diagrams) or kinaesthetically (e.g., re-enacting the role of neurotransmitters in class).

To test your students' knowledge of the key terms, give each member of the class a term/concept/directional arrow from a diagram. Then display the diagram (e.g., like the one opposite from *The Complete Companion*, page 192) but with the terms covered up or deleted.

The task for students is to place their term/concept/directional arrow in the correct place on the diagram.

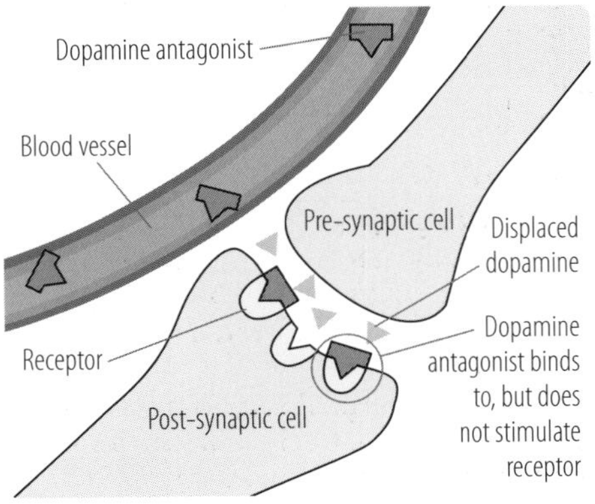

V ✓ A K ☆ O S HANDOUT 184

TOPIC: Psychological therapies: Psychoanalysis

SPOT THE DELIBERATE MISTAKES!

Once you have taught the psychoanalytic therapies for psychopathology, you could test your students' knowledge and understanding by asking them to spot the 10 deliberate mistakes on **Handout 184**. The correct version is shown below.

Correct version: words in bold replace wrong ones on the worksheet.

Repression and the unconscious mind

As a therapy, psychoanalysis is based on the idea that individuals are **unaware** of the many factors that cause their behaviour, emotions and general health. Some of these factors operate at an unconscious level, and are the result of **repressed** memories or **unresolved** conflicts from childhood. During psychoanalysis, the therapist attempts to trace these unconscious factors to their origins and then help the individuals deal with them. The therapist uses a variety of different techniques to uncover repressed material and help the client deal with it.

Free association

One such technique is known as free association, in which the patient expresses thoughts exactly as they occur, even though they may seem unimportant or irrelevant. Freud believed that the value of free association lies in the fact that the associations are driven by the **unconscious** factors which analysis tries to uncover. This procedure is designed to reveal areas of conflict and to bring into consciousness memories that have been repressed. The **therapist** helps interpret these for the **patient**, who corrects, rejects, and adds further thoughts and feelings.

Therapist intervention

Therapists often listen carefully as their patients talk, looking for clues and drawing tentative conclusions about the possible **causes** of the problem. Patients may initially offer resistance to their therapist's interpretations (e.g., changing the subject to avoid a painful discussion), or may even display ***transference***, where they recreate the feelings and conflicts and transfer these onto the therapist (e.g., acting towards the therapist as if they were the despised parent).

Working through

Psychoanalysis is **not** a brief form of therapy. Patients tend to meet up with the therapist four or five times a **week**. Together the patient and therapist examine the same issues over and over again, sometimes over a period of years, in an attempt to gain greater clarity concerning the causes of their neurotic behaviour.

V √ A K √ ☆ O S

TOPIC: Psychological therapies: Psychoanalysis

MAKE YOUR OWN PROJECTIVE TESTS!

This is another fantastic idea from Adrian Frost that we have brought forward from the previous version of *The Teacher's Companion*:

This has got to be the recipe for a perfect lesson, combining as it does cutting, sticking and repressed sexual tension.

I (AF) always teach projective tests as part of the psychodynamic approach, as it gives students something slightly more structured in terms of therapeutic technique and enables them to see how Freud's initial ideas were developed by others.

It can be hard to find more than one or two examples from such tests in textbooks, as these areas often contain only a single illustrative image. You will do better by looking on the Internet, where the whole set of Rorschach inkblots can be found, as well as the 'Blacky the Dog' (an example is shown below) and 'Thematic apperception test' images.

Websites come and go, but you could try:

http://www.deltabravo.net/custody/rorschach.htm

Example of image used in projective tests

Blacky the Dog

Once your students have seen enough examples, they can then start to create their own. Rorschach inkblots are easy; just splash some paint around and then fold and unfold the paper. More interesting is the creation of images similar to those above, perhaps by creating collages of magazine images. This is more difficult than it looks. Students will need to bear in mind the following:

1. The image must contain figures with whom the viewer can *identify*. They can be human or, as in 'Blacky the Dog', animal, but human is probably best. There can be more than one such figure, indeed choice of with whom they identify may be a vital part of the process.
2. The feelings and motivation of the figures should be *ambiguous*. That ecstatic girl from the shampoo ad leaves us in no doubt as to her state of mind and therefore she might not be that useful as she leaves us little space to 'project' our own emotions.
3. The relationships between the figures and the activity in which they are indulging should be open to *multiple interpretations*. For example, one thing to watch out for is age.
4. The material could hint at *key unconscious conflicts* – not just to do with sex, but also power, control, family, insecurity, etc.

All this could be achieved by carefully juxtaposing two or more magazine images.

Students could then have a go at developing a scoring system for their test. This will be much harder and the exercise will probably do little more than illustrate how difficult it is to score responses to such tests objectively.

As usual, you have to be careful that these sorts of exercises don't 'open up a can worms' with some students, but the completed tests will look very nice on the wall!

V √ A K √ ☆ H O S HANDOUT 185

TOPIC: Psychological therapies: Systematic desensitisation and CBT

USING SYSTEMATIC DESENSITISATION

Handout 185 provides students with a succinct description of the behavioural therapy systematic desensitisation.

They are encouraged to consider how this process might work in practice and complete the desensitisation hierarchy dimension line on the left-hand side for a patient with a phobia of spiders.

You may also ask students to attempt the exam-style question.

V✓ A✓ K HOGS HANDOUT 186

TOPIC: Psychological therapies: Systematic desensitisation and CBT

THINKING ABOUT BEHAVIOURAL THERAPIES

Handout 186 could be used to start students thinking about some of the issues involved in this area.

It also provides the opportunity for discussion groups (consider using a collaborative learning structure, see page 3).

Some suggested 'answers' and discussion prompts

1. Patient needs to be briefed well, so can give informed consent. High levels of arousal/ distress possible. Approaches vary in extent to which patient exercised control over events.
2. First approach involves far more rapid (and distressing) exposure to feared stimulus? Less control over events exercised by patient.
3. Quicker analysis than drug therapy or lengthy psychoanalysis? (Cognitive approach also viewed as 'fast-acting' though?)
4. Effect might diminish once removed from lab setting and positive reinforcement from therapist, therefore high chance of relapse?
5. Psychotic, as opposed to neurotic, disorders? Disorders with no clearly identifiable behavioural component? Genetic/physiological/neurochemical disorders?

V✓ A✓ K✓ HOGS HANDOUT 187

TOPIC: Psychological therapies: Systematic desensitisation and CBT

REBT REVISION CARDS

As I (MWG) outlined on page 40, one particularly successful lesson structure for me has been this very simple one:

1. Starter
2. Introduce revision technique to students
3. Students use that revision technique to learn and remember a topic.
4. Plenary – test the students at the end of the lesson with either a quiz or exam-style question.

These lessons seem to work particularly well because students are motivated to learn the material you give them (because they know they will be tested!), but also because they get to evaluate different revision techniques.

Handout 187 contains five revision cards relating to the cognitive behavioural therapy REBT (Rational-Emotive Behavioural Therapy). Students can cut these cards out, and write their answers on the back. They should be able to find the information in their textbooks (page 197 in the *Complete Companion*), or alternatively on the Internet.

When they have finished, they can test themselves and each other (e.g., by picking a card, answering it, and then checking the answer on the back).

At the end of the lesson, provide some kind of test, quiz, or exam-style question that will assess how well the revision technique worked for each student.

SECTION 3

Handouts

FOLDER INDEX

	DATE	TITLE	AIM	☺ 😐 ☹
1				
2				
3				
4				
5				
6				
7				
8				
9				
10				
11				
12				
13				
14				
15				
16				
17				
18				
19				
20				

▶ Lesson notes p.4

DATE	TITLE	AIM	☺ 😐 ☹
21			
22			
23			
24			
25			
26			
27			
28			
29			
30			
31			
32			
33			
34			
35			
36			
37			
38			
39			
40			

▶ Lesson notes p.4

It is absolutely crazy how many students do not read their essays before they hand them in!
Use this form to review your work and assess your own areas of strength and weakness.
This must be handed in WITH your essay in order for your homework to be accepted.

Indicate in the column on the right whether you (1) strongly agree, (2) agree, or (3) disagree.

Self-evaluation form

In this essay I have...

KNOWLEDGE AND UNDERSTANDING (6 marks)

- Read and understood the **knowledge** and **instruction** words in the question and what they require you to do (e.g. discuss, outline, evaluate) ☐
- Included material which is **relevant** to the question and excluded that which is **irrelevant** (e.g., if it says outline findings, don't waste time describing the procedure!) ☐
- **Planned** my essay using an essay plan sheet or mind map ☐
- Used **key terms** to show my knowledge and understanding ☐
- Used those **key terms** accurately and successfully, not just 'dropped' them in ☐
- Selected material which is **relevant** to the question ☐
- **Summarised** detail where I do not have enough time to include it all ☐
- Included **reasonable detail** for 6 marks ☐

EVALUATION AND ANALYSIS (6 marks)

- Included **two (possibly three) evaluation points** ☐
- Used different **signposts** to introduce the evaluations (e.g., this is undermined by, this can be challenged by) ☐
- **Fully elaborated** those two/three evaluation points (e.g., included evidence, examples, supporting statements, counter arguments, etc.) ☐
- Made sure the evaluations are **relevant** to the question (e.g., if the question asks about validity, do not include evaluations on ethics) ☐
- Linked the evaluations back to the question (if necessary – less need for outline/evaluate type questions) ☐

QUALITY OF WRITTEN COMMUNICATION (marked within both sections)

- Used **capital letters** at the start of sentences and for names, etc., (you'd be surprised!) ☐
- Written **clearly** and **concisely** ☐
- Used **paragraphs** ☐
- **Linked** the paragraphs together seamlessly ☐

▶ Lesson notes p.5

Elaboration ladders

Why does that matter?

–

How would that affect the results/ validity?

–

Can I explain my point with an example?

–

Have I got evidence?

–

How could it be improved?

–

Have I got a counter argument?

–

How does this affect the main argument?

Use the prompts above to help you **elaborate** the evaluative arguments on the bottom rung of the ladders.

The more you elaborate your points (without repeating yourself), the more marks you get – hence the smiley face at the top!

▶ Lesson notes p.10

Burger evaluation skills

The 'burger technique' is a way for you to structure an evaluation paragraph where you use a study to support or undermine a theory/explanation. The most important point of the process is the bottom of the burger where you explain how and why that study is relevant. This is where you can really demonstrate your understanding of a) what the theory/explanation would predict, and b) whether or not we should accept that theory based on the research evidence.

Example

A study that undermines the learning theory explanation of attachment is Harlow's (1959) study of rhesus monkeys.

Harlow separated infant rhesus monkeys from their mothers and raised them in isolation. He created two artificial wire mothers that resembled monkeys. One had a feeding bottle attached and the other was wrapped in soft cloth but offered no food. The monkeys spent much of their time clinging to the cloth mother, especially in times of distress.

This undermines the learning theory view of attachment because, according to the explanation, the young monkeys should have attached to the wire monkey which dispensed food because they would associate it with a sense of pleasure and the reduction of their hunger drive. However, the infants tended to cling more to a mother which offered them comfort.

A study that supports/undermines the
[insert name of theory/explanation here]
is....

Describe procedure and findings of a relevant study.

This supports/undermines the
[insert name of theory/explanation here]
because....

▶ Lesson notes p.10

Burger evaluation skills

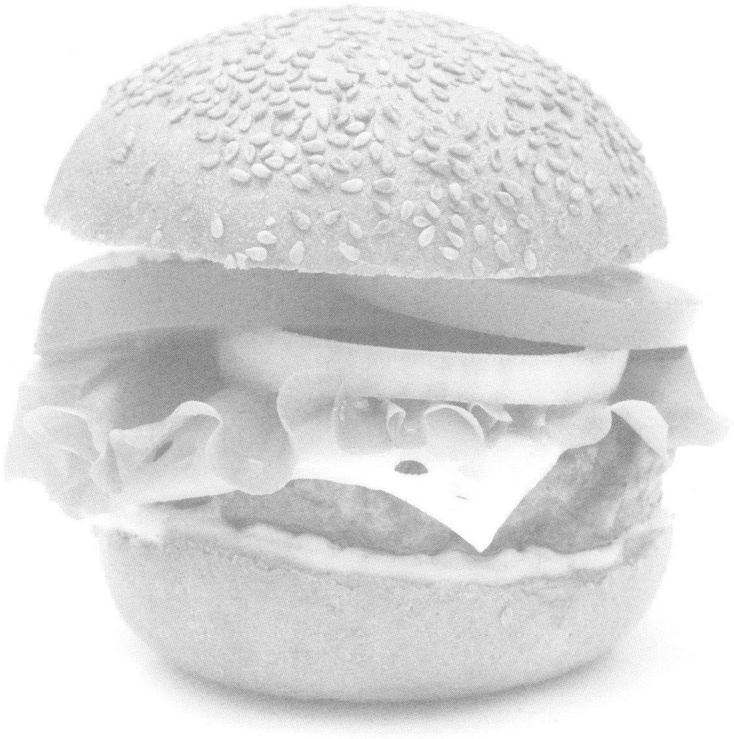

▶ Lesson notes p.10

Extension proforma

READ THE EXTENSION ARTICLE:

1. With highlighters, **select** the most relevant/interesting points in that article (don't fall into the trap of highlighting everything – make considered choices)...

2. **Deconstruct** this article into its three most important points...

☐

☐

☐

3. Can you **assess** and explain the relevance of this article to today's lesson and objectives?

4. Use one of the **higher order thinking** skills in relation to this article and today's lesson objectives *(design, improve, develop, predict, hypothesise, judge the value of, compare/contrast, prove, adapt).*

You must be ready to feedback your considerations to the class without using these notes – be ready to be asked!

▶ Lesson notes p.11

Teacher feedback form

Knowledge and understanding	
6 marks	**Awarded**
Accurate and reasonable detailed description.	
Demonstrates sound knowledge and understanding.	
Appropriate selection of material to address the question.	
Presentation of information is clear and coherent.	
5-4 marks	
Less detailed but generally accurate.	
Demonstrates relevant knowledge and understanding.	
Some evidence of selection of material to address the question.	
Information presented in an appropriate form.	
3-2 marks	
Basic description that lacks detail and may be muddled.	
Demonstrates some knowledge and understanding.	
Little evidence of selection of material to address the question.	
Information presented not in appropriate form.	
1 mark	
Very brief or flawed description.	
Demonstrated very little knowledge or understanding.	
Selection of material is largely inappropriate.	

Evaluation and analysis	
6 marks	**Awarded**
Effective evaluation of the research and use of material.	
Issues/evidence in reasonable depth (or fewer evaluations in greater depth).	
Excellent quality of written communication.	
5-4 marks	
Reasonable evaluation of research, material not always used effectively.	
Issues/evidence presented in less depth.	
Reasonable quality of written communication.	
3-2 marks	
Basic evaluation of research, basic use of material.	
Issues/evidence presented superficially.	
Quality of written communication lacks clarity and accuracy.	
1 mark	
Evaluation is just discernable.	
Rudimentary presentation of evidence/issues.	
Poor quality of written communication.	

Comments.....

Total:

Grade:

▶ Lesson notes p.12

Essay planning

QUESTION:

AO1: KNOWLEDGE AND UNDERSTANDING:

(How will you show knowledge and understanding of this topic? Be very selective. Remember you need 6 marks)

-
-
-
-
-
-

AO2: EVALUATION AND ANALYSIS:

(To gain high marks, you need to make 2–3 points here and the elaborate those points to show 'reasonable depth').

How will you elaborate…

1. →

2. →

3. →

▶ Lesson notes p.12

The duration of STM

Using only the graph shown below try to guess the aims, procedures, findings and conclusions of Peterson and Peterson's study.

Now use the textbook (pages 4-5) of *Complete Companion* to check your ideas, make any corrections and add any missed details. Award yourself an accuracy score for each section out of 10.

STUDY	GUESS	ACTUAL	ACCURACY /10
AIM			
PROCEDURE			
FINDINGS			
CONCLUSION			

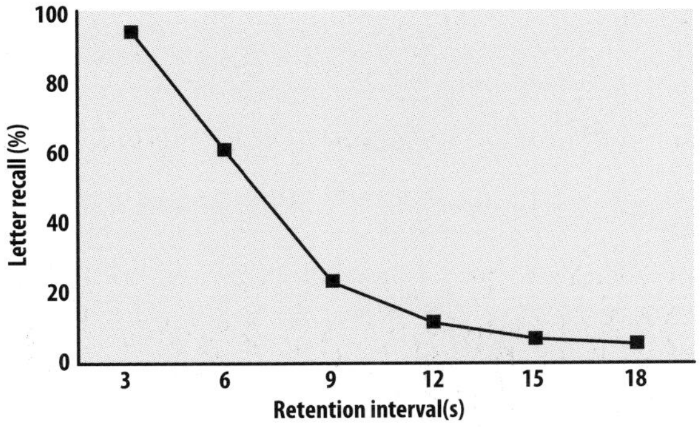

▶ Lesson notes p.15

Encoding in STM and LTM

Read each strip carefully. Decide if each statement refers to A (aim) P (procedure) F (finding) C (conclusion). Cut out each strip and stick them in the correct order. Use pages 7 and 76 of *Complete Companion* to help you.

Participants were given a hearing test before the procedure began.

Baddeley predicted that the STM would show a preference for acoustic encoding while their LTM should prefer semantic encoding.

List A contained acoustically similar words: cat, cab, can, cad, cap, mad, map, man, mat.

In the delayed recall test participants had muddled long-term memories for the semantically similar words but not the acoustically similar ones.

Participants were presented with one of four word lists: A, B, C, D.

To test STM, after each set of five words participants were asked to recall the words they had just heard in the correct order (immediate serial recall).

It was concluded that the dominant form of encoding in STM is acoustic.

List D contained semantically dissimilar words: good, huge, hot, safe, tin, deep, strong, foul.

In the immediate recall tasks participants showed that the most confusion occurred with the acoustically similar words.

The independent variable was the type of list participants received (acoustic or semantic), (similar or dissimilar).

List B contained acoustically dissimilar words: pit, few, cow, pen, sup, bar, day, hot, rig, bun.

It was felt the results showed the most common form of encoding in LTM was semantic.

Each group of participants heard 12 sets of five words from one of the lists.

The dependent variable was how many sets of words they recalled in the correct order.

Baddeley devised a study to investigate encoding in the STM and LTM.

List C contained semantically similar words: great, large, bug, huge, broad, long, tall, fat.

To test LTM, participants' lists contained 10 words and were asked to recall the words 20 minutes later (delayed recall).

The procedure employed an independent measures design.

Extension questions: What are the strengths and weaknesses of using an independent measures design?
Why did Baddeley give his participants a hearing test before the experiment began?

▶ Lesson notes p.15

Capacity of STM

Just how do psychologists investigate how much we can hold in our STM?

In pairs try Jacob's digit span technique

One person is the experimenter. ○
The other is the participant. ○
The experimenter reads out a line of data. ○
The participant then recalls the information immediately in the same order (serial recall). ○

8 6 1 8 9 3
5 3 7 2 9 1 3 7
2 8 4 1 7 3 8 5 8 2

FINDINGS:

FINDINGS:

R W B Q K S
S D V U A F L C
E M Z I H P A W J X

FINDINGS:

table red peace pen button smile
square print cable bin door hurt topic green
vegetable soup nail polish foot ball bread bin hot tub

What have you learnt about capacity of STM?

What have psychologists learnt about the capacity of STM?

Magic number 7 (±2).

Chunking.

▶ Lesson notes p.16

The multi-store model

Task 1: Fill in each box using the key words shown below. Use your textbook to help you.

Short-term memory (STM)	Elaborative rehearsal	Environmental stimuli	Interference
Long-term memory (LTM)	Maintenance rehearsal	Decay	Decay
Sensory memory	Attention	Displacement	

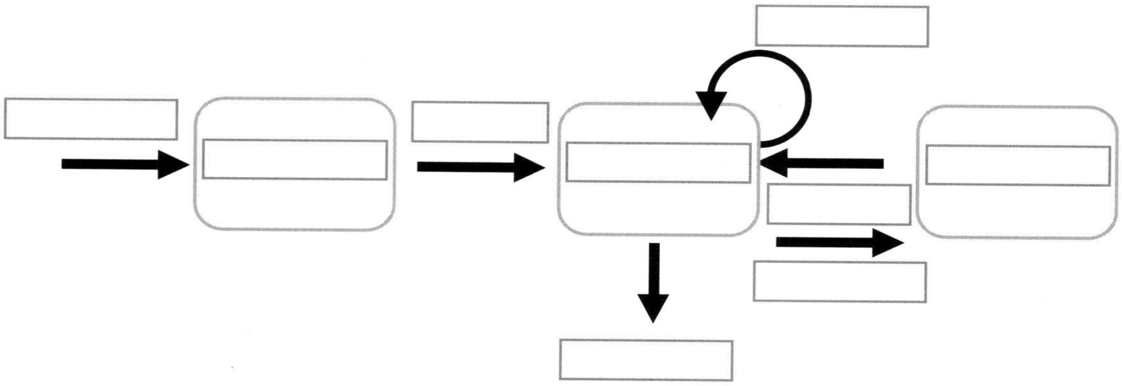

Task 2: For each store fill in the table below:

	Store 1 summary	Store 2 summary	Store 3 summary
Name of Store			
Capacity			
Encoding			
Duration			

Task 3: Now use each summary to write a description of the multi-store model.

Try not to write more than half a page.

▶ Lesson notes p.16

Case studies and the MSM

Studying people who have suffered brain damage has given psychologists further insight into the multi-store model.

HM

can do...

Underwent an operation to remove parts of the brain (which included his hippocampus) in an attempt to control his epileptic fits.

can't do...

How do these findings relate to the structure of memory proposed by the multi-store model?

Clive W

can do...

Suffered a viral infection which attacked his brain, damaging his hippocampus and associated areas.

can't do...

How do these findings relate to the structure of memory proposed by the multi-store model?

KF

can do...

Involved in a motorcycle accident that resulted in brain damage in the left parieto-occipital region (near the back of the brain).

can't do...

How do these findings relate to the structure of memory proposed by the multi-store model?

▶ Lesson notes p.17

Where do you stand?

Place your stickers anywhere along the continua. Remember to explain each one in the box below.

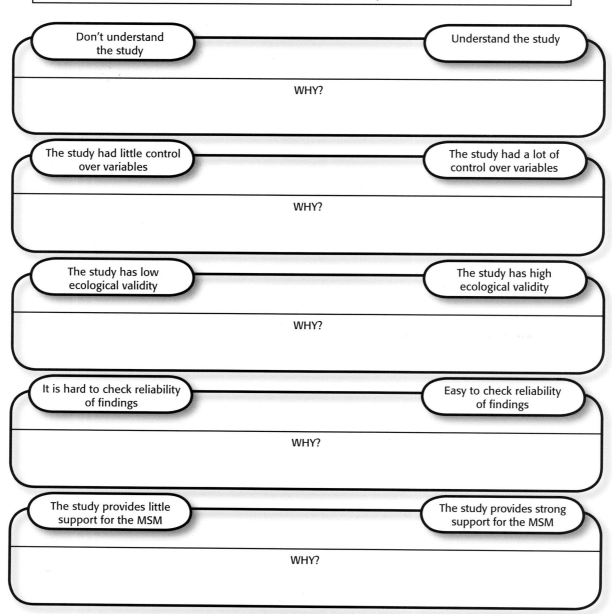

Don't understand the study ——— Understand the study

WHY?

The study had little control over variables ——— The study had a lot of control over variables

WHY?

The study has low ecological validity ——— The study has high ecological validity

WHY?

It is hard to check reliability of findings ——— Easy to check reliability of findings

WHY?

The study provides little support for the MSM ——— The study provides strong support for the MSM

WHY?

KEY WORDS TO HELP YOU

CONTROL	Researchers aim to control all variables in a study that may affect the behaviour of the participants. Usually one variable is manipulated (the IV) and all other variables are controlled for, e.g. age, health of participants, background noise, behaviour and dress of the researcher. If these were not controlled, it would be unclear what caused the behaviour of the participants; the IV or another variable.
ECOLOGICAL VALIDITY	Is the study like real life? Would people be faced with a similar task in their everyday life? If not then can we really apply their behaviour in the study to their behaviour in daily life?
RELIABILITY	If a study is conducted again and the same findings occur then it is considered reliable. Some methods make checking for reliability easy, some make it very difficult. It is impossible to check the reliability of naturalistic observations as no two situations are ever identical so variables present at one observation may not be present the second time you conduct the observation.

▶ Lesson notes p.17

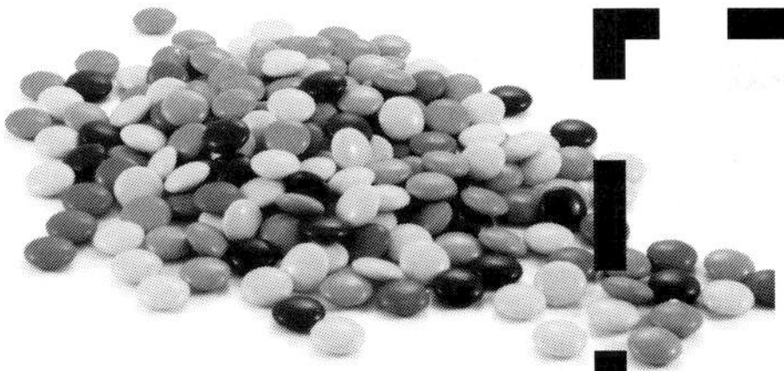

Chocolate bean evidence

Evidence for the multi-store model

TASK 1:

Take one chocolate bean.

Complete the section below that relates to the colour of your bean.

TASK 2:

Now move round the room and find other people to help you complete the other beans. Remember to check you understand the comments you collect.

ORANGE Evidence for sensory memory:

PINK Evidence for two separate stores:

PURPLE PET scan evidence:

RED Case study evidence:

BLUE Issues with lab studies:

YELLOW Issues with case studies:

GREEN Three key words for this section:

BROWN Most interesting point from this section:

▶ Lesson notes p.18

Evaluating the evidence

Just because research seems to support a theory, it doesn't mean we can take the findings as indisputable. We should always question the validity of research.

TASK: Choose one of the following essays to answer

Lab experiments provide better evidence for MSM than case studies because...

- Mention the lab studies that have been conducted and how they have supported the multi-store model.
  For example:
  - Sperling, Logie or
  - Glanzer and Cunitz.
- Explain why we can trust their findings:
  - the level of internal validity
  - the ability to check reliability
  - the type of data collected
  - the number of participants.
- Mention two of the case studies relating to the multi-store model.
  For example:
  - HM, KF or
  - Clive Wearing.
- Criticise the use of case studies. Why is it difficult to trust their findings?
  - the issue of internal validity
  - issues of reliability
  - the type of data collected
  - the number of participants.

Case studies provide better evidence for MSM than lab studies because...

- Mention two of the case studies relating to the multi-store model.
  For example:
  - HM, KF or
  - Clive Wearing.
- Explain why their findings are useful:
  - the level of external validity
  - the amount of data that can be collected
  - the type of data that can be collected.
- Mention the lab studies that have been conducted and how they have supported the multi-store model.
  For example:
  - Sperling, Logie or
  - Glanzer and Cunitz.
- Criticise the use of lab studies. Why is it difficult to trust their findings?
  - the artificial nature of tasks
  - the type of data collected
  - the lack of external validity.

THINK YOU HAVE FINISHED?

Read your work and tick off each of the points listed above.

- Have you included key terminology and used it correctly?
- Have you written in paragraphs?
- Have you clearly explained each idea with a good level of detail?

▶ Lesson notes p.18

Plenary statements

Copy the boxes into your notes then stick each statement in the relevant box.

AO1: Multi-store model outline

AO1: Working memory model outline

AO2: Multi-store model evaluation

AO2: Working memory model evaluation

- A linear model for the whole of memory.
- A more detailed explanation of STM.
- Three stores: sensory memory, STM, LTM.
- Three main components: phonological loop, visuo-spatial sketchpad and central executive.
- Rehearsal moves information to different stores.
- Different components process different types of information.
- Very influential, many now accept this version of STM.
- An explanation of how memory functions instead of how it's structured.
- Doesn't really explain how the central executive works.
- One of the first models that enabled scientific tests into memory to be conducted.
- It is an over simplified model.
- It ignores the different types of information to be remembered.
- Case studies of HM and Clive Wearing suggest memory does consist of separate stores.
- Is rehearsal always needed? For example, vivid memory of 9/11.
- Dual processing tasks seem to show we cannot do two tasks that both require the same component.
- Can be applied to real life, e.g. recruitment tool in air force, learning issues in school.

▶ Lesson notes p.18

Leap frog review

For each statement place a frog on the lily pad that best reflects your thoughts and feelings.

The multi-store model: Be able to give a detailed outline of the model.

I am unsure of most aspects and find recall difficult	I understand some aspects but find it hard to recall	One or two points are confusing	I understand most aspects and can remember some	I have a good understanding and recall of aspects

The multi-store model: Be able to give three evaluation points (positive or negative) for the model.

I am unsure of most aspects and find recall difficult	I understand some aspects but find it hard to recall	One or two points are confusing	I understand most aspects and can remember some	I have a good understanding and recall of aspects

STM and LTM: Be able to explain the difference between STM and LTM (capacity, duration and encoding).

I am unsure of most aspects and find recall difficult	I understand some aspects but find it hard to recall	One or two points are confusing	I understand most aspects and can remember some	I have a good understanding and recall of aspects

STM and LTM: Be able to outline research into STM and LTM.

I am unsure of most aspects and find recall difficult	I understand some aspects but find it hard to recall	One or two points are confusing	I understand most aspects and can remember some	I have a good understanding and recall of aspects

STM and LTM: Be able to evaluate the methodology of research into STM and LTM.

I am unsure of most aspects and find recall difficult	I understand some aspects but find it hard to recall	One or two points are confusing	I understand most aspects and can remember some	I have a good understanding and recall of aspects

What aspects do you feel you need more help with?
What aspects do you think you need to spend longer revising?

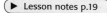

▶ Lesson notes p.19

12-mark question

What are AOs?

- AO1 - Recognise, recall and show understanding of scientific knowledge, select, organise and communicate relevant information in a variety of forms. I know.....
- AO2 - Analyse and evaluate scientific knowledge, apply knowledge and processes to unfamiliar situations, assess the validity, reliability and credibility of scientific information. The strengths/weaknesses are....
- AO3 - Describe ethical, safe and skilful practical techniques and processes, know how to make, record, and communicate valid observations, analyse, interpret, explain and evaluate the methodology and investigative activities in a variety of ways. Psychology is a science...

Work in groups, but keep your own record.

Draw the table in your notes.

Work in groups to complete each column.

I know .... (AO1)	The evaluations I can make about this are .... (AO2)	The scientific aspects shown in the research are ... (AO3)

The 12-mark questions require you to include AO1 and AO2 information.
Outline and evaluate the multi-store model (12 marks).

6 marks for AO1 (half your answer); 6 marks for AO2 (half your answer).

ESSAY EXTRACT

Read and highlight the AO1 and AO2 comments in two different colours.

According to this model information reaches the brain from the senses (sound, sight, etc.). This information enters the sensory memory store. The information that receives our attention is transferred to our STM (short-term memory) for further processing. The MSM (multi-store model) presents the STM as a simple concept, it is often drawn as a box in diagrams. This may be a weakness of the model as some argue STM is much more complex and contains different components that attend to different types of information.

The STM is seen as very limited by the MSM and information must be constantly rehearsed for it to be held in STM for longer than 30 seconds...

Copy the table below into your notes. In each column list words that could be used as signposts in your answers. Use the passage above to help generate ideas.

What do A/B graders need to show?

AO1	AO2	AO3
Accurate & detailed knowledge of research	Can apply ideas to new contexts	Secure knowledge of research principles and design
Correct use of psychological terms and concepts	Effective evaluation of research.	Comment on strengths and limitations of design
Writing is organised and ideas clearly presented.	Detailed analysis of research findings and conclusions drawn.	Comment on reliability and validity of data.

Signposts: How do I show AO2 in my writing?

Strengths	Weaknesses	Comparisons

In pairs write a list of rules for answering 12-mark questions using the information above to help you.
Be positive: try to start rules with DO rather than DON'T.

▶ Lesson notes p.19

Psychology story time

The tale of the working memory model

Once upon a time there lived a very important businessman. He was the **central executive** of a very busy company. Being the central executive was extremely stressful as he had **overall control** of the company's operations and processes.

He was a talented **controller** who had **responsibility** for a wide range of important processes, which included **setting targets, making sure errors did not occur, rehearsing information, dividing attention** between tasks, **preventing unnecessary information** getting in the way. Phew! The list seemed endless. Time was short and the demands were great. You might wonder how one man could cope with all these tasks!

Luckily for the central executive he had **two slave systems** to help him. They had **separate responsibilities** and **worked independently** from each other. This helped **free up** some of the executive's **capacity** so he could deal with **more demanding information processing** tasks. You may not think it is polite to call these systems slaves but as they were under the central executive's control he felt it summed them up nicely.

The two slave systems had different names; one was known as the **phonological loop** and she dealt with speech-based **verbal information**. Any auditory information that came into the business was her responsibility. She felt like she demonstrated two key skills in her work: holding information she heard in a **phonological store** and carrying out **articulatory processing** (repeating information to herself). All day long she busied herself with acoustic tasks.

The other slave system was called the **visuo-spatial sketchpad** and he dealt with **visual information**, what things look like, and **spatial information**, where things are in relation to each other. As he dealt with information very different to the other slave (the loop) they could **work independently** of each other. Should either of the slaves become **overloaded**, the central executive was able to step in and help them out for a short time.

▶ Lesson notes p.20

Baddeley 1975a

Evidence for the phonological loop and articulator process

Aim: to investigate the existence of a phonological loop in STM.

Procedure: Participants saw everyday words displayed very quickly one after the other. They were then asked to write the words seen in serial order (the same order as on the list).

Condition 1 – the list contained five one-syllable English words, e.g. tree, once, pain.

Condition 2 – the list contained five polysyllabic English words, e.g. university, recommendation, establishment.

TASK: Working in pairs.

1. Decide in which condition you will play the role of the researcher (you will play the role of the participant in the other condition).

2. For the condition you are researcher create a list of five words.

3. Write these five words (either all one syllable or polysyllabic depending on the condition) on separate pieces of paper.

4. Carry out the experiment with your participant, showing them one word after the other. Remember to tell them they need to recall in serial order.

5. Record their data. How many words did they recall?

6. Conduct the second condition, this time playing the role of participant.

Your findings. Condition 1: One-syllable words.

I was the researcher / participant (circle)

Your findings. Condition 2: Polysyllabic words.

I was the researcher / participant (circle)

Findings: From analysing several trials Baddeley found participants recalled the shorter, one-syllable words much better than the polysyllabic words. He called this the **word length effect**.

Conclusions: The phonological loop has a role in the capacity of STM. The amount you can hold in your STM is determined by the length of time it takes to say the words NOT the number of items. It seems that the phonological loop holds the amount of information that you can say in 2 seconds.

What do you think happened when the participants were given an articulatory suppression task (e.g., saying 'the the the the' while viewing the words)?

I think: ....

....

▶ Lesson notes p.20

Baddeley 1975b

Evidence for the visuo-spatial sketchpad

Aim: to investigate the existence of a visuo-spatial sketchpad in STM.
Procedure: Participants were asked to complete a visual tracking task at the same time as describing the angles on a letter.

TASK 1: If angle is at the top or bottom line then say YES. If angle occurs anywhere else say NO.

TASK 2: Track the movement of a dot of light with a pointer.

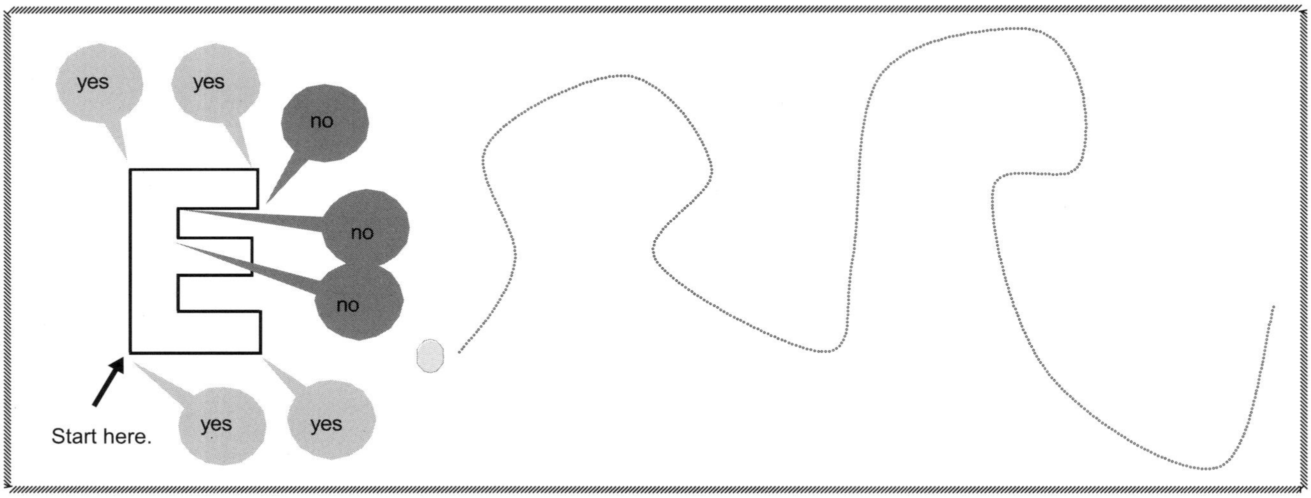

Findings

Participants found it really hard to complete these two tasks simultaneously.

WHY:

Findings

When asked to perform Task 2 while carrying out a verbal task, e.g. saying 'the the the the', participants performed much better.

WHY:

Conclusions: Complete the paragraph.

These laboratory studies could be said to support the existence of separate stores in STM because:

....

....

....

....

....

▶ Lesson notes p.20

Working memory AO2

Should you meet the question 'Outline and evaluate the working memory model', you will need to be able to give a 6-mark evaluation that uses information effectively.

Task 1: Reading for information (*Complete Companion* pages 14-15)

Working in pairs, choose either Strengths of the working memory model (p 14) or Weaknesses of the working memory model (p 15). Identify two key points and rewrite them in your own words using a maximum of 50 words.

Point 1:

Point 2:

Task 2: Snowballing

Join with another pair who looked at the opposite evaluation. Share your ideas and note down their ideas in your own words. Make sure you understand them!

Point 1:

Point 2:

Task 3: Using the information

Now write your own evaluation of the working memory model using the points you have gathered. Try not to exceed half a page as this is all the room you will have on the exam paper for 6 marks of AO2. Make sure you explain your ideas clearly as others will soon be judging your work!

Task 4: Buying an evaluation

Move round the class reading each other's evaluations. Keep a record of evaluations you thought were particularly impressive. Now take your cheque and make it out to the student whose evaluation you liked the most. You can pay up to £100. On the back of the cheque explain why you chose their evaluation.

How much money did your evaluation earn? Who earned the most money?

▶ Lesson notes p.21

Cheques

Students take time to read each other's work. They then decide whose work they found most impressive and award a cheque to them up to the value of £100.

On the reverse they explain why they have chosen to buy their work.

DATE ________________

PAY ____ £

____

MEMO ________________________ ________________________

⑈012⑈ ⑆00345⑆06 ⑈70890

DATE ________________

PAY ____ £

____

MEMO ________________________ ________________________

⑈012⑈ ⑆00345⑆06 ⑈70890

DATE ________________

PAY ____ £

____

MEMO ________________________ ________________________

⑈012⑈ ⑆00345⑆06 ⑈70890

▶ Lesson notes p.21

Expanding evaluations

Baddeley and Hitch use dual task technique experiments to provide evidence for the working memory model. However, are these studies valid? Use your knowledge of validity to complete each evaluation train. Make sure each point is a development of the previous comment.

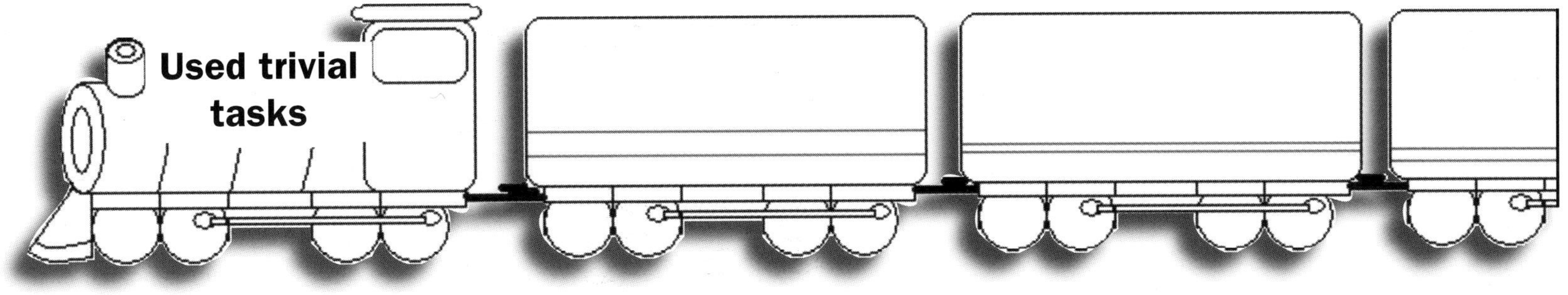

▶ Lesson notes p.21

Considering evaluations

For each evaluative comment decide if it is making a positive statement about the working memory model (a strength) or a negative statement (a weakness). Then decide how convincing you find that statement. The stronger the statement, the longer the line. You could consider issues of validity, cause and effect, implications for real life in your judgements.

Box one has been completed as an example.

A reasonable point as the MSM cannot explain KF who seems to show STM has different components. But, this is only one man and cannot be sure of causes of damage.

Strength of working memory model.

Only some aspects of KF's STM damaged.

The model is vague about the central executive.

The EVR case study casts doubt on central executive.

Baddeley's studies show role of slave systems.

More detailed than the MSM.

Model vague on relationship to LTM.

Weakness of working memory model.

Now pick three of the statements you made and explain in detail the judgements you made for those statements, e.g. as shown in the box above but develop the points further!

▶ Lesson notes p.22

Puddle splash review

For each statement place the Wellington boots in the puddle that best reflects your thoughts and feelings.

The working memory model: Be able to give a detailed outline of the model.

I am unsure of most aspects and find recall difficult	I understand some aspects but find it hard to recall	One or two points are confusing	I understand most aspects and can remember some	I have a good understanding and recall of aspects

The working memory model: Be able to give three evaluation points (positive or negative) for the model.

I am unsure of most aspects and find recall difficult	I understand some aspects but find it hard to recall	One or two points are confusing	I understand most aspects and can remember some	I have a good understanding and recall of aspects

Research: Be able to explain one research study that employs the dual task technique.

I am unsure of most aspects and find recall difficult	I understand some aspects but find it hard to recall	One or two points are confusing	I understand most aspects and can remember some	I have a good understanding and recall of aspects

Research: I can evaluate the validity of laboratory research into the different models of memory.

I am unsure of most aspects and find recall difficult	I understand some aspects but find it hard to recall	One or two points are confusing	I understand most aspects and can remember some	I have a good understanding and recall of aspects

Research: I can evaluate the validity of case study research into the different models of memory.

I am unsure of most aspects and find recall difficult	I understand some aspects but find it hard to recall	One or two points are confusing	I understand most aspects and can remember some	I have a good understanding and recall of aspects

What aspects do you feel you need more help with?

What aspects do you think you need to spend longer revising?

▶ Lesson notes p.22

Loftus and Palmer 1974

Splatter study: Read the outline of Loftus and Palmer's study into the accuracy of EWT then use your knowledge of research methods to complete the boxes.

Summary of aim:

Materials needed:

Sample:

Research design:

Loftus and Palmer were interested in the accuracy of memory after witnessing a car accident, in particular to see if leading questions distorted the accuracy of eyewitnesses' immediate recall.

Forty-five students were shown seven films of different traffic accidents. After each film the participants were given a questionnaire which asked them to describe the accident and then answer a series of specific questions about it. There was one critical question. This was 'About how fast were the cars going when they hit each other?' One group of participants were given this question. The other four groups were given the verbs smashed, collided, bumped or contacted in place of the word hit.

The mean speed estimate was calculated for each group. The group given the word 'smashed' estimated a higher speed than the other groups (about 41 mph). The group given the word 'contacted' estimated the lowest speed (about 30 mph).

Loftus' research suggests that EWT was generally inaccurate and therefore unreliable. The form of questioning can have a significant effect on witness answers to questions. However, this was a laboratory study and may not reflect the recall of those who witness real-life car crashes.

IV:

DV:

Summary of findings:

Type of data collected (qualitative/quantitative):

Summary of conclusions:

Real-life implications:

Development of criticism:

▶ Lesson notes p.22

Post-event information

Complete the table below for either Loftus and Palmer's broken glass study or Yield/Stop sign study. Both studies aimed to investigate whether information received after witnessing an event caused the material to be altered before it is stored resulting in a permanently altered memory.

Aim	
Research design	
Participant grouping	
Materials needed	
Independent variable	
Dependent variable	
Step-by-step procedure	1. 2. 3. 4.
Type of data	***Qualitative / Quantitative (circle)***
Findings	
Conclusion	
Validity	

▶ Lesson notes p.23

Anxiety and EWT

Imagine you are an expert psychologist asked to speak on a radio show about the accuracy of EWT. Summarise relevant research for the listeners.

Topics to consider:

- Research that suggests high levels of stress have a negative impact on accuracy.
- Research that suggests high levels of stress increase accuracy of recall.
- The Yerkes-Dodson law.
- The effect of the presence of a weapon on accuracy.

Everyone **must** complete the following boxes:

Three points you definitely want to include in the radio show.

How you would summarise research findings in this field.

Most of you **should** complete the following box:

One piece of research you want to tell the listeners about.

Some of you **could** complete this box, too:

Why psychologists should be careful when interpreting research gained in lab, natural or field studies.

▶ Lesson notes p.23

Age and EWT

Little Billy is on the stand. He is convinced he saw the defendant 'Burglar Betty' steal the banana. Can the judge and jury believe his testimony?

Defence

Prosecution

Jury's conclusion:

▶ Lesson notes p.23

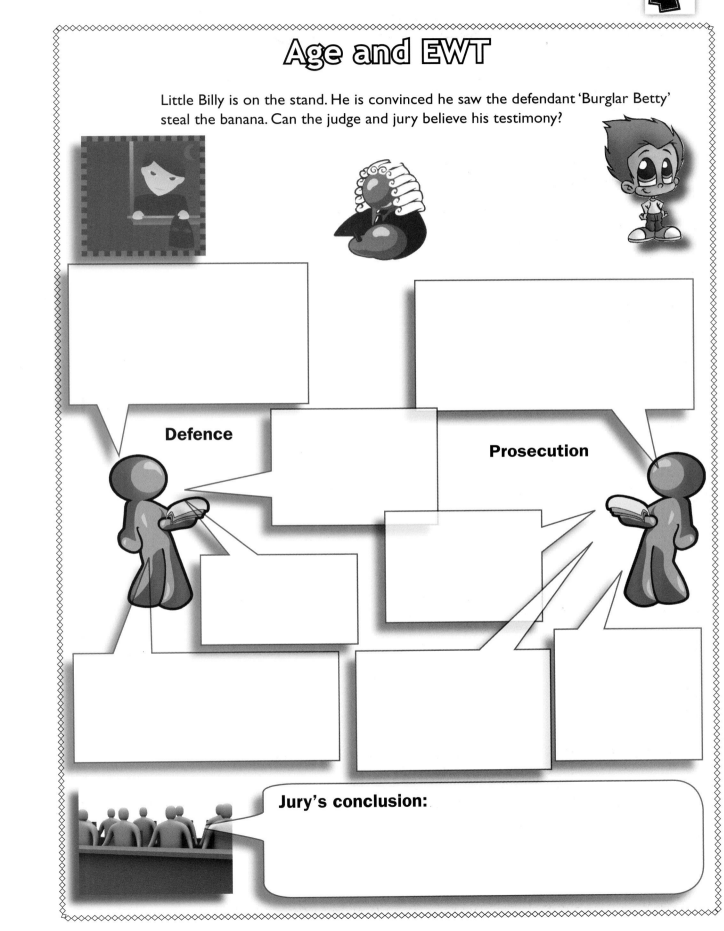

Interviewing witnesses 1

Comparing traditional questioning techniques and the cognitive interview technique.

TASK 1: TRADITIONAL INTERVIEW

In pairs decide who will be the witness and who will be the interviewer.

Interviewers: Leave the room and work in groups of 4 to devise a set of questions to ask the witness regarding the film clip they will watch in your absence.

Witnesses: After the interviewers have left the room you will see a short film clip. Watch carefully as they will question you about the events you have seen when they return.

Question 1:

Response:

Question 2:

Response:

Question 3:

Response:

Question 4:

Response:

Question 5:

Response:

Now watch the film clip together.

Accuracy of the data gathered:

Depth of information:

Usefulness of this interview technique:

▶ Lesson notes p.24

Interviewing witnesses 2

Comparing traditional questioning techniques and the cognitive interview technique.

TASK 2: COGNITIVE INTERVIEW

Now switch roles; the interviewer becomes the witness and the witness becomes the interviewer.

Interviewers: Leave the room and work in groups of 4, practise the cognitive interview question technique. How exactly will you get witnesses to address the four areas of the interview technique?

Witnesses: After the interviewers have left the room you will see a short film clip. Watch carefully as they will question you about the events you have seen when they return.

Report everything:

Response:

Mental reinstatement of original context:

Response:

Changing the order:

Response:

Changing the perspective:

Response:

Now watch the film clip together.

Accuracy of the data gathered:

Depth of information:

Usefulness of this interview technique:

▶ Lesson notes p.24

Cognitive interview AO2

Employing the three-point rule will guarantee you make effective evaluations.

There are three forms your evaluation of the cognitive interview technique could take: Considering the effectiveness, discuss the practical issues or assess their value in real life. Read all the statement boxes and circle whether the box contains point, evidence or example. Then group boxes together, in threes, in the correct order.

The PEE rule:

P = Make the point. *The CI technique seems effective.*
E = Give the evidence for the point. *Köhnken found a 34% increase in recall.*
E = Explain the evidence, (the 'So what' section). *This shows CI is a more effective method.*

Point - Evidence - Explanation
These findings suggest the CI technique could be used to develop a new approach in interviewing witnesses in Brazil. Hopefully, this will lead to a reduction in the amount of miscarriages of justice.

Point - Evidence - Explanation
Kebbell and Wagstaff found many police officers did not use the CI technique in less serious crimes as they did not have the time to carry out this type of interview. Police often used strategies to deliberately limit an eyewitness report to the minimum amount of information deemed necessary by the officer.

Point - Evidence - Explanation
Research into the effectiveness of the CI technique has been useful in improving the interview techniques in Brazil whose police traditionally use interrogation, torture and ill treatment.

Point - Evidence - Explanation
This makes real-life research into the effectiveness of CI difficult as there is not one procedure in operation. It may also mean some CIs are more effective than others.

Point - Evidence - Explanation
Not all police forces use the same procedure or components in their cognitive interviews.

Point - Evidence - Explanation
Thames Valley Police do not use the 'changing perspectives component' in their cognitive interviews, while others tend to use only 'reinstate context' and 'report everything'.

Point - Evidence - Explanation
Therefore, while CI may produce a vast amount of information, it may not always be practical or helpful in terms of allowing the police to efficiently investigate incidents, especially those seen as less serious.

Point - Evidence - Explanation
Stein and Memon showed university cleaning staff a video of an abduction. Compared to standard police interviews the CI showed an increased amount of correct recall. For example, detailed descriptions of the man holding the gun were obtained from the witnesses.

Point - Evidence - Explanation
The CI takes longer to complete than the traditional interview technique.

▶ Lesson notes p.24

Teaching towers

One effective way of learning information is to teach other people.

1 In groups of three use your information to complete your tower.
2 One person now stays with your tower to teach other people about your topic.
3 The others from the group need to split up and visit other towers to learn one topic each.
4 Regroup and teach each other the two new tower topics.

Role of organisation	Role of elaborative rehearsal	Dual coding hypothesis
Key words:	Key words:	Key words:
Summary sentence:	Summary sentence:	Summary sentence:
Research evidence:	Research evidence:	Research evidence:

Rules

- ❑ Make sure the 'teacher' really understands the information to be taught.
- ❑ As a teacher explain the information to your listeners. Don't just read out your work or worse still let them copy your sheet: this isn't teaching or learning, it is just handwriting practice!
- ❑ When listening to a teacher, ask questions if their points are not clear.
- ❑ When you return to your original group, make sure you teach each other. Again don't just let others copy your notes. Again ask questions if your teacher is not clear in their explanations.

▶ Lesson notes p.25

Method of loci

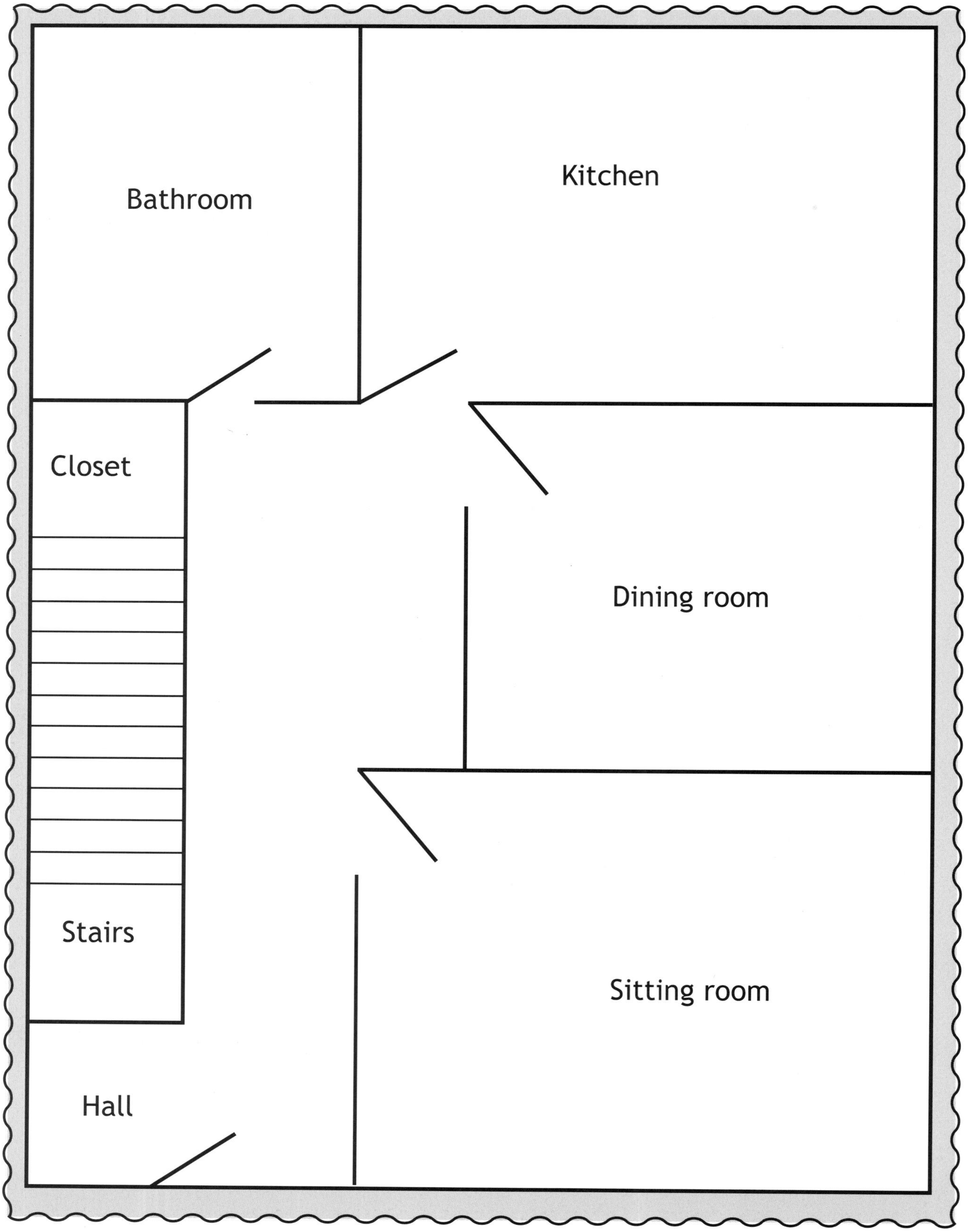

▶ Lesson notes p.25

Assessing mnemonics

This section is great as it should give you lots of ideas for revision in all your studies.

Now you have experienced two mnemonic techniques, complete the table below.

Mnemonic technique 1:	Mnemonic technique 2:
Brief explanation of the technique.	
Explanation of the psychology behind the technique.	
Aspects of the technique I enjoyed or found useful.	
Aspects of the technique I disliked or found difficult.	
Overall feelings towards the technique.	

▶ Lesson notes p.25

Slug to snail review

For each statement turn the slug that best reflects your thoughts and feelings into a snail.

The accuracy of EWT: Be able to outline the factors that are thought to affect EWT's accuracy.				
I am unsure of most aspects and find recall difficult	I understand some aspects but find it hard to recall	One or two points are confusing	I understand most aspects and can remember some	I have a good understanding and recall of aspects

The accuracy of EWT: Can describe procedure and findings of two studies into the accuracy of EWT.				
I am unsure of most aspects and find recall difficult	I understand some aspects but find it hard to recall	One or two points are confusing	I understand most aspects and can remember some	I have a good understanding and recall of aspects

Cognitive interview: Able to explain the techniques employed by police in the cognitive interview.				
I am unsure of most aspects and find recall difficult	I understand some aspects but find it hard to recall	One or two points are confusing	I understand most aspects and can remember some	I have a good understanding and recall of aspects

Cognitive interview: Have an appreciation of the practical issues and effectiveness of the cognitive interview.				
I am unsure of most aspects and find recall difficult	I understand some aspects but find it hard to recall	One or two points are confusing	I understand most aspects and can remember some	I have a good understanding and recall of aspects

Improving memory: Have an understanding of the psychology theories that inform mnemonic techniques.				
I am unsure of most aspects and find recall difficult	I understand some aspects but find it hard to recall	One or two points are confusing	I understand most aspects and can remember some	I have a good understanding and recall of aspects

- What aspects do you feel you need more help with?
- What aspects do you think you need to spend longer revising?

Lesson notes p.25

Matching race 1

Unconditioned Stimulus	A new stimulus that has been paired with an unconditioned stimulus so that an animal/human associates the two together. It used to be the neutral stimulus.
Unconditioned Response	Pavlov, after observing the behaviour of dogs.
Neutral Stimulus	According to learning theory, it is because they have learnt to associate them with food via classical conditioning.
Conditioned Stimulus	Classical and operant conditioning (according to learning theory).
Conditioned Response	A stimulus which causes an unlearnt response. For example, hunger ⇨ salivation.

▶ Lesson notes p.26

Matching race 2

Why are infants happy around their mothers?	An unlearnt behaviour/ action which is caused by a stimulus. For example, screaming ⇨ pain.
Who proposed classical conditioning?	Like a theory: it attempts to account for behaviour which has been observed by psychologists, e.g. why dogs salivate at the sound of a bell.
According to learning theory, all behaviour is the result of...?	A learnt response to a previously neutral stimulus.
In attachment, the conditioned stimulus is...?	This becomes the conditioned stimulus once conditioning has occurred (i.e., it has been paired with an unconditioned stimulus). For example, the bell with Pavlov's dogs.
An explanation is...?	The mother/ caregiver

▶ Lesson notes p.26

Burger evaluation skills

A study that undermines the learning theory explanation of attachment is Harlow's (1959) study of rhesus monkeys.

Harlow separated infant rhesus monkeys from their mothers and raised them in isolation. He created two artificial wire mothers that resembled monkeys. One had a feeding bottle attached and the other was wrapped in soft cloth but offered no food. The monkeys spent much of their time clinging to the cloth mother, especially in times of distress.

This undermines the learning theory view of attachment because according to the explanation, the young monkeys should have attached to the wire monkey which dispensed food because they would associate it with a sense of pleasure and the reduction of their hunger drive. However, the infants tended to cling more to a mother which offered them comfort.

A study that undermines (or supports) the learning theory explanation of attachment is....

Describe procedure and findings of study.

This undermines (or supports) the learning theory explanation of attachment because....

Use these studies and Handout 6 to evaluate the learning theory explanation of attachment using the burger technique.

Fox (1977)

Fox studied 122 children, born and reared in an Israeli Kibbutz. In this system, children are raised communally. Children in this study had lived in a children's house from an early age where they were cared for by a nurse (metapelet). The metapelet was responsible for feeding the infants and taking care of their daily needs. Very little time during the day was spent with parents, perhaps an hour or so a day. By observing separation and reunion behaviour, Fox concluded that the children were strongly attached to their parents, and showed a weaker attachment to the nurses.

Schaffer and Emerson (1964)

Schaffer and Emerson conducted observational study of human infants with the aim to investigate many elements of attachment. One of their findings was that infants would often form multiple attachments. They became most attached to adults who were most responsive to them. In many cases this was not the person who spent the most time with the child, or the person who fed them.

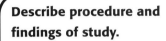

▶ Lesson notes p.26

BOWLBY – 'Connect 5'

Social releasers:

Link...

Adaptive/innate:

Link...

Sensitive period:

Link...

Monotropy:

Link...

Secure base:

▶ Lesson notes p.27

Psychology storytime

'Happy birthday', said Katie's Mum as she handed over a box wrapped in bright pink paper with a matching bow secured to the top.

Katie had been waiting for the date – 1 May 2040 – for what felt like forever. Her tenth birthday had finally arrived and she was silently praying she already knew what lay beneath the pretty pink wrapping.

Tearing off the paper to reveal the familiar, friendly face of the bear staring back at her, Katie said: 'Wow, thanks Mum!'

Excitement bubbled up inside her as she read on the back of the box how she could make her very own, real-life, walking, talking, Edward bear. Katie had become quite attached to her friend Lucy's bear; he was much friendlier than her mother's surly home robot, Robert.

Katie could barely wait for her birthday celebrations to finish so she could focus on the important task ahead of her. With all the industry of a steam train Katie forged ahead with her mission: cutting material, stuffing and sewing, until her work was done.

Inserting Edward's computer chip was the finishing touch. After clicking the chip into place, Katie held the finished article aloft. She eyed her creation as it sprang to life, blinked, and cautiously took in its surroundings. Katie followed Edward's eyes as they scanned the room and came back to rest on her face.

Something about the way Katie had sewn Edward's eyes slightly too close together and the way the stuffing didn't quite reach the full length of his limbs, gave Edward a somewhat haunted, empty look. Edward didn't look like Lucy's bear. His eyes didn't twinkle with cheeky charm, they glinted with what Katie thought, but didn't like to admit, was slightly sinister intent. Disappointed with the fruit of her labour, Katie stuffed Edward into a dark cupboard, leaving him to contemplate his bleak future.

Edward soon began to wonder if dark loneliness was all life had to offer him. He decided to leave Katie's house in search of something more.

Finding himself amongst humans and other robotic creatures was difficult for Edward. If anyone approached him he would respond with anger, pushing any potential friends away until they no longer tried to get to know him. He had also found himself with an inexplicable desire to destroy anything he came into contact with.

Since leaving Katie's house, Edward had taken to watching her from across the road. Seeing Katie playing happily with her friend Lucy and Lucy's bear filled Edward with rage.

Following Lucy home, Edward plotted to put an end to their fun for good.

He was about to remove and destroy the computer chip in Lucy's bear, when the light snapped on, illuminating his dark deed.

Lucy shrieked in horror, immediately summoning Katie to confront Edward.

When Katie arrived she demanded: 'Why have you done this?'

'Because of you', Edward replied.

A shiver ran through Katie as she absorbed his words.

▶ Lesson notes p.27

LOVE Quiz!

A short version of the love quiz

Question 1: Which of the following best describes your parents' relationship with each other?

(a) My parents have a caring relationship and are affectionate with each other.
(b) My parents appear to have a good enough relationship with each other but are not especially affectionate.
(c) My parents have a reasonable relationship and are sometimes affectionate towards each other.

Question 2: Which of the following best describes your relationship with your mother?

(a) My mother treats me with respect and is accepting and not demanding. She is confident about herself.
(b) My mother is humourous, likable and respected by others. She treats me with respect.
(c) My mother treats me with respect but is sometimes cold and rejecting.

Question 3: Which of the following best describes your relationship with your father?

(a) My father is sometimes affectionate but can be unfair.
(b) My father is caring, affectionate and humorous.
(c) My father is reasonably caring.

Question 4: Select the statement that best describes your experiences of intimacy.

(a) I find that others are reluctant to get as close as I would like.
(b) I find it relatively easy to get close to others and am comfortable depending on them and having them depend on me.
(c) I am somewhat uncomfortable being close to others; I find it difficult to trust them completely, difficult to allow myself to depend on them.

Question 5: Select the statement that best describes your experiences of intimacy.

(a) I don't often worry about being abandoned or about someone getting too close to me.
(b) I often worry that my partner doesn't really love me or won't want to stay with me.
(c) I am nervous when anyone gets too close, and often romantic partners want me to be more intimate than I feel comfortable being.

Question 6: Select the statement that best describes your experiences of intimacy.

(a) I enjoy relationships but am generally quite self-sufficient.
(b) I have been lucky in love and most of my relationships are rewarding. I still like the people I was involved with.
(c) At times I wish I could just melt into someone so we could get beyond our separateness.

Question 7: Select the statement that best describes your attitudes towards love.

(a) The kind of head-over-heels love that is depicted in novels and in the movies does not exist in real life.
(b) It is easy to fall in love and I frequently find myself beginning to fall in love, though I am not sure that it really is love.
(c) Love is a positive and real experience.

Question 8: Select the statement that best describes your attitudes towards love.

(a) It is rare to find a person one can really fall in love with.
(b) In some relationships romantic love never fades.
(c) Most of us could love many people equally well, there is no 'one true love'.

Question 9: Select the statement that best describes your attitudes towards love.

(a) I think that romantic feelings do wax and wane.
(b) Romantic feelings wax and wane but at times they reach the intensity experienced at the start of a relationship.
(c) Intense romantic love is common at the start of a relationship but rarely lasts.

▶ Lesson notes p.29

Evaluating Bowlby's theory of attachment

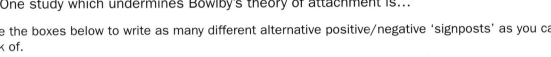

'**Signposts**' are simply ways to introduce your evaluation arguments. They let the reader (or examiner!) know what arguments you are about to make.

For example:

- 'One study which supports Bowlby's theory of attachments is...'
- 'One study which undermines Bowlby's theory of attachment is...'

Use the boxes below to write as many different alternative positive/negative 'signposts' as you can think of.

Positive 'Signposts':

Negative 'Signposts':

Use these 'signposts' to help you write evaluations of Bowlby's theory of attachment (Handout 47).

Remember that your 'signposts' can be more specific by identifying the feature of the theory you wish to evaluate. For example:

- 'One study that supports Bowlby's concept of the internal working model is...'

▶ Lesson notes p.30

Evaluating Bowlby's theory of attachment

Tasks....

1. Cut out the essay fragments and sort into studies/ arguments which **support** or **undermine** Bowlby's theory.
2. Stick down so you have space to write your signpost above, and your commentary below.
3. Introduce each essay fragment with a signpost and make sure it is relevant to the part of the theory you are evaluating, *e.g. One study that supports Bowlby's concept of the secure base is Erickson et al. (1985).*
4. Beneath, explain **how** and **why** the study/argument supports or undermines Bowlby.
5. Extension: Produce counter arguments for each.

Innate and evolutionary emphasis on attachment

Sensitive period

Social releasers

Secure base

Monotropy

Internal working model

Continuity hypothesis

Schaffer and Emerson's (1964) study of 60 infants from Glasgow showed that most infants formed their first attachment with one particular person. But, nearly one third formed multiple attachments (to two or more persons) in which there appeared to be no preferred attachment figure. This became increasingly common as the infants grew older.

Sroufe *et al.*'s (2005) longitudinal study followed participants from infancy to late adolescence and found that early attachment type predicted later emotional and social behaviour. For example, secure infants were more likely to be rated as more popular.

Erickson *et al.* (1985) observed 4 to 5 year olds in pre-school settings. They found that securely attached children were less dependent on the teacher and were more confident undertaking tasks than insecurely attached children.

The Czech twins were 'discovered' at the age of 7. They had been locked up and isolated from the outside world and abused by their stepmother since birth. When discovered, they had no language ability at all. After loving care from two sisters, by the age of 14 the Czech twins showed normal social and intellectual functioning and were able to form meaningful attachments.

Despite rapid advances in genetics, there is no direct evidence of a gene for attachment or genes for attachment.

Hazan and Shaver (1987) found that adults' romantic attachments were closely linked to their infant attachments. Securely attached infants tended to have secure romantic attachments.

The temperament hypothesis (Kagan, 1984) states that we have inborn temperamental differences such as 'easy', 'slow to warm up' and 'difficult'. Psychologists who support this hypothesis believe that these temperaments can affect infant *and* adult relationships.

Hodges and Tizard's (1989) longitudinal study of institutionalised children (living in orphanages) who had formed no attachments in the early parts of their lives and had difficulty forming relationships with peers.

▶ Lesson notes p.30

Insecure attachments – spot the difference!

Don't forget that there are two types of insecure attachment: insecure-avoidant (Type A), and insecure-resistant (Type B). Using the grids provided, complete this 'spot the difference' page with simple drawings (e.g. use stick people) to help you remember and understand those differences!

Insecure-Avoidant	**Willingness to explore**	Insecure-Resistant
Insecure-Avoidant	**Stranger anxiety**	Insecure-Resistant
Insecure-Avoidant	**Separation anxiety**	Insecure-Resistant
Insecure-Avoidant	**Reunion behaviour**	Insecure-Resistant

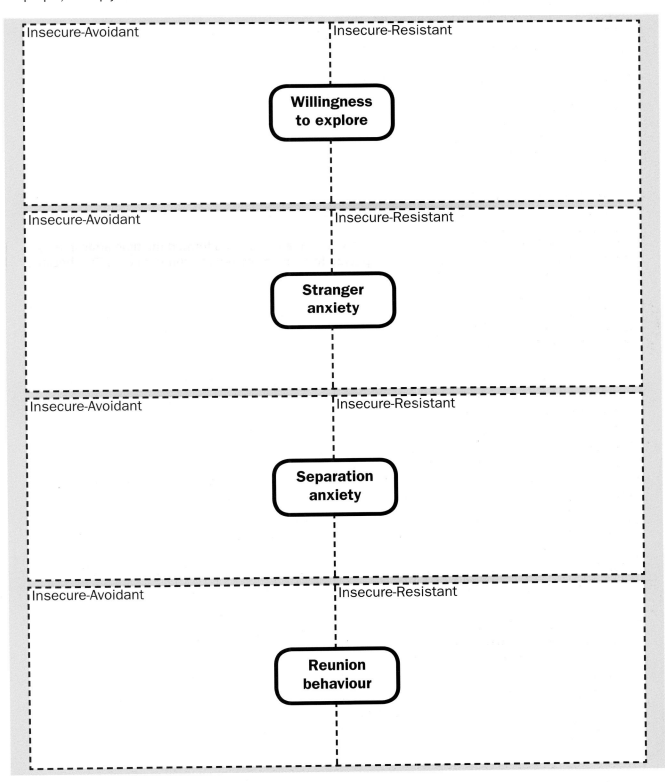

▶ Lesson notes p.32

Caregiver vs. temperament

You can use the information from this sheet to evaluate Ainsworth's Strange Situation conclusions. You could say something like:. 'However, Ainsworth's conclusions have been undermined by the temperament hypothesis....'

Caregiver sensitivity hypothesis	Temperament hypothesis
Ainsworth and Bell (1970)	*Kagan (1984), Thompson and Lamb (1984)*
Securely attached children have mothers who are more effective at: ❍ soothing them ❍ engaging in face to face interaction ❍ having more physical contact. Insecure children have mothers who are: ❍ insensitive to signals (e.g., crying) ❍ inept at handling them.	Thompson and Lamb (1984) ❍ Behaviour of infants in the Strange Situation is dependent on the infants inborn (genetic) temperament not their mother. Kagan (1984) ❍ Children with 'difficult' temperaments (inborn, genetic) who dislike change in routine may have been upset by the Strange Situation, and so may have been seen as insecurely attached.
The mother's behaviour causes the attachment type (nurture).	The inborn temperament of the child affects the behaviour of the infant in the strange situation (nature).

Choose a different colour to shade in each row of the key. Then, shade in each study using this colour code to indicate which viewpoint each of these studies supports. In your notes, explain how/why they support this viewpoint.

Grossmann *et al.* (1985) found NO difference in sensitivity between mothers of securely attached and mothers of insecurely attached children.

Main and Weston (1981) found that children tested in the strange situation with their mother and their father showed different attachment types depending on the parent they were with.

Key:

- **Nature**
- **Nurture**
- **both nature and nurture**

Belsky (1984) found that the weight of evidence seemed to indicate that the caregiver's behaviour has more to do with whether an attachment is formed than infant temperament.

Spangler (1990) found that the mother's responsiveness was influenced by her perception of the infant's temperament. Mothers who saw their children as 'difficult' became less responsive to them by 24 months.

Thomas and Chess (1977) classified 40% of 138 New York infants as having 'easy' temperaments, 10% as 'difficult' and 15% as 'slow to warm up'. The remaining 35% were classed as 'mixed'. Many aspects of these temperaments were evident within the first weeks of life and remained into adulthood.

▶ Lesson notes p.33

Cultural variations in attachment

Israel

Many Israeli infants grow up in a system called the kibbutz.

The kibbutz is a communal society. Nobody owns any individual possessions, clothes or homes – all these things belong to the community as a whole. Everything is shared equally across the whole community.

This idea of sharing even extends to children, so that children born into the community belong to all, with everybody sharing the responsibility to raise them. As such, children are often bought up away from their biological parents, visiting them perhaps for two hours a day.

Japan

Japan is a collectivist country. Child-rearing practices appear to place a much larger value and emphasis on developing close family relationships. As such, Japanese mothers almost never leave their child with a stranger, and are rarely separated from their child. Mothers are generally highly responsive to their needs.

Germany

German cultures require distance between parents and the child.

The ideal is an independent, non-clingy infant who does not make demands on the parents but rather unquestionably obeys their commands.

German parents tend to value independence – they want self-reliant children who can 'stand on their own two feet' and not make demands on them.

▶ Lesson notes p.33

Cultural variations in attachment

It stands to reason that different cultures will place different emphasis on child rearing values. The relationship between child and caregiver will vary across culture because of different beliefs about the qualities that should be nurtured in a child.

Based on the cultural values of these cultures, how do you think the 'average' infant will behave in the 'Strange Situation'? How will this affect the percentages of each attachment type?

Country Israel

SS behavioural categories	**Justification**
Willingness to explore: Low / Medium / High Separation anxiety: Low / Medium / High Stranger anxiety: Low / Medium / High Reunion behaviour: Low / Medium / High	
Based on the above, what percentage of each attachment type do you think Israel will have? Type A: Type B: Type C:	

Country Japan

SS behavioural categories	**Justification**
Willingness to explore: Low / Medium / High Separation anxiety: Low / Medium / High Stranger anxiety: Low / Medium / High Reunion behaviour: Low / Medium / High	
Based on the above, what percentage of each attachment type do you think Japan will have? Type A: Type B: Type C:	

Country Germany

SS behavioural categories	**Justification**
Willingness to explore: Low / Medium / High Separation anxiety: Low / Medium / High Stranger anxiety: Low / Medium / High Reunion behaviour: Low / Medium / High	
Based on the above, what percentage of each attachment type do you think Germany will have? Type A: Type B: Type C:	

▶ Lesson notes p.33

Cross-cultural variations in attachment: Van Ijzendoorn and Kroonenberg

AIM Their main aim was to discover whether there were differences in attachment types between cultures.

PROCEDURE

- **Meta-analysis** (not an experiment or observational study).
- This is when the findings from a variety of studies are drawn together and analysed in order to draw some conclusions.
- They looked through various databases to find multiple studies on attachment.
- They decided to use all those they found which had used the Strange Situation as part of their procedure.
- Altogether they looked at over 2,000 strange situations classifications from 32 studies and 8 countries.

FINDINGS

- Secure attachment was the most common type of attachment across all 8 nations.
- Significant differences were found in distribution of insecure attachments:
  - Western – dominant type was avoidance
  - Non-Western – dominant type was resistance
  - With the exception of China with a 50/50 split between both types of insecure attachment

DO NOT REVISE THIS WHOLE TABLE!! THE TWO BULLET POINTS ABOVE ARE MOST IMPORTANT

COUNTRY	NUMBER OF STUDIES	ATTACHMENT SCALE % Secure	ATTACHMENT SCALE % Avoidant	ATTACHMENT SCALE % Resistant
West Germany	3	57	35	8
Great Britain	1	75	22	3
Netherlands	4	67	26	7
Sweden	1	74	22	4
Israel	2	64	7	29
Japan	2	68	5	27
China	1	50	25	25
United States	18	65	21	14
Overall average		**65**	**21**	**14**

CONCLUSIONS

- The global pattern across cultures appears to be similar to that in the US. Secure attachment is the 'norm' – the most common form of attachment.
- This supports the idea that secure attachment is the 'best' for healthy social and emotional development.
- Van Ijzendoorn and Kroonenberg suggest that cross-cultural similarities might be explained by the effects of mass media (e.g. TV and books), which spreads ideas about parenting so that all children across the world are exposed to similar experiences.

▶ Lesson notes p.33

Cultural variations in restaurants!

France

In France, restaurant food is taken very seriously, and they really value the quality of food. In addition, they tend to believe that visiting a restaurant should be an all round social experience – and not just to simply 'eat food'.

As a result, people are far more likely to want to wait longer for their food so that they can enjoy their conversations and be safe in the knowledge that the chefs are taking good care, time and preparation over their food.

United States

Just like the British, Americans also have a tendency to like a bargain – so the price of food is important.

In addition, Americans tend to lead very busy lives and so the speed of service is often vital. People in restaurants are very quick to complain if the food is taking too long to appear and customers are far less likely to tip if that happens.

Choice is also important, and restaurants will often offer foods from America, China, Italy, Mexico and other regions from around the world.

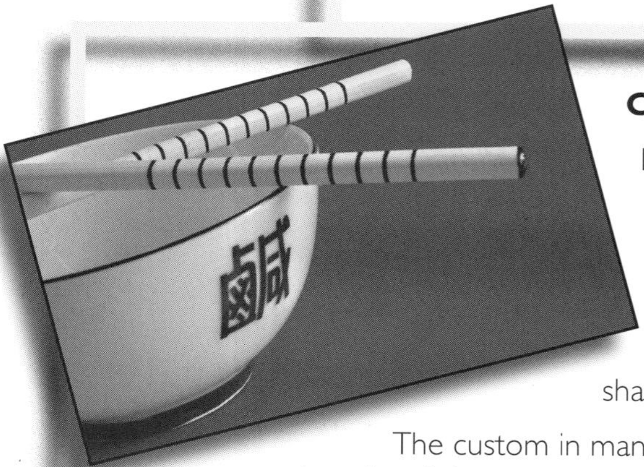

China

In China, sharing the meal is very important and individual meals/portions are a rarity. This reflects their culture as a whole, which is collectivist and values the idea that everything is equal and shared.

The custom in many Chinese restaurants is to call for service when it is required, as opposed to waiting for somebody to serve you. This can lead to confusion when Western people travel to China because they can end up waiting and become frustrated that no one is serving them!

▶ Lesson notes p.34

World Restaurant Cup!

World Restaurant Competition Launched!

Today, the first 'World Restaurant Cup' will be launched by the USA. Thousands of restaurants from across the globe will be visited and assessed by 'mystery shoppers'.

The competition organisers have said that the restaurants will be assessed out of 50 points using the following criteria (in order of importance):

1. Speed/quality of service (20 points)
2. Cost of food (15 points)
3. Quality of food (10 points)
4. Choice/variety of food (5 points)

The American organisers hope that by launching this competition they can find the country which is the 'World's Indisputable Champion of Restaurants'.

However, some countries have already expressed their concern about the ethnocentric bias in the competition's judging criteria...

Using Handout 53, evaluate the criteria being used to judge the 'World Restaurant Cup' from the perspective of each country. Are the criteria a fair way to judge the standard of restaurants in that country? Fully explain and elaborate your arguments.

France:

USA:

China:

Overall conclusions:

▶ Lesson notes p.34

Evaluating Van Ijzendoorn and Kroonenberg

World Attachment Competition Launched!

Today, the first 'World Attachment Cup' will be launched by the USA. Thousands of attachments between mothers and infants have been assessed across the world to determine which country has the most 'secure' attachments.

The competition organisers have said that the attachments will be assessed using Ainsworth's Strange Situation technique, and the criteria for judging each type of attachment are shown on the right.

However, some countries have already expressed their concern about the ethnocentric bias in the competition's judging criteria...

Summary of attachment behaviours

Classification of behaviour in the Strange Situation	Secure attachment (Type B)	Insecure attachment Avoidant (Type A)	Insecure attachment Resistant (Type C)
Willingness to explore	High	High	Low
Stranger anxiety	Moderate	Low	High
Separation anxiety	Some, easy to soothe	Indifferent	Distressed
Behaviour at reunion with caregiver	Enthusiastic	Avoid contact	Seeks and rejects

Using Handout 50, evaluate the criteria being used to judge cross-cultural variations in attachment from the perspective of each country. Are the criteria a fair way to judge the attachment types/amount of secure attachments in that country? Explain your answers (make sure you make reference to cultural values, and how they might affect the behaviour of infants in the strange situation).

Israel:

Japan:

Germany:

Overall conclusions:

▶ Lesson notes p.34

Extension

evaluating Van Ijzendoorn and Kroonenberg 1

*There are many **flawed arguments** (i.e., arguments which contain problems) when it comes to cross-cultural judgements of attachment. Your job here is to explain why those arguments are flawed. To help you, similar flawed arguments about food across cultures are made and discussed. Remember to use evidence from handouts and textbooks where you can.*

FLAWED ARGUMENT 1

'All Germans eat sausages, and sausages are their favourite foods.'

Problem:

Whilst German culture is quite famous for enjoying different varieties of sausage, it is far too simplified to suggest that *all* Germans eat and enjoy sausages. This is because there are differences *within* cultures. For example, you may well find that younger Germans (a subculture) prefer more Americanised foods because they are influenced by channels such as MTV. Therefore, the argument is not representative of the whole German culture.

FLAWED ARGUMENT 1

'(All) Germans are less likely to form secure attachments.'

Problem:

FLAWED ARGUMENT 2

'Yorkshire puddings, beef and roast potatoes are the ideal foods to have on Sunday! Therefore, the Japanese who eat sushi are clearly wrong!'

Problem:

This argument is made from a British cultural viewpoint (it is ethnocentrically biased). The person who makes this argument has been socialised to think this. However, it is unfair to judge other cultures' customs and traditions based on our own. Every culture values and appreciates different things (including food, morals, values and beliefs).

FLAWED ARGUMENT 2

'Secure attachments (as described by the SSC designed in the USA) are the ideal attachment to have. Therefore, China's parenting is poor.'

Problem:

▶ Lesson notes p.34

Extension

evaluating Van Ijzendoorn and Kroonenberg 2

FLAWED ARGUMENT 3

'You should asses the quality of a restaurant by how fast the service is, and how cheap the prices are.'

Problem:

This might be an accurate way to classify the quality of restaurants in cultures such as Britain and the USA because those cultures value speed of service and good, competitive prices. However, other cultures do not. In other cultures, expensive prices and lengthy service are seen as indicators of quality because time and effort has been spent on producing that food. As such, restaurants in these cultures are likely to score poorly on British and US measures of restaurant quality.

The use of speed and cheap prices to judge quality of restaurants would therefore judge British and US restaurants to be excellent, but foreign culture restaurants to be poor. However, these so-called 'poor' restaurants may well be highly valued and respected in their own cultures.

FLAWED ARGUMENT 3

'You should assess the quality of an attachment by measuring separation anxiety, stranger anxiety, and willingness to explore.'

Problem:

▶ Lesson notes p.34

The effects of physical separation 1

Extract from *The Complete Companion* p 48:

The work of James Robertson, and his wife Joyce, increased our understanding of the effects of separation and, in particular, how the negative effects might be avoided. The Robertsons (1967-73) made a landmark series of films of young children in situations where they were separated from their primary attachment figure.

A two year old goes to hospital

In the first film, James Roberston used a cine camera to meticulously record his observations of daily life in a hospital ward, focusing on one little girl, Laura, who was admitted to hospital for an eight-day stay. The film shows Laura alternating between periods of calm and distress. She is visited occasionally by her parents and begs to go home, but as time goes on she tries to cope with the disappointment of having to stay. Laura's obvious struggle to control her feelings over the course of the film is hard to watch.

Jane, Lucy, Thomas and Kate

Jane, Lucy, Thomas and Kate were all under three years of age and placed in foster care for a few weeks with the Robertsons while their mothers were in hospital. The Robertsons endeavoured to sustain a high level of substitute emotional care and keep routines similar to those at home. Fathers' visits were arranged regularly to maintain emotional links with home. Kate was taken to visit her mother in hospital and was much more settled after this. All the children seemed to adjust well. They showed some signs of distress, for example Thomas rejected attempts to cuddle him, but in general they slept well and did not reject their mothers when reunited. Some were reluctant to part with the foster mother, demonstrating the formation of good emotional bonds.

John

John's experiences were quite different. John was placed in a residential nursery for nine days while his mother was having a baby. His father visited regularly. During the first two days in the nursery the film shows John behaving fairly normally. Gradually this changes as he makes determined efforts to get attention from the nurses, but cannot compete with the other, more assertive children. The nurses are always very friendly but also always busy. When John fails to find anyone who will respond to him, he seeks comfort from an over-sized teddy bear, but this also isn't enough. Over the next few days he gradually breaks down and refuses food and drink, stops playing, cries a great deal, and gives up trying to get the nurses' attention. The nurses change shift regularly so there is no constant care.

In his first week he greets his father enthusiastically but by the second week he just sits quietly when his father is there and doesn't say anything. For long periods of the day he lies with thumb in mouth, cuddling his large teddy bear. On the ninth day, when his mother comes to take him home, John screams and struggles to get away from her.

For many months afterwards he continued to have outbursts of anger towards his mother.

Tasks

Read the extract above and for each case study:

1. Highlight any details of the separation from the primary attachment giver in one colour (e.g., duration, location, reason, etc.).
2. Highlight any mediating variables in another colour (e.g., visits from father, type of care given during separation).
3. Highlight the short-term effects of the separation in another colour (i.e., effects during the separation).
4. Highlight the long-term effects of the separation in another colour (i.e., reunion behaviour and thereafter).
5. Use this information to complete Handout 59.

▶ Lesson notes p.35

The effects of physical separation 2

LAURA

SEPARATED FROM MOTHER WHEN ADMITTED TO HOSPITAL FOR AN EIGHT-DAY STAY.

Mediating variables	*Short-term effects of separation*

JANE, LUCY, THOMAS AND KATE

ALL UNDER 3 YEARS OF AGE AND PLACED IN FOSTER CARE WHILE THEIR MOTHERS WERE IN HOSPITAL.

Mediating variables	*Short-term effects of separation*	*Behaviour on/after reunion (long-term effects)*

JOHN

UNDER 3 AND PLACED IN A RESIDENTIAL NURSERY FOR NINE DAYS WHILE HIS MOTHER HAD A BABY.

Mediating variables	*Short-term effects of separation*	*Behaviour on/after reunion (long-term effects)*

In your notes, or on the back of this worksheet, use evidence from above to explain how these case studies show that:

1. The absence of substitute emotional care can disrupt the long-term attachment between infant and main caregiver.
2. The negative effects of physical separation between infant and caregiver can be reversed.

▶ Lesson notes p.35

Applying your knowledge

Alana is just under 3 years of age and has been hospitalised for an unknown illness. It is possible that she could be in hospital for 2–3 weeks and her parents are concerned about the negative effects that this could have on their emotional bond with Alana. It is possible that the separation of Alana from her mother could disrupt their mutual attachment.

Outline **two** strategies Alana's parents and the hospital could use to minimise the negative effects of this separation. *(3 +3 marks)*

This question requires you to **apply** your knowledge of psychology. You must use your knowledge and understanding to answer the question.

Notice that for each strategy 3 marks are available, so you must **elaborate** on your answers, whilst at the same time not writing too much! Use this writing frame to structure your answers, but do not write any more than space provides – so don't waffle!

STRATEGY 1:

Explain why this will minimise the negative effects:

Briefly provide evidence (from a study/theory) to support your idea:

STRATEGY 2:

Explain why this will minimise the negative effects:

Briefly provide evidence (from a study/theory) to support your idea:

▶ Lesson notes p.36

Case study – GENIE 1

1 Outline the background details to Genie's case study, i.e. her experiences before she was 'discovered'.

2 What were the **physical effects** of Genie's failure to form attachment?

3 What were the **psychological effects** of Genie's failure to form attachment, i.e. intellectual, emotional and social development?

4 How does this case study help test Bowlby's 'critical period' hypothesis?

▶ Lesson notes p.37

Case study – GENIE 2

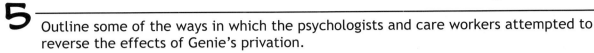

5 Outline some of the ways in which the psychologists and care workers attempted to reverse the effects of Genie's privation.

6 Explain whether you feel Genie recovered from the effects of her privation. If so/not, in what ways?

7 Why have people cast doubt on the validity of Genie's case study as a study of the effects of privation?

8 Comment on the usefulness and generalisability of this case study.

9 Identify and explain some of the ethical issues raised in the research of Genie.

▶ Lesson notes p.37

Failure to form attachment – assessment exercise

Taken from *The Complete Companion*, p 63.

Discuss research into the effects of failure to form attachment (privation). (8 marks)

Alice's answer

Hodges and Tizard used a longitudinal approach to study the effects of early experiences and later development. They found that children who were raised in an institution during the sensitive period were unlikely to form an attachment, even when restored to their biological parents.

The Czech Twins (Koluchová, 1976) were detained in a basement by their stepmother until the age of seven. Although they were severely affected, they had a normal social and intellectual capability by the age of 14, and at the age of 20 they were above average intelligence.

A weakness to Hodges and Tizard's research is that parents may not have invested emotionally the same in their children. The biological parents in Hodges and Tizard's sample may not have been as interested in their children, which is why they were less attached.

Although the Czech twins suffered from privation, this did demonstrate that a person without a bond with a primary caregiver could then go out and function adequately in society.

Rutter's study shows that recovery from extreme privation can be achieved given adequate care, although adoption (at age two) was still within Bowlby's 'sensitive period'.

Tom's answer

It has been found by psychologists that absence of a primary caregiver can have many effects, for example the Robertsons looked at how children were affected when their mothers had to spend time in hospital. They filmed a number of children under the age of 3 in foster care or in a hospital nursery. The children were OK if they were cared for emotionally. These were case studies. Other work includes Genie who was a victim of severe neglect. She suffered from privation and couldn't speak properly. Her state of mind may not have been because she was a victim of no attachment but because she was retarded. This was another case study. There are also the Czech twins who were locked in a cellar but rescued when they were 7 and then raised by two kind sisters. Later in life they appeared to be fine, which shows that privation doesn't always have negative effects.

Note: This is an essay question but only worth 8 marks not 12. These can come up in your exam!

Tasks...

1. Highlight **description/knowledge** of *research into the effects of failure to form attachments* for both essays.
2. Highlight **evaluation/discussion** of *research into the effects of failure to form attachments* for both essays.
3. Underline irrelevant information for '*failure to form attachments*' if there is any *(hint: disruption of attachment is a different topic).*
4. Circle any description of results and conclusions included (most important in a shorter essay to convey what psychologists have learnt about the topic).
5. Mark knowledge/understanding out of 4 (consider detail, accuracy and relevance of work).
6. Mark evaluation/discussion out of 4 (consider effectiveness, elaboration, and expression of ideas).

▶ Lesson notes p.37

Day care and sociability – a correlational study

In order to collect suitable data you will need the following!

ONE A way to assess the 'time spent in day care' for each participant. An easy way to measure this might be to ask each participant to estimate the number of months they spent in day care before starting school.

TWO A way to **operationalise** the co-variable 'sociability' so that we can measure it. One way to do this would be to design a **questionnaire survey**. This might consist of questions such as, 'How many close friends do you have?' or 'Do you prefer to spend time on your own, with one close friend or in a group of people?' The key thing is that your questionnaire is able to produce a score for each participant that measures their sociability.

You might use closed questions such as shown in the box opposite. Using **closed questions** makes it easier to use the data because there are only a few possible answers. Also, it is much easier to devise a scoring system which enables you to directly compare each participant. On the other hand, **open questions** allow for people to give a more exact answer to suit their circumstances. An example of an open question would be 'How do you feel around large groups of people?'

How many close friends do you have?

- 0–3 close friends
- 4–7 close friends
- 8–11 close friends
- 12–15 close friends
- 15 + close friends

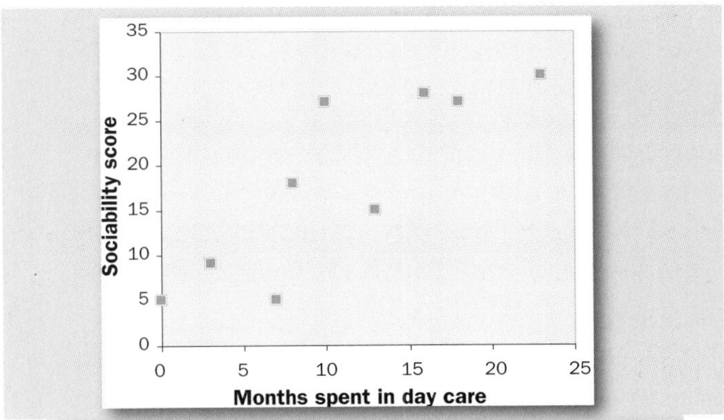

Analysing the data

When you have collected the data you can calculate two scores for each participant: one for 'time spent in day care' and the other for 'sociability'. Now plot these on a scattergraph, like the one above. If you have time, you could produce the scattergraph and calculate the correlation coefficient using the 'Do it yourself' box on the right (from *The Complete Companion,* page 54).

What type of correlation do you find? Positive, negative, or zero correlation? What does this mean?

Do it yourself

Playing with correlation coefficients: The Excel method
Using Excel (the Microsoft Office application) you can enter and alter pairs of numbers to see how this affects a scattergram and correlation coefficient. Both are produced by Excel:

1 Open a new document in Excel (select <file> <new> <blank workbook>).
2 Select <insert><chart><XY (scatter)> and press <next>.
3 Place cursor at very top left of the page, click and drag across two rows and then down 16 rows. Press <next><next><finish>.
4 Now enter your pairs of scores (these can be invented or you could try entering a real set of numbers — such as height and shoe size of your class) to see if they are correlated. Do not enter data in the top row.
5 To calculate correlation coefficient: Place the cursor in an empty box. Select <insert><function>. In top box type 'correl' and press 'go' and then <OK>.
6 Screen now says 'array1' and 'array2'. Click in 'array1' and then move cursor to top of first column of your numbers, click and drag to bottom of column. Do the same for array2.
7 Try changing some of the numbers and see how this alters your scattergram and the correlation coefficient.

You can also play with correlations on various websites such as www.stattucino.com/berrie/dsl/regression/regression.html

▶ Lesson notes p.39

Day care research

Extract from The Complete Companion, p 54.

Aggression and day care

There are two other findings from the NICHD study that haven't received quite as much media attention as the aggression/day care link. First, one of the NICHD workers, Sarah Friedman, has pointed out that the results related to aggression can be stated differently – the study found that 83% of children who spend 10 to 30 hours in day care did *not* show higher levels of aggression. Friedman claims that the study results so far actually tell us very little (reported in Lang, 2006).

The second finding to consider is that the NICHD data actually showed that a mother's sensitivity to her child was a better indicator of reported problem behaviours than was time in childcare, with more sensitive mothering being linked to few problem behaviours. Higher maternal education and family income also predicted lower levels of children's problem behaviours. These findings put the aggression findings into perspective (NICHD, 2003). The 2006 data again suggest that children's development is more strongly affected by factors at home than those in day care (Belsky *et al.*, 2007).

A final important consideration is that the findings are not causal – that data cannot show that day care *caused* aggression. Instead, the data show that day care and aggressiveness are linked in some way. The American Psychological Association (Dingfelder, 2004) suggests that the results are meaningless unless one knows the processes by which aggression is increased; for example, it could be that aggression only increases when children are inadequately supervised.

Peer relations and day care

The issue about correlation versus cause (see above) applies to the peer-relations and day-care link. We cannot assume that experiences in day care *cause* later sociability – we have merely uncovered a link. It might be, for example, that shy and unsociable children have mothers who are also shy and unsociable (because temperament is inherited) and such mothers prefer to stay at home to care for children. Therefore it is more outgoing children who attend day care, which explains why day-care children are more sociable!

Use this information to complete the evaluation revision cards (Handout 66).

▶ Lesson notes p.40

Evaluating day care research – Revision cards

Which two other findings from the NICHD study haven't received as much attention?

Day care evaluation card 1

Why might the results of the NICHD study be meaningless?

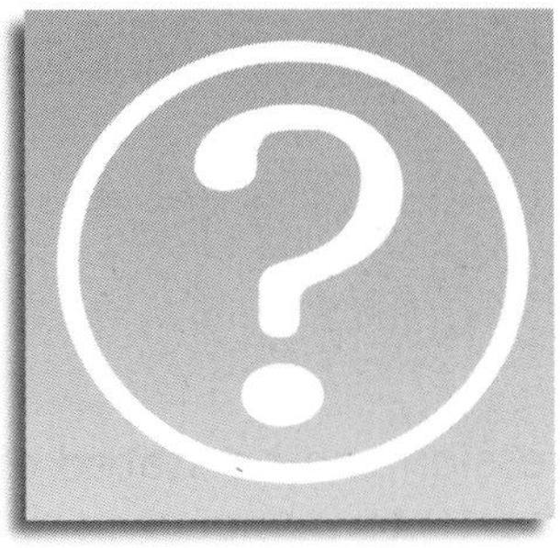

Day care evaluation card 2

What else could explain the correlation between positive peer-relations and day care?

Day care evaluation card 3

What is the major issue with correlational research?

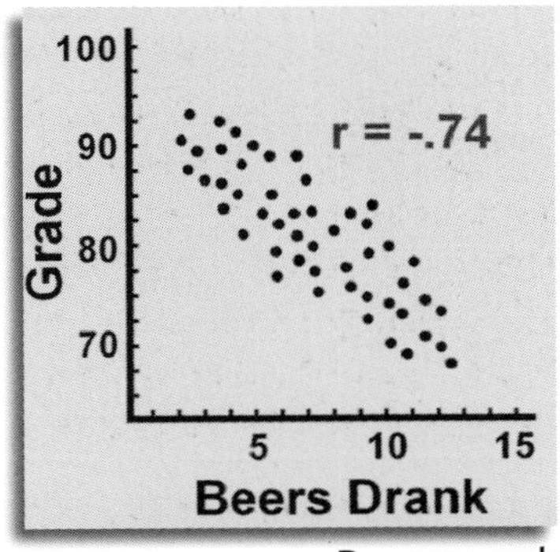

Day care evaluation card 4

Can you think of any positive points about the day care research?

Day care evaluation card 5

▶ Lesson notes p.40

Reviewing day care

evidence 1

Having studied day care, you will know that there are arguments both for and against the possible effects of day care on a child's social development. This exercise is to help you sort out the main arguments and/or evidence in order to write an essay, and to sort out the effects on peer relations and aggression.

Essay 1

Step 1

The following studies/arguments can be used to provide evidence 'for' or 'against'. Of course there are many others you can also use but you won't need more than two/three for either side of the debate. Complete the table below with research studies from your textbook. These will be studies you use for your A01. Your textbook might have the following studies:

- NICHD – longitudinal study
- Sroufe *et al.* (2005) – Minnesota longitudinal study
- Field (1991) – correlational study
- Clarke-Stewart *et al.* (1994) – day care and social development
- Melhuish (2004) – nursery care
- Belsky and Rovine (1988) – time spent in day care

For	Against
•	•
•	•
•	•

In your essay, ensure that you explain why the studies are for or against day care.

Step 2

To evaluate the arguments for and against, four main factors can be considered, i.e. individual differences, child's age, quality of care, and methodology used in the studies. Write the number of each of the following statements into the correct box below.

1. Negative effects are more likely to be found in children who are placed in day care before 18 months old (Gregg *et al.*, 2005).
2. Day care can show a correlation with the outcomes but it can't tell us about the causes.
3. Some children find day care harder to cope with than others, shy children in particular (Pennebaker *et al.*, 1981).
4. Insecure children may feel more benefits from day care because they need compensatory emotional care from adults, whereas securely attached children do not (Egeland and Hiester, 1995)
5. In day care situations where the staff-to-child ratio is poor, children will not be able to form consistent secondary attachment figures (NICHD, 1997).
6. If suitable substitute emotional care is provided, there may be no ill effects (Robertson and Robertson, 1967–73).
7. Some studies are over 10 years old so may not be relevant today.

Individual differences	Child's age	Quality of care	Methodology
•	•	•	•
•	•	•	•

Step 3

Now use the material in the two tables and write an answer to this question:

- **'Outline and evaluate research into the effects of day care on social development.'**

Remember that you should aim for an essay that is about 240–300 words long.

▶ Lesson notes p.40

Reviewing day care

evidence 2

Essay 2

Step 1

Now repeat the exercise given in Handout 67 but separate your studies into those relevant to 'aggression' and those relevant to 'peer relations'. You may find that some studies might be relevant to both. You will only ever need 2/3 of each – bear that in mind when you complete the table.

Study	'Peer relations', or 'aggression'	What effects were found?

Step 2

Use the material to write an essay on:

- **'Outline and evaluate research into the effects of day care on either peer relations or aggression.'**

AO1.

Outline the relevant studies from the table and explain why they are for or against day care.

AO2.

Either evaluate the studies used for A01 with evaluations outlined in your textbook, or, use material from step 2 on Handout 67 to evaluate the evidence.

Remember that you should aim for an essay that is about 240–300 words long.

Also remember that you will only have time in the exam to cover two/three studies in your description of the research (not including studies which you might use to evaluate the research).

▶ Lesson notes p.40

Implications of attachment research on childcare practices

- How has research into attachment been used to change childcare provision in the UK?

Bowlby's sensitive period

- ❑ In the past, mothers who were going to give up a baby for adoption were encouraged to nurse the baby for a significant period of time.
- ❑ However, by the time the baby was adopted, the sensitive period (3–6 months) for attachment formation may have passed, making it difficult for the adoptive caregiver to form secure attachments.
- ❑ As such, Bowlby's theory led to changes in adoption procedures. Today, most babies are adopted within the first week of birth, and research indicates this has had a positive impact on the amount of secure attachments being formed.

Research into the disruption of attachment

- ❑ Robertson and Robertson's research showed that the negative effects of physical separation from the main caregiver could be avoided if **substitute emotional care** was provided as well as links with existing attachment figures (such as visits from them whilst in hospital).
- ❑ This research led to major changes in the visiting arrangements for parents with children in hospital.
- ❑ It also affected institutional care of children, for example in foster homes.

Bowlby's attachment theory

- ❑ Bowlby's theory of attachment states that whilst a child has a *primary attachment* figure (monotropy), secondary attachments are also formed which are important for emotional development.
- ❑ As such, the Soho Family centre believes that childcarers must function as these secondary attachment figures who support the main caregiver.
- ❑ In order to ensure this, each carer is assigned a maximum of only three children. Thus each child is ensured close emotional and consistent relationships.

▶ Lesson notes p.41

Implications of day care research on childcare practices

- How has research into day care been used to change childcare provision in the UK?
- Most often, it has been used to improve the quality of day care...

Low staff-to-child ratios

- ❑ The NICHD (1999) study found that day care staff could only provide sensitive care if the ratios were as low as 3:1.
- ❑ As such, day care centres now strive to have low ratios.
- ❑ The UK government also has a requirement that there must be 1 member of staff for every 8 children.

Minimal staff turnover

- ❑ Schaffer (1998) identified consistency of care as one of the most important factors in good outcomes for children.
- ❑ When staff come and go, children may fail to form attachments with staff.
- ❑ As such, day care centres try to ensure that their staff are consistent.

Qualified staff

- ❑ Sylva *et al.* (2003) reported that quality of day care was associated with the qualifications of day care staff.
- ❑ The higher the qualifications of the staff, the better the outcomes for the children in terms of social development.
- ❑ As a result, the government try to encourage leaders of day care centres to have a relevant qualification.

▶ Lesson notes p.41

Experiment planning

Group names ____________________

Idea to be investigated

Aim – What do you want to find out?	**IV** – What are you manipulating?
Hypothesis – What do you think you will find? (directional / non-directional) *do not use 'I'	**DV** – What are you measuring?

Sourcing and sorting participants

Sampling method and reasons for choice Random sampling, opportunity sampling, volunteer sampling	**Experimental design and reasons for choice** Independent measures, repeated measures, matched pairs
Number of participants/age/gender and reasons for choice	

Planning the procedure

What do participants have to do?	**Ethical issues** Informed consent Deception Protection from harm	**Dealing with ethics** Right to withdraw Confidentiality Debrief
Type of data to be collected		

▶ Lesson notes p.42

Experiment analysis

Group names ______________________________

Analysis of the findings

Data gathered

Measures of central tendency

- ☐ Mean – (total/number of participants)
- ☐ Median – (the middle value in the data)
- ☐ Mode – (the most commonly occurring score)

Measures of dispersion

- ☐ Range – (the difference between the highest and lowest score)
- ☐ Standard deviation – (the spread of data around the mean)

Conclusion – What does the data suggest in relation to the aim and hypothesis?

Evaluating the procedure

What went well?	What needs to be improved?
Internal validity (Did you measure what you set out to measure?)	External validity (Population and ecological validity)

▶ Lesson notes p.42

Threats to internal validity

Participant reactivity and investigator effects

Definitions – which box helps define participant reactivity and which defines investigator effects?

Participants react to cues, often unintentional, in an experimental situation.

Participants are not passive; they actively react to the research situation they are involved in.

This can lead to the participants' fulfilment of the investigator's expectation.

This can include anything the investigator does which affects the performance of a participant in a study other than what was intended.

Subconscious cues from an investigator that encourage certain behaviours from the participants.

The reaction of participants can affect the validity of any conclusions drawn from the data gathered.

Examples – does the study demonstrate participant reactivity or investigator effects?

Loftus found using leading questions can affect an interviewee's behaviour. Participants who were asked 'How fast do you think the car was going when it **smashed** into the other car?' estimated a higher speed than those who were asked 'How fast was the car going when it **connected** with the other car?'.

Another way participants' behaviour can be affected is known as the **Greenspoon effect**. Greenspoon (1955) found that he could alter participant's behaviour by saying 'mm-hmm' after certain responses, e.g. the investigator could subconsciously utter 'mm' after the participant does a desired behaviour and so the participant is more likely to do it again.

Social desirability bias – participants want to present themselves in a good light so may lie/not give their true opinions/behave in a different way so others will think good of them.

Factory workers at the Hawthorne Electric factory took part in a study into the effect of lighting on work rate. No matter what lighting they worked in (bright to practically black), production levels continued to increase. The researchers (Roethlisberger and Dickinson, 1939) realised it wasn't the IV (light levels) having an effect but the increased attention the workers were getting as part of being in a study.

If attention gained from being in a study affects behaviour it is known as the **Hawthorne effect**.

Orne (1962) observed that participants act in unusual ways if they think they are part of a psychology experiment, e.g. participants were asked to add up numbers on a sheet, tear the paper up then start again. Some continued the task for over 6 hours. Orne developed the idea of **demand characteristics** – people taking part in studies want to please the researcher (participants unconsciously seek cues about how to behave) and want their performance to be helpful and so they don't act in the way they normally would, which affects the data.

▶ Lesson notes p.42

Word wall

Colour code each brick so that it relates to the correct key term displayed at the top of the wall. Use all bricks of one colour to write a definition of that key word.

Each term has four related bricks.

External validity	Internal validity	External reliability	Internal reliability

Includes ecological, population and historical	Inter-interviewer reliability is important	Can be affected by observer bias	
Check by making comparisons of findings	Inter-observer reliability should be checked	Repeat the test at a later date	
Concurrent validity	Test – retest method	Representativeness	
Measures what it intends to measure	Generalisable	Split-half method	Face validity
Consistency within itself	Can be applied to other situations	Consistency over occasions	

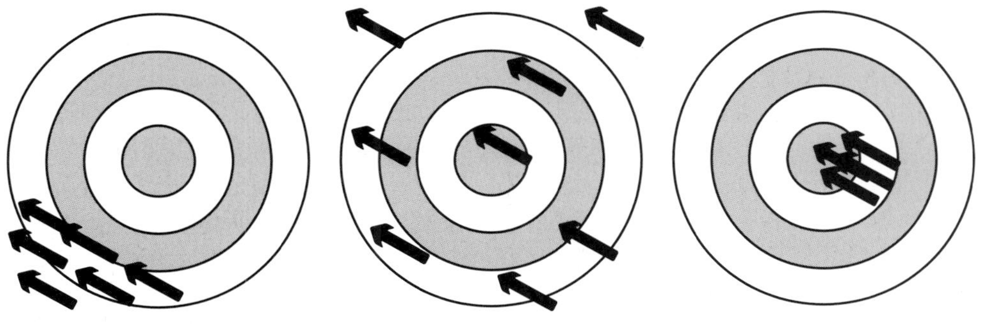

Reliable, but not valid

Not reliable, not valid

Reliable and valid

Define the four key words by using the words and target diagram to help. Choose at least one of the key words. Try to include what the term means, why it is important and how investigators can ensure their findings are valid or reliable.

▶ Lesson notes p.42

Ethical considerations: proposal

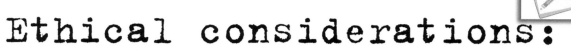

Now you have planned your experiment you need to present your proposed methodology to an ethical committee.

All institutes where research takes place have an ethical committee, and the committee must approve any study before it begins. It looks at all possible ethical issues raised in any research proposal and at how the researcher suggests that the issue will be dealt with, weighing up the benefits of the research against the possible costs to the participants. In some cases the cost-benefit balance is seen to be reasonable, in other cases it is decided that the costs are simply too great, or the research simply not of sufficient value.

Task: Complete the research proposal for the experiment you have planned.

This will be submitted to an ethics committee composed of your fellow class mates.

Ethical issue 1	**Related ethical guideline**	**Proposed method of dealing with this issue**

Ethical issue 2	**Related ethical guideline**	**Proposed method of dealing with this issue**

Ethical issue 3	**Related ethical guideline**	**Proposed method of dealing with this issue**

▶ Lesson notes p.43

Ethical considerations: committee

Read the ethical proposal you have received and decide whether the research should be carried out.

Use the British Psychological Society's Code of Ethics and Conduct (2006) to help you reach your decision. Visit **http://www.bps.org.uk/the-society/code-of-conduct/ethical-principles-for-conducting-research-with-human-participants.cfm**

Your textbook will also help you consider the ethical issues the proposal has identified and the effectiveness of the proposed measures of dealing with the issues.

Ethical issues identified	Suggestions for how to deal with the issue
Issue 1:____________________ Suggested ways of dealing with it: Is this acceptable?	
Issue 2:____________________ Suggested ways of dealing with it: Is this acceptable?	
Issue 3:____________________ Suggested ways of dealing with it: Is this acceptable?	

Should the research take place? **Yes/No**

If No, please state what changes need to be made to ensure the method will be ethically acceptable.

If Yes, please state why you feel the method is ethically acceptable.

▶ Lesson notes p.43

What if?

What if ethical guidelines did not exist in psychology?

Try to think of 20 outcomes if this were true.

▶ Lesson notes p.43

Directional or non-directional?

Psychologists use a **directional** hypothesis when past research (a theory or a study) suggests that the findings will go in a particular direction.

Psychologists use a **non-directional** hypothesis when there is no past research or past research is contradictory. The findings could go in either direction.

Read the following hypotheses and highlight the independent variable in one colour, and the dependent variable in a second colour. Then decide if they make directional or non-directional statements.

- CHAMPIONSHIP FOOTBALLERS SCORE MORE PENALTIES THAN SECOND DIVISION PLAYERS.
- *There is a difference in memory scores between students who have received a lecture on revision techniques than students who have not received this lecture.*
- Women solve a jigsaw puzzle faster than men.
- **Children aged 5-10 are able to name more cartoon characters than teenagers aged 13-18.**
- Participants do better on a test when tested in the same room where they were taught rather than tested in a different room.
- Participants perform differently depending on whether they are tested in the same room where they were taught rather than tested in a different room.
- **There is a significant difference between IQ scores of male and female pensioners.**
- There is an increase in performance of a dramatic scene after a rehearsal session compared to performance before the session.

▶ Lesson notes p.43

Writing hypotheses

A hypothesis states what you believe is true. It is a precise and testable statement of the relationship between two variables. It is a statement, not a question or a prediction. Follow the example on the left to develop the hypothesis on the right into a fully operationalised, testable statement.

Possible hypothesis
People remember more when they study in short bursts.

Possible hypothesis
People remember more when they revise using mnemonics.

The independent variable needs to have at least two conditions to make a comparison. These conditions are known as the levels of the independent variable. A good hypothesis should always include two (or more) levels of the IV or a condition where the IV is absent.

Levels of the IV 'time spent studying'
- short bursts
- longer sessions

Possible hypothesis
People remember more when they study in short bursts than when studying for longer sessions.

Levels of the IV 'revision technique'
- mnemonics
- ____________________

Possible hypothesis
____
____

A good hypothesis must be in a testable form, i.e. a way that makes clear the specific way the experiment tests the hypothesis. In particular we need to operationalise the IV and DV.

Operationalising the variables
IV: short bursts = 10 mins repeated three times over three hours.
Longer sessions = one 30 min session.

Operationalising the variables
IV: mnemonics = ____________________
____
____________ = ____________________
____

Operationalising the variables
DV: remember more = will get more questions right on a test of recall

Operationalising the variables
DV: ____________ = ____________
____

Fully operationalised hypothesis
People get more questions right on a test of recall when they study in short bursts (ten minutes at a time repeated three times) than when studying for longer sessions (one 30-min session).

Fully operationalised hypothesis

▶ Lesson notes p.43

Experimental design

Experimental design: A set of procedures used to control the influence of factors such as participant variables in an experiment.

Repeated measures: each participant takes part in every condition under test.

A strength of repeated measures is:

Therefore, a weakness of independent measures is:

Independent measures: each participant takes part in only one condition under test.

A strength of independent measures is:

Therefore, a weakness of repeated measures is:

Overcoming issues

Repeated measures design can use counterbalancing. This is when:

This overcomes the problem of:

Independent measures design can be changed to matched pairs design.
This is when:

This overcomes the problem of:

▶ Lesson notes p.43

Defending the design

Experimental design: A set of procedures used to control the influence of factors such as participant variables in an experiment.

Arguments for the use of independent measures design in this study.

Gavin wants to investigate encoding in STM. He intends to compare recall of visual items (pictures of everyday objects) with recall of acoustic items (common nouns, e.g. table, letter).

Arguments for the use of repeated measures design in this study.

Arguments for the use of matched pairs design in this study.

Laura wishes to research the effect of using mnemonics to revise for the driving theory test compared to revising by just reading through a theory test handbook.

Arguments against the use of matched pairs design in this study.

Weaknesses of using repeated measures design.

Hugo is interested in memory performance at different times of the day. He wants to compare participants' results on a test taken in the morning with another test taken in the afternoon.

Possible ways of dealing with the weaknesses identified.

▶ Lesson notes p.44

Sort it out

Extraneous variables can seriously impact on the internal validity of a study. If they are not controlled, they can confound the results because the change in the dependent variable (DV) may be due to the extraneous variables rather than the independent variable (IV).

Sort the note cards based on one of the following categories:

- Participant variables / Participant reactivity / Situational variables
- Easier for the researcher to control / More difficult for the researcher to control
- Easy for researcher to identify / More difficult for the researcher to identify
- More risk of occurrence in experiments / More risk of occurrence in questionnaires

AGE	**TIME OF DAY**	**SOCIAL DESIRABILITY**	**MOTIVATION**
HAWTHORNE EFFECT	**INTELLIGENCE**	**ORDER EFFECTS**	**TEMPERATURE**
NOISE	**EXPERIENCE**	**DEMAND CHARACTERISTICS**	**GENDER**

Dealing with extraneous variables

For the terms below produce	a definition and	identify the EV they aim to overcome.
Single bind		
Double bind		
Experimental realism		
Standardised procedures		
Counterbalancing		

▶ Lesson notes p.44

Teacher time

Teachers love marking! Join in the fun by marking the passage below.

What is meant by the term extraneous variables and how might they affect the validity of a study?

Extraneous variables (evs) can be split into four types; participant variables, participant effects (reactivity) and setuational variables. It is important these are controlled because if not they can confirm the results of a study because they change the DV rather than the IV causing the outcome seen. Any characteristics of an individual participant can become a participant variable if in an independent measures design. Therefore a way to overcome this is to use a repetitive measures design. However, repeated measures design can suffer from order effects order effects are an example of situational variables. After completing 1st condition participants may be board or fatigued so do worse than they normally would on the second condition or perform better as they have had a practise. Participant reactivity occurs when participants actually seek cues about how to behave. If you don't know you are being watched you will not show reactivity but this may be uneconomical. The hawthorne effect is when people respond to the extra attention they receive as they no they are being watched. If Participants try to present themselves in the best possible way they may alter there responses to that which they feel is most socially acceptable this is called social desirability bais.

Marking codes:

Sp and word underlined = spelling error, write correct version above.

WW and word underlined = wrong word used, write correct version above.

// or **NP** = new paragraph

Large letter over small = capital letter needed.

P and error underlined = punctuation error.

? = sentence doesn't make sense, write correction above.

^ = word missed out.

Development

When teachers mark work they don't just point out what you have done wrong but also give you areas for improvement.

Suggest what else the student could have included in their answer so that their response is accurate and detailed.

All must give 1 suggestion.

Most could give 2 suggestions.

A few should give 3 suggestions.

▶ Lesson notes p.44

Central tendency: mode and median

Measures of central tendency: These give average values of a set of data.

Measures of central tendency – 3 types:

1. *Mode = the most frequently occurring value in a set of data.*
2. *Median = the middle value of scores arranged in numerical order.*
3. *Mean = the mathematical average score.*

Study details	*Rich carried out a study into remembering the names of paint colours. He decided to compare painters and decorators with postmen.* *All participants were shown 50 colours and asked to learn the names of each paint colour. After an interval of 24 hours participants were shown the colours with the names removed and asked to write the name of each colour.* *Colours that were named incorrectly or left blank were ignored. The number of colours they named correctly was recorded.* *He thought painters and decorators would have better recall as their prior knowledge would help them.*
Results for painters and decorators	*7, 18, 22, 25, 25, 26, 29, 32, 34, 38, 41, 42, 47*
Results for postmen	*1, 4, 10, 12, 13, 13, 13, 15, 18, 20, 21, 23, 40*

The mode: e.g. 2, 3, 6, **8, 8, 8,** 10, 12, **mode = 8.**

The modes in Rich's study were:
Painters and decorators =
Postmen =

The median:
e.g. 2, 3, 5, **6,** 8, 11, 12, **median = 6**
e.g. 2, 3, 5, **6, 8,** 11, 12, 13, **median = (6 + 8) ÷ 2 = 7**

The medians in Rich's study were:
Painters and decorators =
Postmen =

▶ Lesson notes p.44

Central tendency: mean

The mean:

e.g. 2 + 3 + 5 + 5 + 6 + 6 + 6 + 8 + 8 + 11 = **62 ÷ 10 = 6.2 = mean**

Study details	Rich carried out a study into remembering the names of paint colours. He decided to compare painters and decorators with postmen. All participants were shown 50 colours and asked to learn the names of each paint colour. After an interval of 24 hours participants were shown the colours with the names removed and asked to write the name of each colour. Colours that were named incorrectly or left blank were ignored. The number of colours they named correctly was recorded. He thought painters and decorators would have better recall as their prior knowledge would help them.
Results for painters and decorators	7, 18, 22, 25, 25, 26, 29, 32, 34, 38, 41, 42, 47
Results for postmen	1, 4, 10, 12, 13, 13, 13, 15, 18, 20, 21, 23, 40

The means in Rich's study were:

Painters and decorators =

Postmen =

Reviewing central tendency measures

The measure of central tendency most useful to the data was ________________ because:

The measure of central tendency least useful to the data was ________________ because:

The measure of central tendency I found easiest to calculate was ________________

From the measures of central tendency calculated, I can conclude about Rich's data:

....

....

▶ Lesson notes p.44

Dispersion: range and SD

Measures of dispersion *look at the spread of scores in a data set. They help us understand whether the data collected (e.g., scores) are very similar to each other or whether great differences can be seen.*

The range

e.g. 3, 6, 7, 8, 10, 11, 12, 13, 15, **range = 12 (3 to 15)**

STRENGTHS

WEAKNESSES

The ranges for Rich's data (Handout 84) were: ***Painters and decorators =***	***Postmen =***

The Standard Deviation (SD)

Measures the spread of data collected around the mean of the data set.

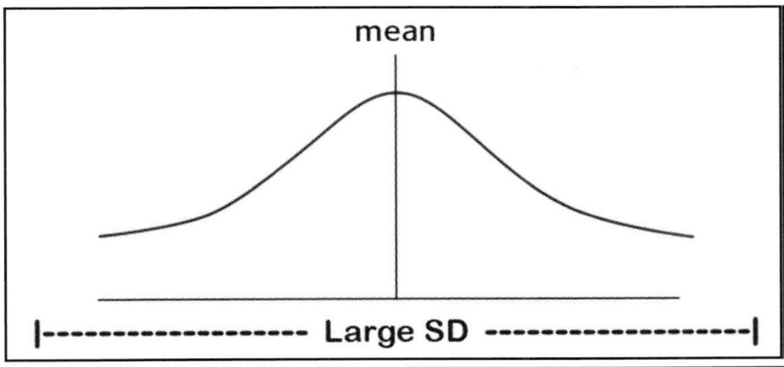

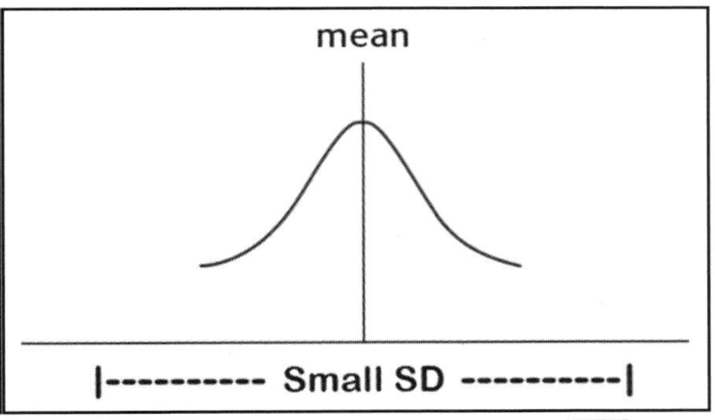

STRENGTHS

WEAKNESSES

The exam will NOT ask you to calculate standard deviation but you do need to know what standard deviation means. For your data use the standard deviation button on your calculator to work it out.

The standard deviations for Rich's data (Handout 84) were: ***Painters and decorators =***	***Postmen =***

A small standard deviation means the data from each participant was very similar.

A large standard deviation means the data from each participant was different to each other.

▶ Lesson notes p.44

87

Blending brains

Sometimes it is useful to share your thinking with somebody else's ideas to produce an answer that is not only accurate but detailed too.

Participants were tested in their teaching room and given nonsense trigrams (e.g. SXT) and then asked to count backwards until told to stop. Then participants were asked to recall the trigram. The counting interval was used to prevent the trigram being rehearsed. When the counting interval was three seconds, participants could recall most trigrams; when it was 18 seconds they couldn't recall many trigrams (Peterson and Peterson, 1959).

Answer each question alone. Then share ideas with a partner and add any extra points raised in the second column. Lastly, use both your ideas and your partners to produce a final answer.

Identify the IV and DV

My answer	Extra points from partner	Final answer

Was the task required of participants contrived?

My answer	Extra points from partner	Final answer

Was the setting high or low in mundane realism?

My answer	Extra points from partner	Final answer

Was the study a laboratory, field or natural experiment?

My answer	Extra points from partner	Final answer

What relevant variables might not have been controlled?

My answer	Extra points from partner	Final answer

▶ Lesson notes p.45

Which word?

The extract below outlines a study into eyewitness testimony. When you meet bold text circle the correct word or phrases.

Christianson and Hubinette (1993) questioned 58 real witnesses to bank robberies. Those witnesses who had been threatened in some way were more accurate in their recall, and remembered more details, than those who had been onlookers and less emotionally aroused. This continued to be true even 15 months later.

The **independent variable** / **dependent variable** in this study was the level of emotional arousal; either high as directly threatened or lower as an onlooker. The **independent variable** / **dependent variable** in this study was the accuracy of recall relating to the robbery witnessed.

This is an example of a **laboratory experiment** / **field experiment** / **natural experiment** because the researcher made use of naturally varying IV instead of deliberately manipulating it. Sometimes these experiments are called quasi-experiments because the researcher **does** / **does not** deliberately change the **IV** / **DV** to observe the effect on the **IV** / **DV**.

This type of experiment is advantageous when researching areas that cannot be artificially created for ethical or practical reasons. For example, it would be **unethical** / **impractical** to take children away from their parents at birth to study **privation** / **deprivation**. However, as the researcher does not manipulate the IV directly **causal relationships** / **correlational relationships** cannot be identified. In addition, participants are not randomly allocated to conditions which may reduce **reliability** / **validity**.

For the following studies decide whether they are an example of a laboratory, field or natural experiment and give either one advantage or one disadvantage of this experiment type for the study outlined.

Two primary schools use different reading schemes. A psychological study compares the reading scores at the end of the year to see which scheme was more effective.

Laboratory experiment	*Field experiment*	*Natural experiment*

One advantage / disadvantage for this study is...

Participants' ability to recall details from a specific scene in a comedy film is compared to participants' ability to recall details from a specific scene in a horror film.

Laboratory experiment	*Field experiment*	*Natural experiment*

One advantage / disadvantage for this study is...

▶ Lesson notes p.45

Psycho babble

Complete the conversation between psychologists discussing the different forms of experiments

I PREFER TO CONDUCT LABORATORY EXPERIMENTS BECAUSE…

I THINK…

But aren't you worried the situations you create are artificial? I find natural experiments…

Have you considered the benefits of field experiments? They…

It seems to me you are forgetting...

I seem to recall a study into ...

I see your point but...

▶ Lesson notes p.45

Say what you see

In an observational study participants are observed engaging in whatever behaviour is being studied and the observations recorded. This can take the form of naturalistic or controlled observation.

Task 1: Read the two passages below and decide which one to summarise using pictures and a maximum of three words in the box below.

Naturalistic observation

Behaviour is studied in a natural setting where everything has been left as it normally is. Ainsworth (1967) observed the interaction between Ugandan women and their children. She used structured observation; spending short periods of time noting down specific behaviours. The behaviour under study was not interfered with as Ainsworth simply recorded what she saw occurring in her participants' natural environment.

Controlled observation

Some variables are controlled by the researcher meaning the naturalness of the study is reduced. Ainsworth and Wittig's (1969) Strange Situation involved structuring the behaviour of the participants and the observers. The participants had to follow eight episodes in which a child was left alone with their mother or a stranger and the observers used a checklist of five behaviours (proximity and contact-seeking, contact-maintaining behaviour, proximity and interaction-avoiding behaviour, proximity and interaction-resisting behaviour and search behaviour). They rated these every 15 seconds.

Create your picture here

Task 2: Share your picture with a partner. In the box below describe your partner's drawing in your own words. Consider what information they did not include and add this to your description.

Description of what your partner drew.

Further information they could have included.

▶ Lesson notes p.46

Levels of thinking

Bloom's taxonomy demonstrates the wide range of thinking skills that can be employed when considering information. These range from the simple, lower order thinking skills through to challenging higher order thinking skills.

Ainsworth and Wittig (1969) devised the Strange Situation to be able to test the nature of attachment systematically. They aimed to identify how infants aged between 9 and 18 months behaved under conditions of mild stress (stranger anxiety and separation anxiety) and novelty (a new situation to encourage exploration). The procedure consisted of eight episodes with a group of observers recording the infants' behaviour every 15 seconds. Observers noted down which of the following behaviours were displayed, and scored each behaviour on an intensity scale of 1 to 7: (1) proximity and contact seeking, (2) contact-maintaining, (3) proximity and interaction-avoiding, (4) contact and interaction-resisting, (5) search behaviours. From observations of 106 middle class infants, three main types of attachment were identified: Type A (insecure-avoidant), Type B (securely attached) and Type C (insecure-resistant).

Ainsworth (1967) spent two years observing 26 Ugandan women and their infants in a naturalistic setting. The women and their infants were from six villages surrounding Kampala. She spent short periods of time noting down specific behaviours. She observed some of the women were more sensitive to their infants' needs and these mothers tended to have securely attached infants.

In your notes answer the following questions.
Each question is more challenging than the one before as they progress along Bloom's taxonomy of thinking skills.

Lower order thinking skills

Knowledge
List the five behaviours observers were asked to record in the Strange Situation.

Comprehension
Did the observers in the Strange Situation use time or event sampling?

Middle order thinking skills

Application
How do the observations in the Strange Situation and Uganda study relate to the notion of individual differences in attachment?

Higher order thinking skills

Analysis
What are the similarities and differences between the Strange Situation observations and the Uganda observations?

Synthesis
Design a study to observe attachment types in children attending their first day at nursery.

Evaluation
Discuss the strengths and weaknesses of observational research in developing our understanding of individual differences in attachment.

▶ Lesson notes p.46

Organising an observation

In order to make systematic and objective observations, researchers need to develop behavioural categories. This method is called a coding system or behavioural checklist.

Using a **coding system** means that a code is invented to represent each category of behaviour.

A behavioural checklist is essentially the same thing though a code for each behaviour may not be given.

See your textbook (page 88 in *Complete Companion*) for examples of behavioural checklists and coding systems.

Task: Devise a behavioural checklist or coding system to enable you to carry out an observation in your school or college cafeteria.

Consider:
What do you wish to find out?
E.g. Differences in queuing behaviour between genders or ages? Differences in food choices between genders?

Think about:
The Hawthorne effect
How will you minimise the effect your presence has on those being observed?

Plan:
How will you record data?
Event or time sampling?
Coding system or checklist?
What categories will you have?
Inter-observer reliability

Remember:
Ethical considerations
Are you invading peoples' privacy?
Will your observation be overt or covert?

Record your initial ideas here before forming a group and developing a complete procedure.

▶ Lesson notes p.46

Naturalistic observation

Naturalistic observation: Carried out in a naturalistic setting, in which the investigator does not interfere in any way but merely observes the behaviour in question, though this is likely to involve the use of structured observations.

Situation to be observed:

Characters to be observed:

Behaviours to be observed
Operationalised :

Event/time sampling:

Data collected:

A strength of this method is:

A weakness of this method is:

▶ Lesson notes p.46

Roll with it

Below are a set of questions relating to the evaluation of observational research. Take it in turns to roll two dice to identify the question you have to answer and teach to the rest of your group. Either take the number shown on one die, or the two numbers added together (e.g. 2 + 3 = 5).

1 What is meant by the term inter-observer reliability?

2 Are population validity and ecological validity examples of external or internal validity? Explain your answer.

3 Why does observer bias reduce the validity of observations?

4 Observations that take place without the participant knowing (covert) could be said to be unethical. Explain which ethical issues are involved in such studies.

5 Why is it important to train observers?

6 What is meant by the term reliability?

7 Give one advantage of using observational research.

8 Give one disadvantage of using observational research.

9 Explain how psychologists can improve the validity of their observations.

10 How can psychologists improve the reliability of the observations they make?

11 Can a study lack reliability but still be seen as valid? Explain your answer.

12 Why is it important that a researcher clearly categorises the behaviours to be observed?

▶ Lesson notes p.47

Selecting participants

Define each type of sampling then identify the strengths and weaknesses associated with each method.

Random sample

Stratified/quota sample

Opportunity sample

Volunteer sample

The easiest method as you use the first participants you can find, which means it takes less time to locate your sample than if you used another technique.

Each sub-section could be biased in other ways, for example if you use opportunity sampling you only have access to certain sections of the target population.

Unbiased, all members of the target population have an equal chance of selection.

Will be biased because sample is drawn from a small part of the target population, e.g. if selecting participants by walking round town centre on a Monday morning, it would be unlikely to include professional people as they are at work.

Access to a variety of participants (e.g. all the people who read a newspaper) which would make the sample more representative and less biased than opportunity sampling.

Sample is biased because participants are likely to be more highly motivated and/or with extra time on their hands (known as volunteer bias).

More representative than an opportunity sample because there is equal representation of sub-groups.

The researcher may end up with a biased sample (e.g., more boys than girls) because the sample is too small.

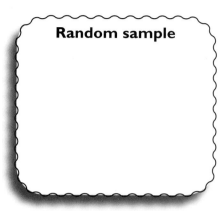

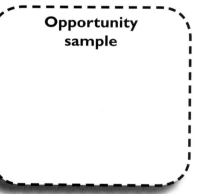

▶ Lesson notes p.47

Sampling techniques

For each example state the sample technique used and give the strengths and weaknesses of that sampling method for the context in which it was used.

Strengths for the researcher: ....

E.g. this technique did not take long to do. The researcher probably did not have access to a lot of young children so this was a quick way to gather his sample.

A researcher wishes to study memory in children aged between 5 and 11. He contacted the headmaster of his local primary school and arranged to test the children in the school.

Sample technique:

Weaknesses for the researcher: ....

Strengths for the university department: ....

A university department undertook a study of mobile phone use in adolescents, using a questionnaire. The questionnaire was given to a group of students in a local comprehensive school, selected by placing all the students' names in a container and drawing out 50 names.

Sample technique:

Weaknesses for the university department: ....

Strengths for the psychology students: ....

A class of psychology students conduct a study on memory. They put a notice on the notice board in the sixth form common room asking for participants who have an hour to spare.

Sample technique:

Weaknesses for the psychology students: ....

▶ Lesson notes p.47

Taboo

Read each taboo statement and decide which taboo word they are describing.
Then rewrite the definition using the related words.

These ask people to choose an answer from a number of set responses. They are quick to complete and can be easily analysed to produce graphs and statistics. This makes it easy to compare participants.

These allow participants to provide their own answers. They often include who, what, when, where, why, how. The data gathered is lengthy and contains a lot of information. It can be difficult to compare people's answers.

These are included to distract the respondent from the true aim of the questionnaire, so participants are less likely to give the answers they think the researcher wants to hear. They are questions not related to the main topic under study.

The order of questions is considered. Simple questions are placed first to ease the participant into the questionnaire. More challenging questions are included later in the questionnaire. This is used to encourage completion of the questionnaire.

Taboo word
Filler questions
Related words
Irrelevant questions, Demand characteristics

Taboo word
Sequence for the questions
Related words
Easier questions, Anxious or defensive

Taboo word
Closed questions
Related words
Range of responses, Quantitative data

Taboo word
Open questions
Related words
In-depth, insightful Qualitative data

Now try to create your own taboo statements from the definitions shown below.

Taboo word **Structured interview**
Related words
Pre-determined, before

Structured interview — any interview where questions are pre-determined. The researcher decides what they want to ask before beginning the interview.

Taboo word **Unstructured interview**
Related words
Structure, guided

Unstructured interview – the interviewer begins the study with general aims and maybe a few questions but there is no structure. The interviewer is guided by the respondents' answers.

▶ Lesson notes p.47

SELF-REPORT VENN DIAGRAM

Use the Venn diagram to record the similarities and differences between interviews and questionnaires.

AO1

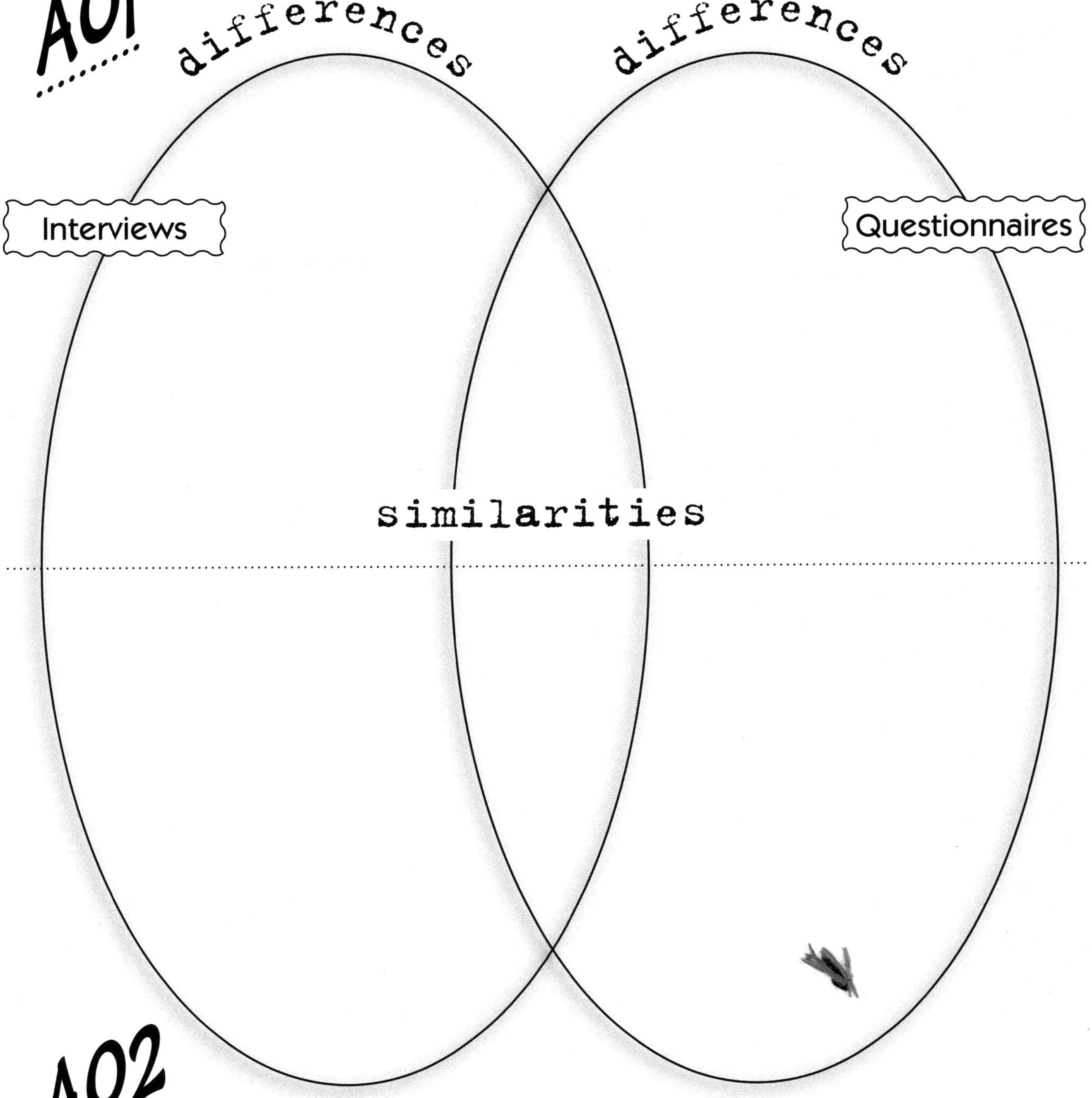

AO2

▶ Lesson notes p.48

Evaluating self-report techniques

Read the extract below then answer the questions relating to the use of self-report techniques.

Hazan and Shaver (1987)

Aim – to investigate Bowlby's (1969) suggestion that later relationships are a continuation of an infant's early attachment style, as the mother's behaviour creates an internal working model of relationships, which leads the child to expect the same in later relationships.

Procedure – a love quiz was placed in a newspaper asking about early experiences (to classify attachment type), current love experiences and attitudes towards love (internal working model).

Findings – early attachment type was associated with patterns of later romantic behaviour, e.g. secure attachment as a child was linked to later stable relationships showing trust in others. Respondents classified as insecure-avoidant reported a fear of closeness; insecure-resistant attachments were linked to later experiences in trouble finding true love in adulthood.

Conclusion – findings seem to support Bowlby's theory. Early attachment type does seem to impact on attitudes towards later relationships in adulthood.

How could the internal reliability of the Love quiz be assessed?

How could Hazan and Shaver have assessed the internal validity of the Love quiz?

How could the external reliability of the Love quiz be assessed?

How could Hazan and Shaver have assessed the external validity of the Love quiz?

Advantage of placing Love quiz in a newspaper

Disadvantage of placing Love quiz in a newspaper

▶ Lesson notes p.48

Conducting correlations 1

Is there a correlation between exam stress score and exam confidence score?

Procedure:

- You need to ask 10 participants to complete the attached questionnaire on exam stress and exam confidence. (5 min)

Before you start you need to write a **hypothesis**.

Type up your hypothesis using a word processor. Remember a hypothesis means a prediction, e.g.

There is a positive correlation between… *(write the two variables in your study).*

There is a negative correlation between… *(write the two variables in your study).*

There is no correlation between… *(write the two variables in your study).*

- Next you need to carry out the study! (10 min)

When you have the data you need to put it into **Excel** and then calculate a **correlation coefficient analysis**. (Insert/function/correl)

- You now need to produce a scattergraph. (5 min)

• Highlight your data. Click on <insert> <chart> <XY scatter>
and press <next> and <next> again.

• Add a suitable title, and axis titles, then select <finish>.

Copy and paste into your word processed document.

- When you have done this you need to write a conclusion stating what the findings of your results were (including the correlation coefficient) and if there is a relationship between these two variables. (10 min)

Is it positive, negative or is there no correlation?

Can you accept your hypothesis? (Was the prediction right?)

Use your information sheet to check whether your results are significant (if they are/are not, explain what this means).

▶ Lesson notes p.48

Conducting correlations 2

Use the questionnaires below to gather data for your correlation.

Exam stress questionnaire

Rate your reaction to the following statements:

1 = not at all like me/never -- 7 = exactly like me/all the time

	1	2	3	4	5	6	7
I feel a high level of anxiety before I enter an exam room							
I find exams the most stressful aspect of my AS course							
I often become ill with colds and sore throats after my exams							

Exam confidence questionnaire

Rate your reaction to the following statements:

1 = not at all like me/never -- 7 = exactly like me/all the time

	1	2	3	4	5	6	7
I know with adequate revision I can do well in my exams							
I see exams as an opportunity to demonstrate what I know							
I eagerly await my exam results to see how well I have done							

Exam stress questionnaire

Rate your reaction to the following statements:

1 = not at all like me/never -- 7 = exactly like me/all the time

	1	2	3	4	5	6	7
I feel a high level of anxiety before I enter an exam room							
I find exams the most stressful aspect of my AS course							
I often become ill with colds and sore throats after my exams							

Exam confidence questionnaire

Rate your reaction to the following statements:

1 = not at all like me/never -- 7 = exactly like me/all the time

	1	2	3	4	5	6	7
I know with adequate revision I can do well in my exams							
I see exams as an opportunity to demonstrate what I know							
I eagerly await my exam results to see how well I have done							

▶ Lesson notes p.48

Using case studies

Experiments are not the only method psychologists have used to investigate memory.

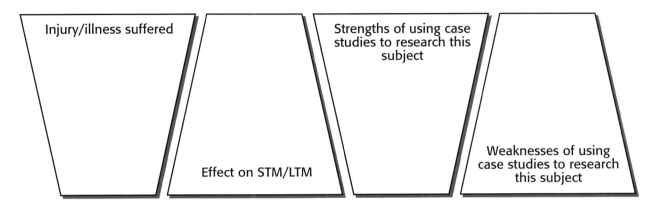

CASE STUDY 1

Injury/illness suffered

Effect on STM/LTM

Strengths of using case studies to research this subject

Weaknesses of using case studies to research this subject

CASE STUDY 2

Injury/illness 2

Effect on STM/LTM

Differences from case study 1

Task 1 Complete the passage:

Having considered the use of case studies to research memory and the strengths and weakness of the method I feel that:

What to include:

- *All students* ***must*** *explain one strength and one weakness of using case studies to research memory then make their own conclusion relating to their usefulness in researching memory.*
- *Most students* ***should*** *explain two advantages and two disadvantages of using case studies to research memory then make their own conclusion relating to their usefulness in researching memory.*
- *Some students* ***could*** *explain two advantages and two disadvantages of using case studies to research memory and consider their validity before reaching their own conclusion relating to their usefulness when researching memory.*

▶ Lesson notes p.49

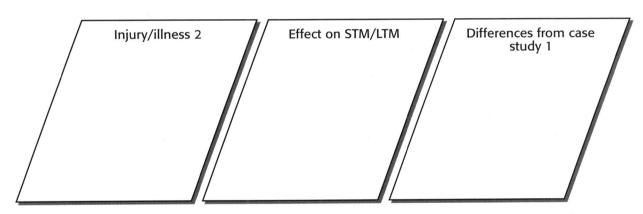

Case study critique

Consider the strengths and weaknesses of case studies as a method of investigation.

Case studies offer rich, in-depth data, so information that may be overlooked using other methods is likely to be identified.

- ☐ Strongly agree
- ☐ Agree
- ☐ Disagree
- ☐ Strongly disagree

Reason for choice:

Can be used to investigate instances of human behaviour and experience that are rare, for example investigating cases of children locked in a room through childhood to see what effects deprivation has on emotional development.

- ☐ Strongly agree
- ☐ Agree
- ☐ Disagree
- ☐ Strongly disagree

Reason for choice:

It is often necessary to use recollection of past events as part of the case study and such evidence may be unreliable.

- ☐ Strongly agree
- ☐ Agree
- ☐ Disagree
- ☐ Strongly disagree

Reason for choice:

It is difficult to generalise from individual cases as each one has unique characteristics.

- ☐ Strongly agree
- ☐ Agree
- ☐ Disagree
- ☐ Strongly disagree

Reason for choice:

▶ Lesson notes p.49

Content analysis: TV today

Content analysis: *A kind of observational study in which behaviour is observed indirectly in written or verbal material such as interviews, conversations, books, diaries or TV programmes. Behaviour is categorised (qualitative analysis) and may be counted (quantitative analysis).*

Task: Produce a content analysis of the television available in today's society using the television guide from a recent newspaper or magazine.

Decisions to be made:

Channels to be included in the analysis are:	**These were selected because:**
The time frame for programmes is:	**This time frame was selected because:**
The programme types are: 1. Human interest documentary 2. Soap opera 3. Situation comedy (sitcom) 4. Local and national news 5. Film (plus state genre) 6. 7. 8. 9. 10.	**Definition of each programme type:** 1. 2. 3. 4. 5. 6. 7. 8. 9. 10.

After you have collected the data

Analysis of the findings

Give a detailed description of your findings from the content analysis. Begin by looking at the overall programme types across all channels. You could develop this further by identifying whether certain channels show more of one programme type or whether time of day has an impact on the type of programme available to watch. The data will be quantitative so you could represent your findings using bar charts.

Evaluation of findings

What did you find easy?
What aspects did you find difficult?
Do you feel there were any threats to the internal or external validity of your study?
Could reliability of your study easily be checked?
Were there any ethical issues?
If you were to repeat the study what improvements could be made?
Any ideas for future research?

▶ Lesson notes p.49

One word review

Qualitative data aims to produce an in-depth understanding of behaviour, and, because of the open-ended nature of the research, produce new explanations. The goal is to understand behaviour in a natural setting and also to understand a phenomenon from the perspective of the research participant and understand the meanings people give to their experience. The researcher is concerned with asking broad questions that allow the respondent to answer in their own words, or to observe behaviour.

Qualitative research uses smaller samples than quantitative research but usually involves the collection of a large amount of data. The challenge when presenting qualitative data is to find ways to summarise it so that a conclusion can be drawn. Data is categorised (pre-existing categories or emergent categories) and then these behavioural categories used to summarise the data. From this a conclusion can be drawn.

Task 1: Read the passage and highlight single words you feel are central to the explanation of qualitative data.

Task 2: Choose one single word that 'sums up' the passage and explain your choice below. This word can be one you highlighted from the passage above or a new word.

WORD CHOSEN:	REASONS FOR CHOICE:

Collect other people's ideas.

WORD CHOSEN:	REASONS FOR CHOICE:

WORD CHOSEN:	REASONS FOR CHOICE:

▶ Lesson notes p.50

Work it out word search 1

Answer each clue to identify the words that can be found in the grid.

Methods

- *Combining results of several studies that have similar aims/hypotheses, e.g. Deffenbacher et al.'s (2004) work on EWT (p 16) or Van Ijzendoorn and Kroonenberg's (1988) combination of 32 studies into attachment (p 45 in* Complete Companion*)* ____/ ________
- *A study conducted over a long period of time, e.g. Hodges and Tizard's (1989) study of institutionalised children (p 50 in* Complete Companion*)* ____________/ _____
- *Research in which psychologists compare behaviour in different cultures to determine whether cultural practices affect behaviour, e.g. Ainsworth's (1967) study of infants in Uganda (p 44 in* Complete Companion*)* _____/ ________/ _____
- *This approach combines all sorts of different techniques and methods to investigate the target behaviour, e.g. Schaffer and Emerson's (1964) study of infant attachment (p 38 in* Complete Companion*)* _____/ ______
- *A form of controlled observation in which participants are asked to take on a certain character and their interactions with other characters is recorded, e.g. Zimbardo (1973) prisoners and guards (pp xii and 45 in* Complete Companion*)* ____/ ____
- *A study where different ages are compared at the same point in time rather than following one group as they age* _____/ _________

Problems

- *A technique or theory developed in one culture and then used to study behaviour of people in a different culture which has different norms, values, expectations, etc., e.g. Ainsworth and Wittig's (1969) Strange Situation (p 40 in* Complete Companion*). A problem associated with cross-cultural studies*

  _______/ ____
- *Where one group of participants has unique characteristics because of time-specific experiences during the development of its members, e.g. being a child in the Second World War. A problem found in longitudinal studies and cross-sectional studies* ______/ ______
- *A measure of the strength of the relationship between two variables. Used in meta-analysis*

  _____/ ____
- *The loss of participants from a study over time which is likely to leave a biased sample or a sample that is too small. A problem with longitudinal studies* _________

Answers can be found in the grid running forwards, backwards, horizontally, vertically and diagonally.

▶ Lesson notes p.50

Work it out word search 2

Find the words in the grid.

A	T	B	O	L	V	Q	R	N	K	L	C	T	L	X
V	H	Y	R	O	L	E	P	L	A	Y	R	I	T	Q
S	P	R	B	N	N	F	U	M	T	Z	O	P	W	L
W	D	F	K	G	L	Z	E	B	T	Q	S	N	Y	C
D	P	M	J	T	W	B	J	H	R	N	S	Q	R	L
X	K	U	E	I	P	L	E	T	I	H	C	D	V	M
E	W	L	O	T	T	G	H	O	T	G	U	F	F	U
T	Y	T	O	U	A	P	W	B	I	D	L	V	X	P
Y	I	I	B	D	S	A	I	Y	O	R	T	H	I	T
M	B	M	T	I	G	J	N	M	N	U	U	W	M	C
K	D	E	Y	N	D	F	I	A	Y	L	R	I	U	E
Q	L	T	N	A	P	L	X	J	L	P	A	Z	Q	F
C	Q	H	Q	L	W	T	V	B	W	Y	L	X	T	F
X	M	O	I	S	E	F	F	E	C	T	S	I	Z	E
P	I	D	M	T	A	I	X	C	R	C	T	I	P	T
L	O	Q	N	U	Z	P	K	D	N	X	U	P	S	R
C	I	T	E	D	E	S	O	P	M	I	D	R	Y	O
D	W	Y	R	Y	T	Q	K	B	P	I	Y	P	W	H
Q	L	Y	G	G	O	P	S	J	T	Y	L	W	M	O
A	L	A	N	O	I	T	C	E	S	S	S	O	R	C

Reflection

Words I could easily identify from the clues were:

Words I had to look up were:

Words I am still unsure of are:

What I need to do to further my understanding of these words is:

▶ Lesson notes p.50

Work it out word search 3

Answers

				L							C			
			R	O	L	E	P	L	A	Y	R			
				N					T		O			
				G					T		S			
		M		T					R		S			
		U	E	I					I		C			
		L		T					T		U			
		T		U	A				I		L			
		I		D		A			O		T			T
		M		I			N		N		U			C
		E		N				A			R			E
		T		A					L		A			F
		H		L						Y	L			F
		O		S	E	F	F	E	C	T	S	I	Z	E
		D		T							T	I		T
				U							U		S	R
C	I	T	E	D	E	S	O	P	M	I	D			O
				Y							Y			H
														O
	L	A	N	O	I	T	C	E	S	S	S	O	R	C

▶ Lesson notes p.50

True or false?

Decide whether the statement is true or false then either correct the statement or expand it.

SCHAFFER AND EMERSON (1964) USED A MULTI-METHOD APPROACH IN THEIR STUDY OF INFANT ATTACHMENTS.	T	F
Correction /expansion		

KÖHNKEN *ET AL.* (1999) CONDUCTED A META-ANALYSIS OF 53 STUDIES RELATED TO THE COGNITIVE INTERVIEW. THEY USED THE EFFECT SIZE AS THE IV IN ORDER TO ASSESS OVERALL TRENDS.	T	F
Correction /expansion		

IMPOSED ETIC REFERS TO A TECHNIQUE OR THEORY DEVELOPED IN ONE CULTURE AND THEN USED TO STUDY THE BEHAVIOUR OF PEOPLE IN A DIFFERENT CULTURE WHICH HAS THE SAME NORMS, VALUES, EXPERIENCES, ETC.	T	F
Correction /expansion		

ATTRITION IS A PROBLEM IN LONGITUDINAL STUDIES WHICH CAN RESULT IN A BIASED SAMPLE.	T	F
Correction /expansion		

COHORT EFFECTS CAN HAVE AN IMPACT ON BOTH CROSS-SECTIONAL AND LONGITUDINAL STUDIES.	T	F
Correction /expansion		

▶ Lesson notes p.50

Let me tell you...

One of the best ways to check you understand a concept is to explain it to someone else.

The body's response to acute (sudden) stressors

The *sympatho*medullary pathway

When a stressor is present, the sympathetic branch of the autonomic nervous system (SNS) arouses an animal to be ready for fight or flight. Neurons from the SNS travel to virtually every organ and gland within the body.

The SNS also regulates the SAM (sympathetic adrenal medullary) system. Some of the SNS' neurons travel to the adrenal medulla (the middle of the adrenal gland which is located above each kidney). When activated by the SNS the medulla releases adrenaline into the bloodstream. Responses include an increase in heart rate, blood pressure and cardiac output, increased pupil size and metabolic changes such as fat and glycogen into the blood stream.

The body's response to chronic (on-going) stressors

The **hypothalamic**-pituitary-adrenal system

The hypothalamus is found deep within the brain. When physical or emotional stress is detected in the pituitary gland it causes this gland to release adrenocorticotrophic hormone (ACTH). ACTH travels in the blood to the adrenal glands (found at the top of the kidneys). The outside of the gland, called the adrenal cortex, releases cortisol, which has a number of stress related effects in the body. We experience a quick burst of energy, a lowered sensitivity to pain but also a lowered immune response. Prolonged release of ACTH causes the adrenal cortex to increase in size to enable it to cope with increased cortisol production. Long term ACTH deficiency causes it to shrink.

Working in pairs, decide how you would explain the two systems to the following people:

- ☐ ***A Year 7 secondary school student.***
- ☐ ***An AS Psychology student who needs help.***

Now on your own try to write a 150-word summary for each stress response explaining each system for an examiner.

Remember to be accurate and detailed

▶ Lesson notes p.51

Definition doctor

Understanding the body's response to stress is difficult as there are many medical terms used in the explanation of the body's stress reaction. Defining the key terms will help your AO1 writing.

The sympathomedullary pathway

The sympathetic branch of the autonomic nervous system (SNS)

↓

adrenal medulla

↓

adrenaline

↓

- increase in oxygen and glucose supply to the brain and muscles
- suppression of non-emergency bodily processes such as digestion

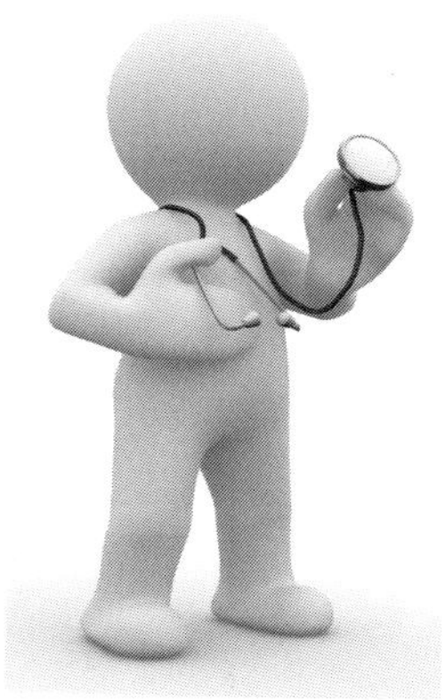

The hypothalamic-pituitary-adrenal system

hypothalamus

↓

adrenocorticotrophic hormone (ACTH)

↓

adrenal cortex

↓

cortisol

- quick burst of energy, lowered sensitivity to pain
- higher blood pressure
- lowered immune response

For each term, write a one-sentence definition of the term. Be sure to use your own words, rather than those in your textbook, to fully develop your understanding.

Sympathomedullary pathway –

(Hypothalmic) Pituitary-adrenal system –

Adrenal gland (medulla and cortex) – Tip: Middle – Medulla, Coating/cover - Cortex

Adrenaline – Tip: Adrenaline - adrenal medulla

Cortisol – Tip: Cortisol – adrenal cortex

Lesson notes p.51

Immune issues

Does the stress associated with being a student or in a relationship put you at risk of illness due to the impact of the body's stress reaction on the immune system?

Research into:	
Study 1	Measure
Study 2	Measure

Research into:	
Study 1	Measure
Study 2	Measure

Confounding variables. *Why is it hard to identify a clear relationship between stress and immune functioning?*

Individual differences. *Why might differences between age and gender make it difficult to generalise research findings to the wider population?*

Conclusion. *What impact do you think stress has on the immune system?*

▶ Lesson notes p.51

Health scare

The media can create health scares in society by partially reporting research. Using your knowledge of stress and the immune system consider how the following groups would react.

The Daily Digest

Immune system special

Daily news and research reviews

Psychology in the real world

School and love bad for your health!

Shock research into effects of stress

Story by Roving reporter C. O. R. Tisol

The devastating effects of stress on your mental stability and health of the heart has been extensively documented. Now scientists are warning of a new assault on our well-being. Our immune system is under siege from stress.

Stress has once again shown to be a deadly assassin targeting our body. The hustle and bustle of daily life results in a

Research conducted on students sent shock waves through educational establishments earlier this week when it was suggested exam-related stress had a severe impact on pupils' immune functioning.

Education worries

'How will we assess students now?' One teacher was heard to complain.

Quarrelling couples be warned. As you bicker, your body's stress response in the form of adrenaline and noradrenaline is coursing through your veins. The various components of the immune defence are crippled under this prolonged attack, leading to increased susceptibility to viruses and infection.

Consider how the following people would react to this news article:

- Newly married couples.
- AS Psychology students facing their Unit 2 exam.
- AS students who have not studied Psychology.
- Doctors.
- A psychologist who has carried out research into this area.

Taking the role of one of the people mentioned above, write a letter to the editor of The Daily Digest clearly explaining your response to their reporting of the relationship between stress and immune functioning.

▶ Lesson notes p.52

Stress and the heart

Explain the link between stress, the cardiovascular system and cardiovascular disorders.

This activity will help you develop your summary skills.

Read the information below and highlight the five most important words in the text relating to the question '**Explain the link between stress, the cardiovascular system and cardiovascular disorders**'.

Acute and chronic stress may affect many different aspects of the cardiovascular system (i.e., the heart and circulatory system), for example: hypertension (high blood pressure), coronary heart disease (CHD) caused by atherosclerosis (the narrowing of the coronary arteries) and stroke (damage caused by disruption of blood supply to the brain). Although such cardiovascular disorders are affected by lifestyle, diet, smoking, etc., stress has become increasingly implicated in the development of all the disorders listed above. A number of suggestions have been put forward to explain how stress might cause cardiovascular disorders. For example:

- Stress activates the sympathetic branch (SNS) of the autonomic nervous system, leading to a constriction of the blood vessels and a rise in blood pressure and heart rate.
- An increase in heart rate may wear away the lining of the blood vessels.
- Stress leads to increased glucose levels, leading to clumps blocking the blood vessels (atherosclerosis).

Five key words the class selected:

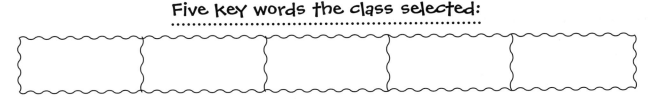

Now write a summary in your own words, explaining the link between stress, the cardiovascular system and cardiovascular disorders. Make sure you include the five words identified by the class.

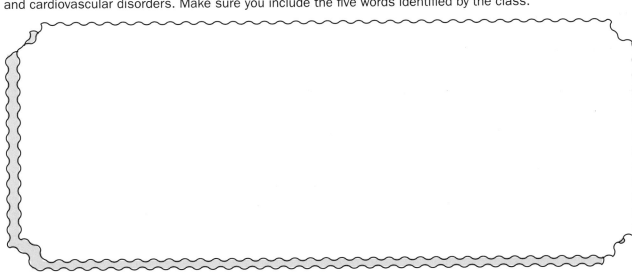

▶ Lesson notes p.52

Match making

Use *Complete Companion* p 122 to help you match the correct words to each study into cardiovascular disorders.

acute stressor

blood pressure

co-habiting women

left ventricle

existing conditions

35%

2.9

pathologists

heart disease

hot headed

GPs

Williams (2000)	Russek (1962)

Sheps (2002)	Orth-Gomér (2000)

18%

chronic stressor

low-stress

public speaking

2 1/2 times

6 years

256

3.2%

existing conditions

MARITAL CONFLICT

dermatologist

erratic heartbeats

fatal

44%

doctors

high-stress

anger

married

anaesthetists

coronary artery disease

recurrent events

11.9%

ischemia

173

heart-attack

▶ Lesson notes p.52

Triplets

All the words below relate to research in stress-related illness. For each set select three words by writing their number on each line and explain how they are connected to each other.

1. Kiecolt-Glaser	9. Women	17. Students
2. Increase	10. Disease	18. Exam
3. Acute	11. Marital conflict	19. Conflict
4. Work	12. Year	20. Stress
5. Questions	13. Immune system	21. Test
6. Depression	14. Relationship	22. Heart
7. Blood	15. Healing	23. Chronic
8. Wounds	16. Survey	24. Men

Set A ___ ___ ___ ______________________________

Set B ___ ___ ___ ______________________________

Set C ___ ___ ___ ______________________________

Set D ___ ___ ___ ______________________________

Set E ___ ___ ___ ______________________________

▶ Lesson notes p.53

Smiley scale

For each topic decide where you fall on the smiley scale. Decide what you need to do to move yourself along the smileys or keep yourself at the top spot.

The body's response to stress: sympathomedullary pathway and pituitary-adrenal system.

I am unsure of most aspects and find recall difficult	I understand some aspects but find it hard to recall	One or two points are confusing	I understand most aspects and can remember some	I have a good understanding and recall of aspects

How can I move along the smileys or remain at the top spot?

Stress-related illness: Outlining research into stress-related illness and the immune system.

I am unsure of most aspects and find recall difficult	I understand some aspects but find it hard to recall	One or two points are confusing	I understand most aspects and can remember some	I have a good understanding and recall of aspects

How can I move along the smileys or remain at the top spot?

Stress-related illness: Evaluating research into stress-related illness and the immune system.

I am unsure of most aspects and find recall difficult	I understand some aspects but find it hard to recall	One or two points are confusing	I understand most aspects and can remember some	I have a good understanding and recall of aspects

How can I move along the smileys or remain at the top spot?

▶ Lesson notes p.53

True or False?

Decide whether each statement is true or false. If false, write the correct statement below.
Extension – for correct statements add further details to develop the point.

Holmes and Rahe observed that many of their patients' illnesses seemed to have occurred after a number of major life changes.	T F
Extension/correction (circle)	
Only negative life changes were included on the Social Readjustment Rating Scale (SRRS).	T F
Extension/correction (circle)	
The SRRS contains 40 life events and was based on the analysis of over 3000 patient records.	T F
Extension/correction (circle)	
400 participants scored each event in terms of how much readjustment would be required by the average person.	T F
Extension/correction (circle)	
LCU stands for lucky chance units.	T F
Extension/correction (circle)	
Rahe *et al.* (1970) used the SRRS with the US Navy to test the hypothesis that the number of life events experienced would be positively correlated with illness.	T F
Extension/correction (circle)	
Rahe's findings were not significant.	T F
Extension/correction (circle)	
It seems change, not whether the event is seen as positive or negative by the individual, is the important factor in whether stress will be experienced.	T F
Extension/correction (circle)	

▶ Lesson notes p.53

Chat about changes

Read the information in your textbook (page 124 in *Complete Companion*). Make a list of 10 key points to help you with this activity. Move round the room chatting to others to help you complete this worksheet.

__________ said a key word from the passage is __________ __________

__________ summarised one key point by saying __________ __________ __________ __________

__________ advised me to remember that __________ __________ __________ __________ __________

__________ told me that __________ __________ __________ __________ __________ __________

__________ thought __________ __________ __________ __________ __________

__________ explained that __________ __________ __________

__________ defined __________ __________ as __________ __________ __________ __________

__________ feels an important issue is __________ __________ __________ __________

▶ Lesson notes p.54

The six hats

Edward de Bono's six hats is a way of looking at an issue from a number of different perspectives. Use this technique to consider the view that daily hassles play a significant role in psychological well-being.

White hat 	What data is available regarding daily hassles as a cause of stress?
Red hat 	What do you feel about the suggestion 'daily hassles cause stress'. How do you feel when experiencing hassles/uplifts?
Black hat 	What problems does the theory face? Who disagrees that daily hassles cause stress? Are there any weaknesses with the explanation?
Yellow hat 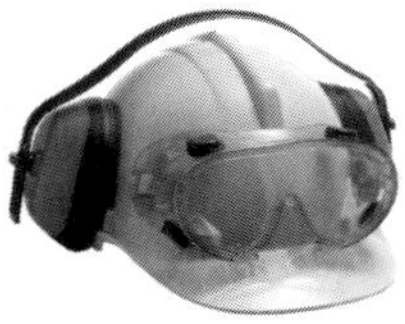	What are the strengths of the theory? Who supports the suggestion 'stress results from daily hassles'?
Green hat 	How can this theory be used in the real world to improve people's psychological well-being?
Blue hat 	How would this theory be viewed by Holmes and Rahe (SRRS)?

▶ Lesson notes p.54

Opinionated octopus

Complete the octopus placards to show your opinion of the suggestion that daily hassles play a major role in our psychological well-being.

Daily hassles are relatively minor events that arise in the course of a normal day. They involve the everyday concerns of work, such as a disagreement with a colleague, or issues arising from family life. Although such issues and their associated emotional effects are usually short-lived, they may linger if left unresolved, and the 'after-effects' of unresolved issues may then intensify over time as they accumulate with subsequent hassles. The negative effects of daily hassles can in turn be offset to some degree by the more positive experiences that we have every day. Such daily uplifts, such as a smile from someone in the street or an e-mail from a long lost friend, are thought to counteract the damaging effects of stress.

The Hassles and Uplifts scale (Delongis et al. *1982) measures respondents' attitudes towards daily situations. Instead of focusing on the more highly stressful life events, the HSUP provides a way of evaluating both the positives and negative events that occur in each person's daily life.*

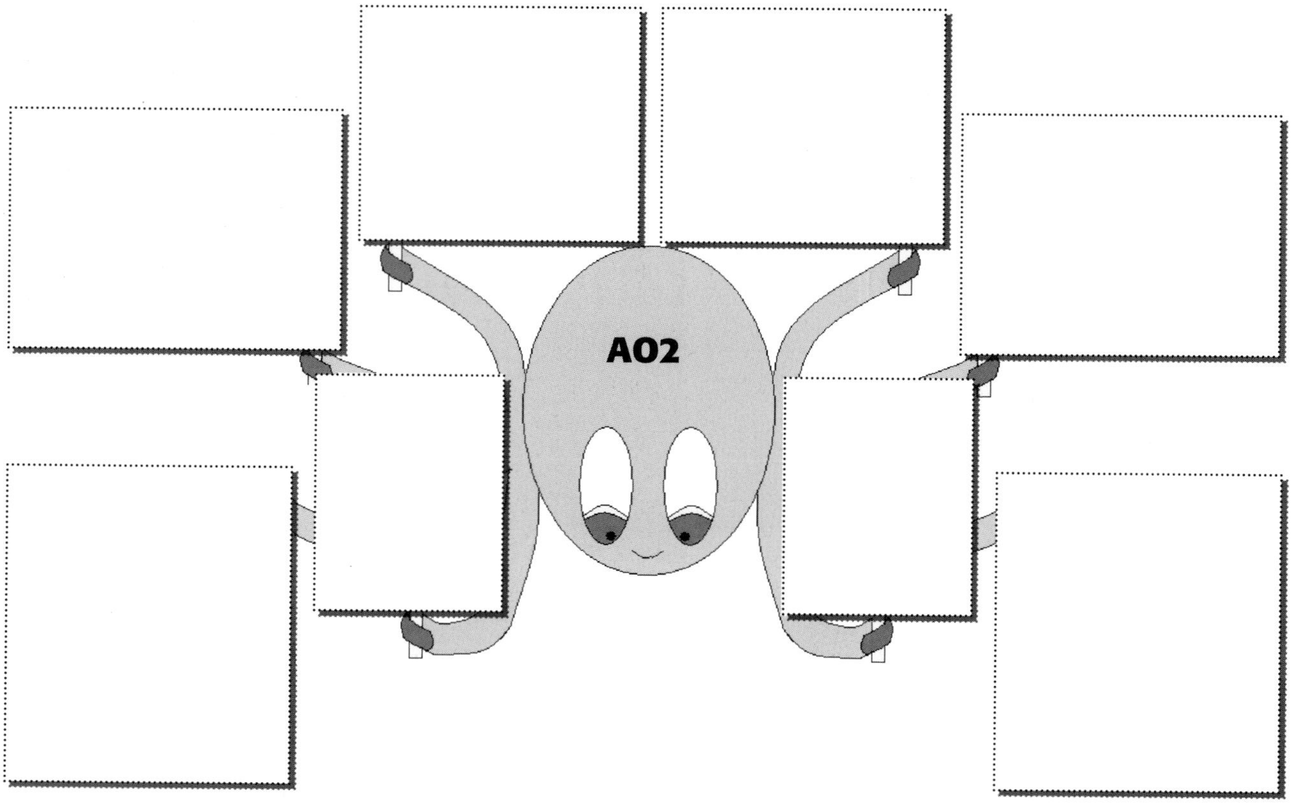

You might consider studies by Bouteyre *et al.* (2007) and Gervais (2005), comparisons made between daily hassles and life events scales, methodological issues in research and real world applications. Information can be found in your textbook

(pp 126–127 *Complete Companion*).

▶ Lesson notes p.54

Stress and work

Complete the questionnaire yourself about school or a part-time job, alternatively ask a friend or relative to consider their full-time job.

For each statement award yourself a score: 1 = not at all/never occurs, 5 = very much like me/ occurs often.

Section A: Workload

- ☐ I find my job repetitive (do the same tasks all day).
- ☐ I feel a lot of responsibility for others in my job daily.
- ☐ I never have the time to pause for a second in my job.

Section B: Control

- ☐ I am unable to prioritise the tasks I have to complete.
- ☐ I feel unable to make my own decisions concerning my daily tasks.
- ☐ It seems others set the agenda of my working day.

Section C: Role conflict

- ☐ I have to take work home at the end of the day.
- ☐ I feel torn between my work life and my home life.
- ☐ I feel guilt for neglecting different areas in my life.

Ethics

Remind your participant their answers will be kept confidential and they can withdraw at any time.

If someone has a particularly high stress score, advise them this is only a simple questionnaire. If they are worried they should seek help.

Score out of 45 ___
High score = stressed

Summary of psychological research underlying the questionnaire.

Workload: Marmot/Johansson	***Control:*** Marmot	***Role conflict:*** Pomaki

Extension - Use your knowledge. Write a report on your interviewee. Include: their stress score, what aspects of work seem to be causing them most stress and offer advice to the worker and the workplace to reduce their employee's stress.

▶ Lesson notes p.55

Essay plan

Planning sheet for workplace stressors.

Outline and evaluate two or more factors that lead to stress in the workplace (12 marks).

a) *AO1: Factor 1 (50 words)*

b) *AO2: Evaluation – support (25 words)*

c) *AO2: Evaluation – weaknesses (25 words)*

d) *AO1: Factor 2 (50 words)*

e) *AO2: Evaluation – support (25 words)*

f) *AO2: Evaluation – weaknesses (25 words)*

Peer review – what do you need to do? (Record the relevant section, a–f, in the boxes below)

☐☐☐☐ *Add more detail.*
☐☐☐☐ *Reduce the amount of words.*
☐☐☐☐ *Rewrite as it is hard to understand.*
☐☐☐☐ *Check whether information is accurate.*
☐☐☐☐ *Check your spelling.*
☐☐☐☐ *Check your work is detailed.*

▶ Lesson notes p.55

Exam practice

Not only do you need to know how the workplace may affect stress, you need to know how to use that information to gain maximum marks in the exam.

Discuss how factors in the workplace may affect stress (8 marks).

Alice's answer

Two factors are workload and control. High amounts of workload and low levels of control are thought to increase levels of stress. However, Marmot's research with civil servants found that those workers who were high on workload did not suffer unduly from stress. His research did, however, support the claim that low levels of control produce high levels of stress. Workers who were in jobs where they had very little control over what happened to them were more likely to experience cardiovascular disorders such as high blood pressure. However, this may have more to do with the fact that, compared to workers in the higher grades, these workers were lower paid, and had lower levels of social support, something which is known to help people resist the harmful effects of stress.

Read Alice's answer and highlight

AO1 comments (identification and brief explanation of a factor) *in one colour. In a second colour highlight* ***AO2 comments (evidence to challenge/support the factor).***

Alice received a score 3 out of 4 for AO1 and 3 out of 4 for AO2. What advice would you give her to improve her mark?

Tom's answer

There are three main factors which may affect whether people suffer from stress at work. Workload has been studied by Marmot et al. (1997), who found no relationship between level of workload and stress, and Johansson et al. (1978), who did, with workers in a sawmill who experienced the highest workloads also suffering from the most stress-related illnesses. The second factor is control. In Marmot et al.'s study, civil servants in higher grade positions, who experienced more control over their jobs than civil servants in lower grade positions, experienced lower levels of stress at work. The third factor is role of conflict, where work and home demands interfere with each other, which has been found to contribute to stress.

Lazarus (1995) criticises studies in this area, saying there are individual differences in how people are affected, and that this research doesn't take into account modern types of workplace (each working from home).

Read Tom's answer and highlight

AO1 comments (identification and brief explanation of a factor) *in one colour. In a second colour highlight* ***AO2 comments (evidence to challenge/support the factor).***

Tom's answer was clearly organised and contained three factors (AO1) – enough in a question worth 8 marks. He was awarded 4 out of 4.

On the down side, his evaluation (AO2) is fairly basic. He received 2 marks out of 4. What advice would you give him to improve his AO2 comments?

Now try to answer the 12-mark question yourself.

Outline and evaluate the contribution of two or more factors to stress in the workplace. Use Tom and Alice's answers to help you structure your answer and to help you identify what research to include.

▶ Lesson notes p.55

Personality

Producing a summary sheet of information will help you organise your thoughts in preparation for essay writing.

Type A Alex

Alex sees life as a competition. Everyone is an opponent. She constantly strives for perfection. With so much to do she is always impatient and hates wasting time. At times she can be quite aggressive and hostile, especially to those she feels are standing in her way. Alex's doctor worries about her high blood pressure.

Hardy Harriet

Harriet feels in control of her life. She has a strong sense of purpose and loves to get involved in events and activities. Harriet feels problems in life are really challenges that can be overcome. She enjoys the opportunities life events present.

Alex and Harriet have different stress levels due to their personality. Produce a 200-word summary for each study that supports this notion.

FRIEDMAN AND ROSENMAN – TYPE A AND B

KOBASA – HARDINESS

There are problems with the suggestion personality affects stress levels. Produce a 100-word summary of two criticisms for each study into personality and stress.

FRIEDMAN AND ROSENMAN – TYPE A AND B

1.

2.

KOBASA – HARDINESS

1.

2.

Use your notes to answer the question: ***Discuss what psychological research has shown about the way personality affects a person's experiences of stress (12 marks).*** *You need to write 240–300 words in 15 minutes. You will not have time to discuss all the information recorded on this sheet so highlight the points you are going to include.*

▶ Lesson notes p.56

Critical questioning

Read about Friedman and Rosenman's research into personality, then complete the questions.

Identify the facts: What happened?

Reasoning: How is the Type A personality related to increased stress?

Personal response: How do you feel about the findings?

Summarising: What are the main ideas in Type A research?

Friedman and Rosenman (1959) set up the Western Collaborative Group Study in 1960 to investigate the hypothesis that CHD is related to Type A personality. Approximately 3000 men aged 39 to 59, living in California, were examined for signs of CHD (those who were already ill were excluded) and their personalities assessed using a structured interview. The interview included questions about how they responded to everyday pressures. The interview was conducted in a provocative manner to try to elicit Type A behaviour.

After 8 ½ years, twice as many Type A participants had died of cardiovascular problems. 12.8% of Type As had experienced a heart attack compared to 6% of Bs. Twice as many Type As (2.7%) had died of cardiovascular problems compared to Bs (1.1%).

Analysing: Explain the impact of Type A on development of CHD.

Who disagrees with the idea Type A is related to CHD?

Application: How could this research help society?

Testing for truth: Is the research valid?

Alternative views: How do other people view personality?

Ethics: Did the research have any ethical issues?

▶ Lesson notes p.56

Reading Race

Compete against your class mates to reach the finish line.

Remember, your answers need to be accurate and detailed for you to receive the next question.

Accurate | Detailed

Question 8

Accurate | Detailed

Question 7

Accurate | Detailed

Question 6

Accurate | Detailed

Question 5

Accurate | Detailed

Question 4

Accurate | Detailed

Question 3

Accurate | Detailed

Question 2

Accurate | Detailed

Question 1

▶ Lesson notes p.56

Reading race Q & A

Questions and answers for reading race activity.
Next question available if previous answer can be ticked for accurate and detailed.

1 What characteristics did Friedman and Rosenman (1959) associate with the Type A personality?

- Competitiveness and achievement striving
- Impatience and time urgency
- Hostility and aggression

2 Describe the sample Friedman and Rosenman gathered in their Western Collaborative Group Study.

- Approximately 3000
- Californian Males
- Aged 39–59
- Healthy (examined for signs of CHD, any who were already ill were excluded)

3 How was personality assessed?

- Structured interview
- Questions designed to assess how participant would respond to everyday pressures
- Interviewer spoke slowly and hesitantly to illicit Type A behaviour

4 Why does the data suggest a relationship between Type A behaviour and CHD?

- 8½ years later Type A participants showed greater rate of heart attacks (12.8%, compared to 6.0% for Type B)
- Twice as many Type As (2.7%) had died compared to Type Bs (1.1%)
- Recurring heart attacks (A = 2.6%, B = 0.8%)
- Type As showed higher blood pressure and cholesterol
- Type As more likely to smoke and have family history of CHD

5 Which seems to be a greater contributing factor to CHD; personality or lifestyle?

- Ragland and Brand (1988) carried out a follow-up study, 22 years later 15% (214 men) had died of CHD
- Confirmed importance of CHD risk factors (age, smoking and high blood pressure)
- But found little relationship between Type A behaviours and mortality
- Challenges conclusion that Type A personality was a significant risk factor

6 How can our understanding of risk posed by Type A personality be refined?

- Myrtek's (2001) meta-analysis of 35 Type A studies
- Found relationship between one component of Type A (hostility) and CHD
- This is only evidence of an association between Type A and CHD

7 How can the resistance of some people to CHD be explained?

- Kobasa *et al.* (1982) suggested these people are more psychologically 'hardy' than others.
- Their characteristics; control, commitment, challenge, defend against the negative effects of stress

8 Which of your answers can be used to address AO1 exam questions and which can be used to address AO2 exam questions?

- AO1 – answers to questions 1, 2, 3, 4
- AO2 – answers to questions 5, 6, 7

▶ Lesson notes p.56

Coping card

Folkman and Lazarus (1980) define coping responses as 'cognitions and behaviours that a person uses to reduce and to moderate its emotional impact'. Their Ways of coping questionnaire (WCQ) indicates that people use two major types of coping strategy to deal with stressful events.

Ways of coping

Problem-focused coping Deals with stressor itself.	**Emotion-focused coping** Deals with emotions generated by stressor.

AO1: Using two different colours, highlight which strategy belongs to which way of coping

- Cope by taking control of situation.
- Cope by denying stressor exists.
- Cope by distancing self from stressor.
- Cope by evaluating options to deal with stressor.
- Cope by focusing on or venting emotions, e.g. crying.
- Cope by suppressing competing activities.
- Cope by indulging in wishful thinking.

AO1: Produce your own summary of each way of coping

Problem-focused coping:	Emotion-focused coping:

AO2: Using different colours, highlight which research finding belongs to which way of coping

- Nursing students who used problem-focused coping showed a positive correlation with overall health outcomes. Negative emotion-focused coping showed a negative correlation with overall health outcomes (Penley *et al.*, 2002).
- Breast cancer patients who used avoidance and distraction as a way of coping with their illness showed high psychological distress. Those who used strategies such as social support found this helped lessen their distress (Gilbar, 2005).
- Exam students used more problem-focused coping before their exams and more emotion-focusing coping when waiting for their results (Folkman and Lazarus, 1985).
- The threat a person feels seems to affect the way of coping employed. If a significant degree of threat is felt when facing the stressor, people employ emotion-focused coping first to deal with anxiety, once under control problem-focused coping can be used (Rukholm and Viverais, 1993).

AO2: Produce your own evaluation of each way of coping
(Give two strengths and two weaknesses of each method)

Problem-focused coping:	Emotion-focused coping:

▶ Lesson notes p.57

Describe/Distinguish

The AQA specification requires you to distinguish between problem-focused and emotion-focused coping. As well as distinguishing between the two you also need to be able to describe each way of coping.

Decide who has described the different ways of coping and who has distinguished between the ways of coping.

The main difference between emotion-focused and problem-focused coping is that emotion-focused only deals with the emotions that arise in the stressful situation, whereas problem-solving is a more active type of coping and involves dealing with the problem itself. For example, if someone gets a big bill that they can't pay, they might hide it in a drawer (denial) or ring up the company and arrange to pay a smaller amount each month (problem-focused).

Emotion-focused approaches to coping with stress include denial, which is where you don't admit to yourself that something is happening. For example, someone might still lay the table for their husband, even after he has died. Problem-focused approaches include dealing with the problem, for example the bereaved wife might start dating again and stop being lonely that way.

What words were used by the author to show the examiner they were making a distinction between the two forms of coping? Can you think of any other words they could have used?

Have a go for yourself….

Explain the difference between problem-focused and emotion-focused approaches to coping with stress (4 marks).

▶ Lesson notes p.57

Cut it out

You have limited space and time in the exam to describe theories and/or research. The art of précis is a vital skill to develop.

Stress inoculation training

Meichenbaum (1985) believed that although we cannot (usually) change the causes of stress in our life (e.g., a stressful job is still a stressful job), we can change the way that we *think* about these stressors. As negative thinking (e.g., 'I failed to hit a deadline, people must think I am hopeless') may lead to negative outcomes such as anxiety and depression; positive thinking (e.g., 'my boss will still be delighted by what I've achieved') leads to more positive attitudes and feelings. These reduce the stress response and help us to cope better in the future.

Meichenbaum's therapy, called stress inoculation training (SIT), is a form of cognitive behavioural therapy developed specifically to deal with stress. It is different from other stress treatments because Meichenbaum suggested that an individual should develop a form of coping before the problem arises. He suggested that a person could *inoculate* themselves against the 'disease' of stress in the same way that they would receive inoculations against infectious diseases such as measles.

Cut it out Reduce the passage to 100 words:

Cut it out Reduce the passage to 50 words:

▶ Lesson notes p.57

Build it up

Add details to the précis of Meichenbaum's stress inoculation training shown below.

50 word précis (*well, 58 words – count them!*)

SIT consists of three phases. Firstly, the conceptual phase where trainer and client establish a relationship and client is educated about stress. The next phase is skills acquisition and rehearsal. The client learns coping skills and practises them in the clinic and then real life. Lastly, application, gives clients opportunity to apply the new skills to different situations.

Build it up

Add detail to create a 100-word summary:

Build it up

Give full details to fill the box:

▶ Lesson notes p.57

'Image-in' it

Test your thinking, reading and drawing skills in this activity on Meichenbaum's stress inoculation training.

Circle the section assigned to your group:

- A general description of cognitive behavioural therapy (CBT). (AO1)
- An explanation of Meichenbaum's view of stress and aims of SIT. (AO1)
- Outline of the three phases of SIT. (AO1)
- The strengths of SIT. (AO2)
- The weaknesses of SIT. (AO2)

Task 1: represent your information in four pictures. Draw them in the boxes below. Your group then needs to reproduce four pictures on plain paper to share with the class later.

Task 2: As a group pick four new pictures, each one from a different group. In the boxes below recreate each picture and explain the information it represents.

▶ Lesson notes p.58

Crystal ball

Psychology involves making predictions (hypotheses) and investigating whether they are correct.

Now you have an understanding of the drug therapies available to manage stress, develop your own ideas regarding the strengths and weaknesses of this form of stress management.

Strengths

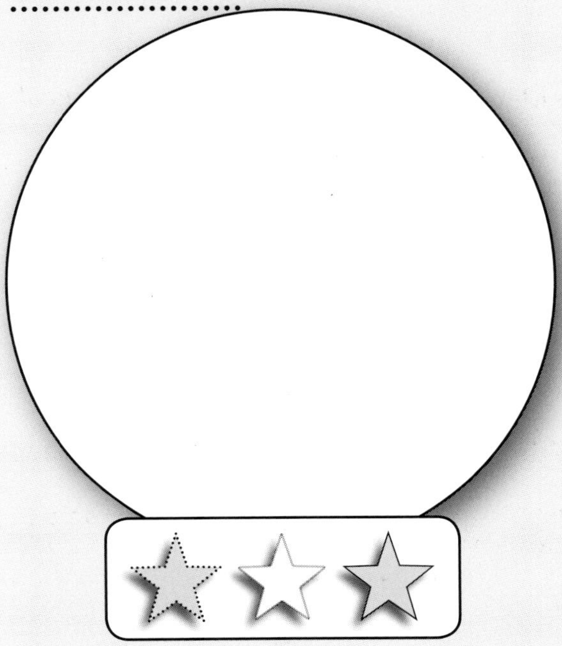

See how many of your ideas were the same as those in your textbook.

I was correct about:

I was incorrect about:

Weaknesses

See how many of your ideas were the same as those in your textbook.

I was correct about:

I was incorrect about:

▶ Lesson notes p.58

Sort it out

The strips below describe the action of Benzodiazepines (BZs) and Beta-blockers (BBs).

Cut out each strip and organise them into two separate paragraphs.

As an extension try using the strips to write 100 words about each type of drug.

Valium and Librium belong to this group of drugs that are most commonly used to reduce anxiety and stress as they slow down the activity of the central nervous system.

As the receptors are now blocked, it becomes harder to stimulate the heart, so its beat slows and blood vessels do not contract as easily, so blood pressure is reduced.

The actions of this drug on the neurons reduce the brain's output of excitatory neurotransmitters. As a result the person feels calmer.

These drugs work by binding to receptors on the cells of the heart and other parts of the body that are usually stimulated during arousal.

GABA reacts onto neurons' receptors and allows chloride ions into the neuron, which makes it hard for the neuron to become excited. The drug enhances GABA's action by increasing the flow of chloride ions into the neuron.

The action of these drugs is to reduce the activity of adrenaline and noradrenaline which form part of the sympathomedullary response to stress.

This reduces the strain on the heart, makes the person feel calmer and less anxious. These benefits mean this drug is often used by people who have to give a performance of some kind.

The neurotransmitter serotonin has an arousing effect in the brain. As the drug reduces any raised serotonin activity, the anxiety a person feels is reduced.

The body produces its own form of anxiety relief; a neurotransmitter called GABA – 40% of the brain's neurons respond to this neurotransmitter.

When stress occurs, the sympathetic nervous system becomes aroused. This leads to an increase in blood pressure, heart rate and cortisol levels.

▶ Lesson notes p.58

Debating drugs

The exam may ask you to consider the effectiveness of physiological approaches to stress management in either an 8- or 12-mark question.

A01

Drug therapies are an effective form of stress management.

Reasons why:

1.

2.

3.

Drug therapies are not a particularly effective form of stress management.

Reasons why:

1.

2.

3.

A02

Evidence that supports the suggestion that drug therapy is effective:

1.

2.

3.

Evidence that supports the suggestion that drug therapy is a particularly ineffective form of stress management:

1.

2.

3.

▶ Lesson notes p.58

Suggesting solutions

Read the case studies below and suggest a stress management technique or combination of techniques that best suits each individual. Be sure to explain your decisions.

Miss X

Miss X is an 18-year-old university student in the first year of her degree. Recently she has become anxious about meeting all her deadlines. She is ambitious and wants to continue studying after her degree but feels stressed by the workload. Talking to a psychologist highlighted her desire to feel in control of her studies and feel more confident in her ability to achieve good marks.

Mr Z

During a routine health check with his GP, Mr Z was found to have dangerously high blood pressure. His heart rate was elevated and he had raised cortisol levels. Mr Z's GP realised he was feeling anxious, and talking with him discovered he felt his workload had dramatically increased over the past year as a result of his promotion to team leader.

Mr Y

Mr Y appears extremely stressed. He worries about a lack of time to complete his work and spend time with his family. He feels he cannot think clearly and sees no solution to his problems. 'I'm just so stressed' is a phrase Mr Y utters often. The physical indicators of anxiety are clear to see in Mr Y – pounding heart, shallow breathing.

Mrs W

Talking to Mrs W reveals her to be a woman who doubts her ability to cope with her busy lifestyle as a part-time worker and mother to 5-year-old twins. She demonstrates negative thinking patterns, claiming 'I'm a rubbish mother', 'people at work must think I leave everything to the last minute'. Although she feels stressed, she doesn't want to leave her job and cannot afford to pay for extra childcare. She just wants help coping with the demands of a busy lifestyle.

▶ Lesson notes p.59

Stress A to Z review

For each letter write one word that begins with that letter.
Then assign a happy, sad, or neutral face to each word based on how well you understand the term.

A ______

B ______

C ______

D ______

E ______

F ______

G ______

H ______

I ______

J ______

K ______

L ______

M ______

N ______

O ______

P ______

Q ______

R ______

S ______

T ______

U ______

V ______

W ______

X ______

Y ______

Z ______

Review your knowledge by answering the following:

Which letters did you fill first?

Why?

Which letters did you find difficult?

Why were these letters difficult?

For the letters you assigned a sad face, take time to define them and use each one in an a separate sentence.

▶ Lesson notes p.59

Asch: Stimulus lines 1

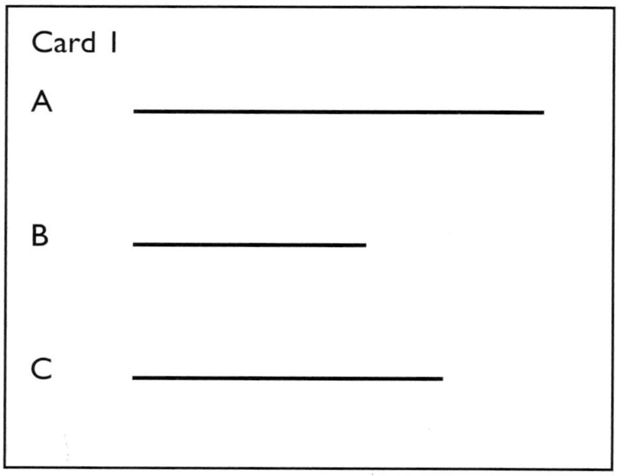

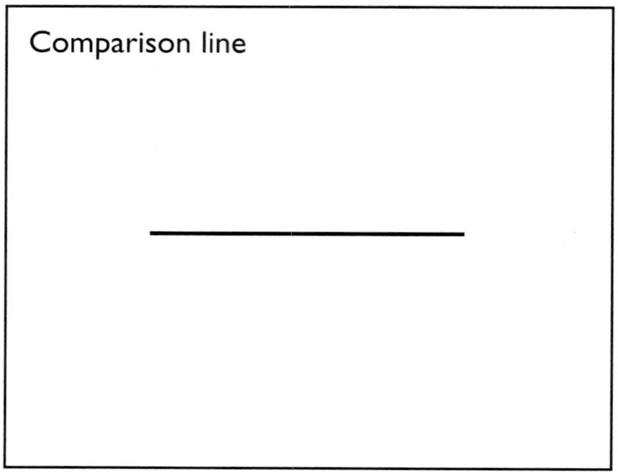

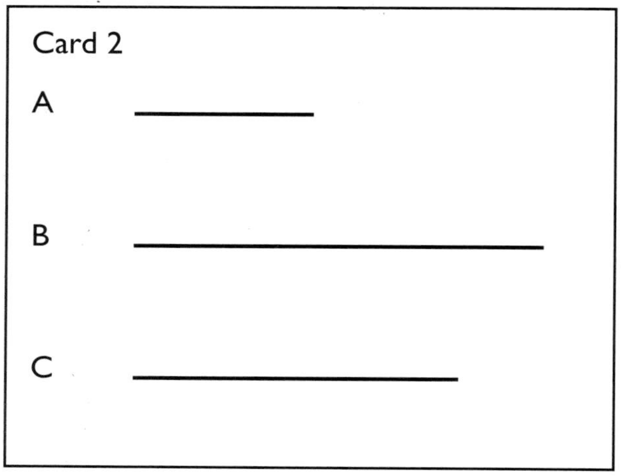

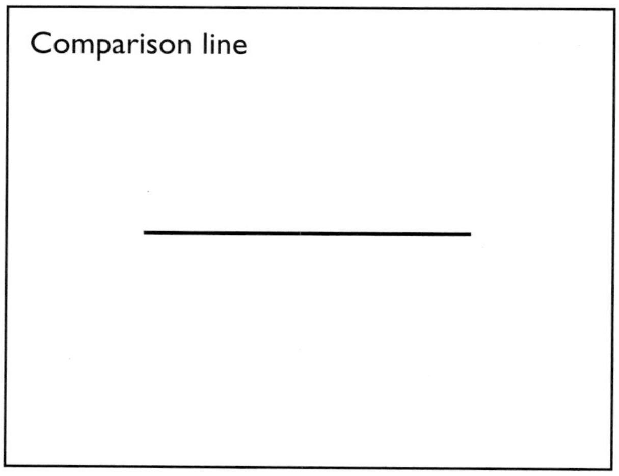

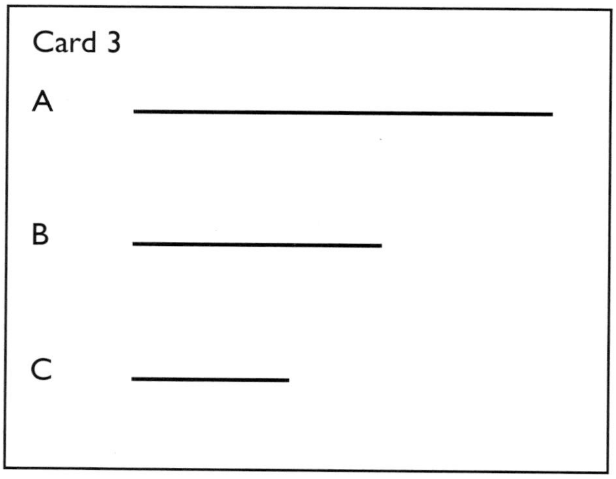

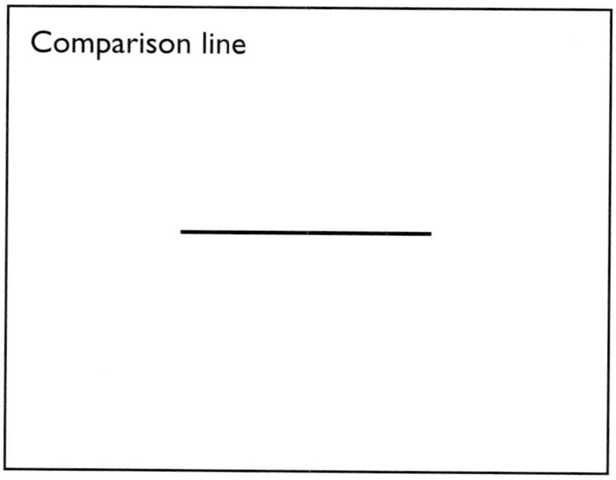

▶ Lesson notes p.61

Asch: Stimulus lines 2

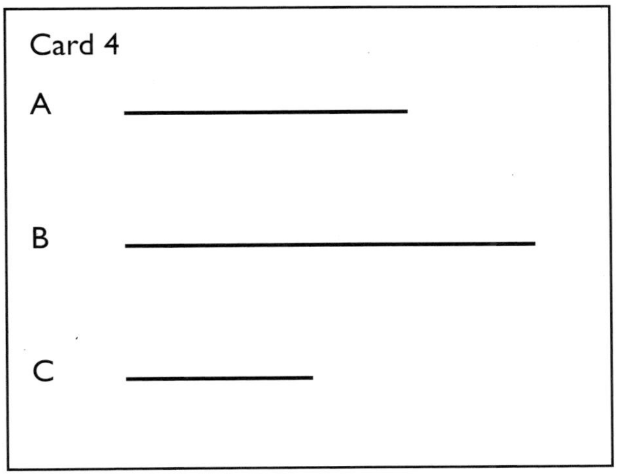

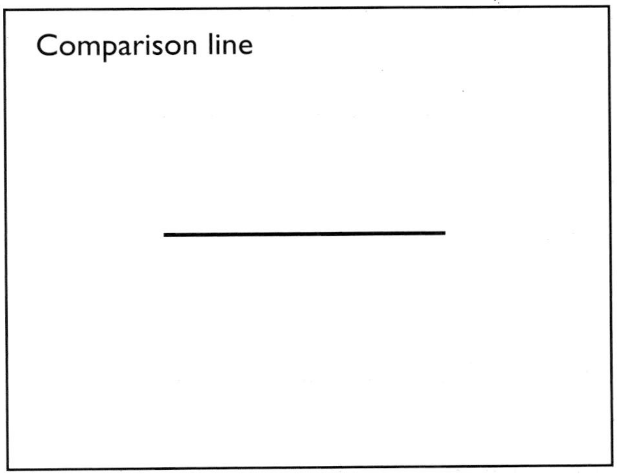

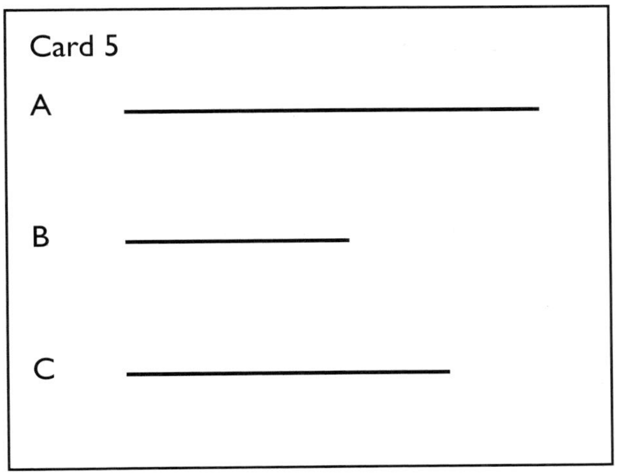

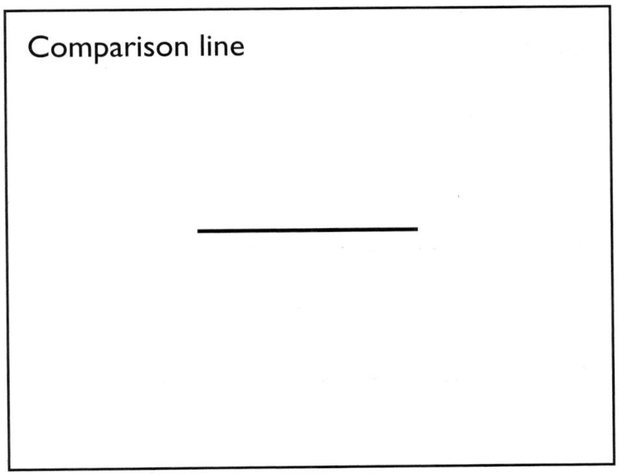

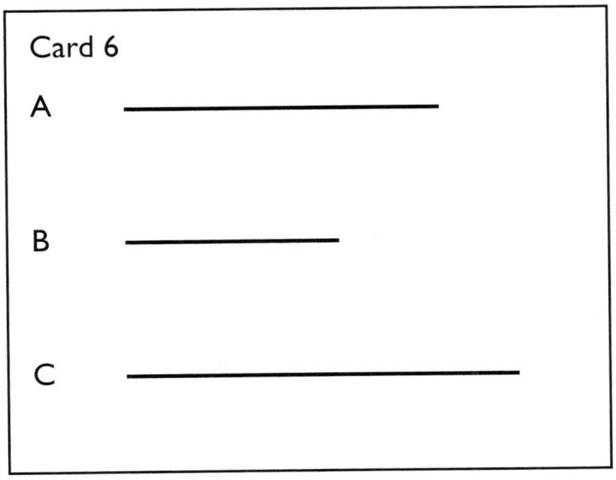

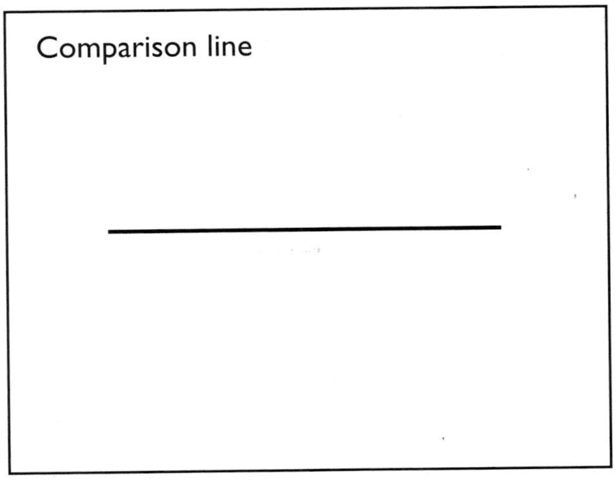

▶ Lesson notes p.61

Asch: Stimulus lines 3

Card 7

A

B

C

Comparison line

Card 8

A

B

C

Comparison line

Card 9

A

B

C

Comparison line

▶ Lesson notes p.61

Asch: Stimulus lines 4

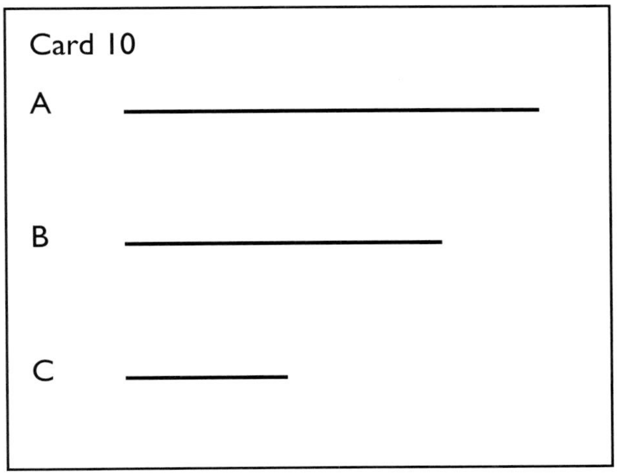

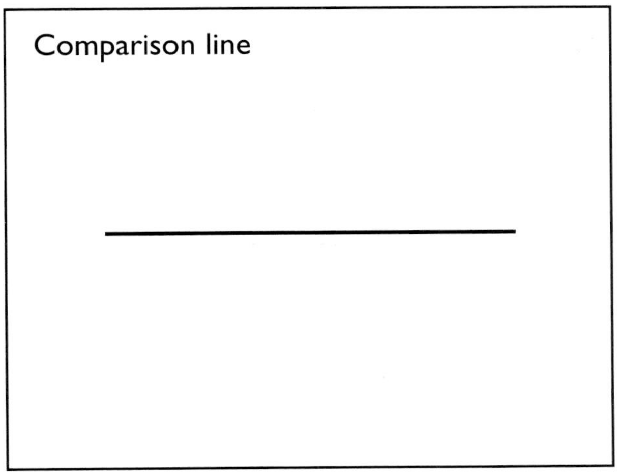

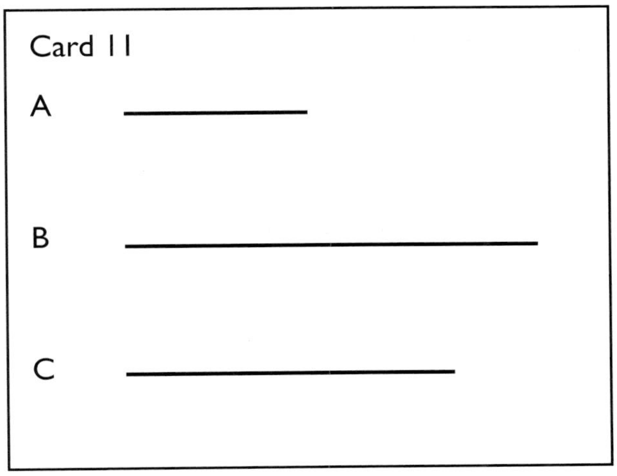

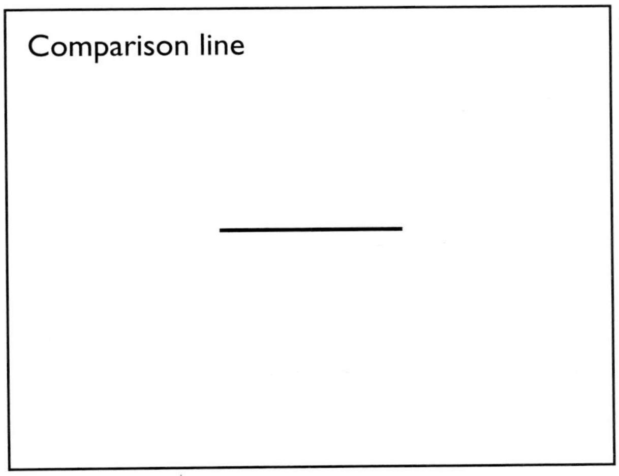

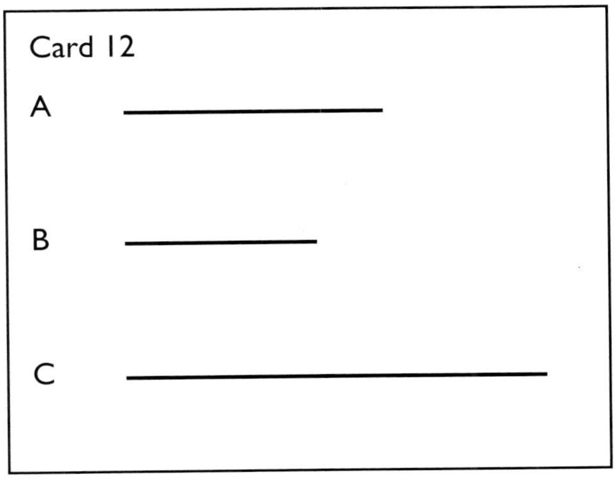

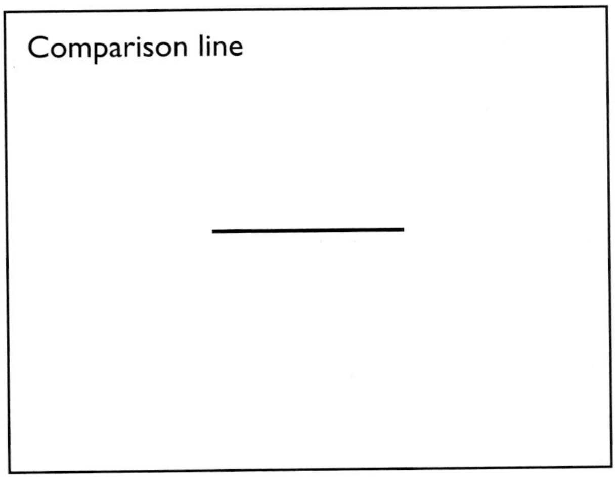

▶ Lesson notes p.61

Asch: Stimulus lines 5

Card 13

A

B

C

Comparison line

Card 14

A

B

C

Comparison line

Card 15

A

B

C

Comparison line

▶ Lesson notes p.61

Asch: Stimulus lines 6

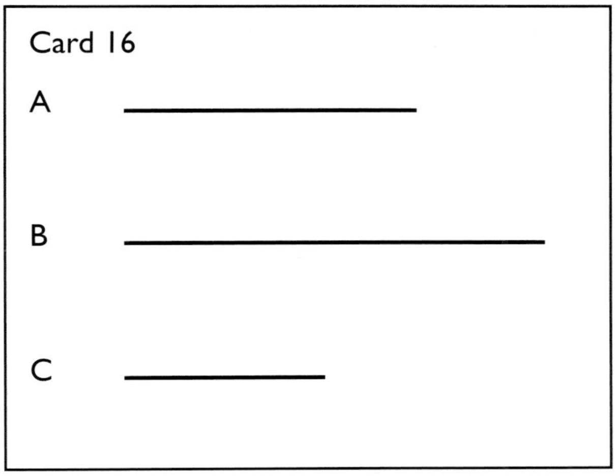

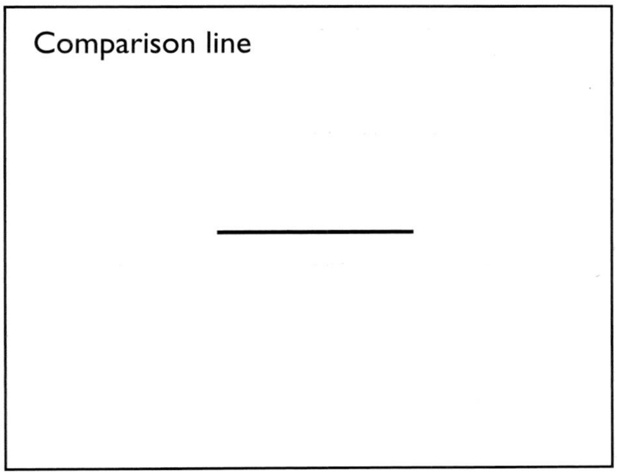

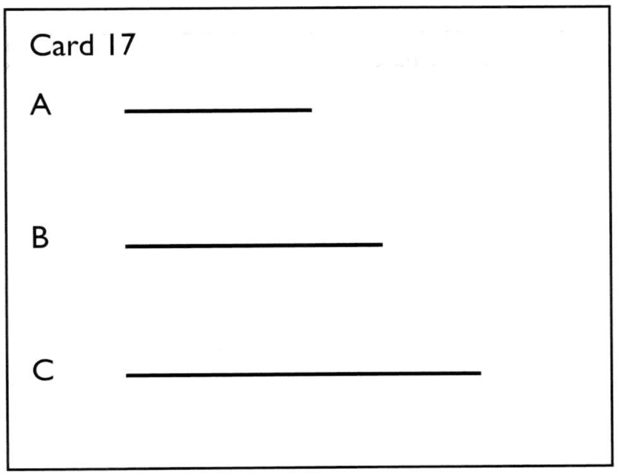

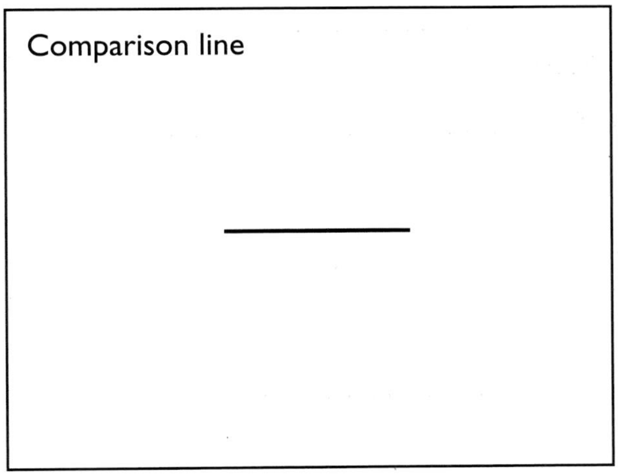

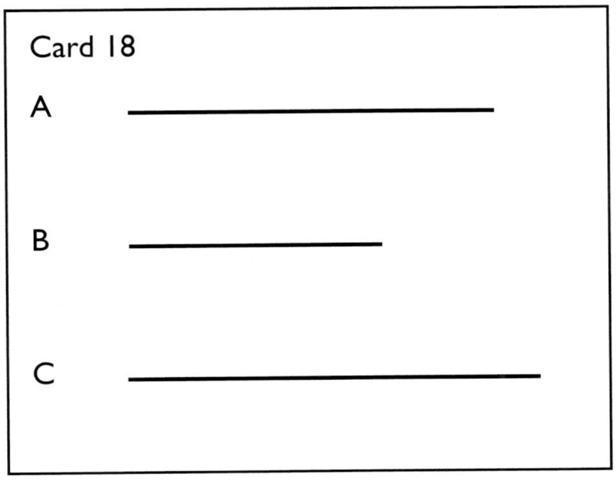

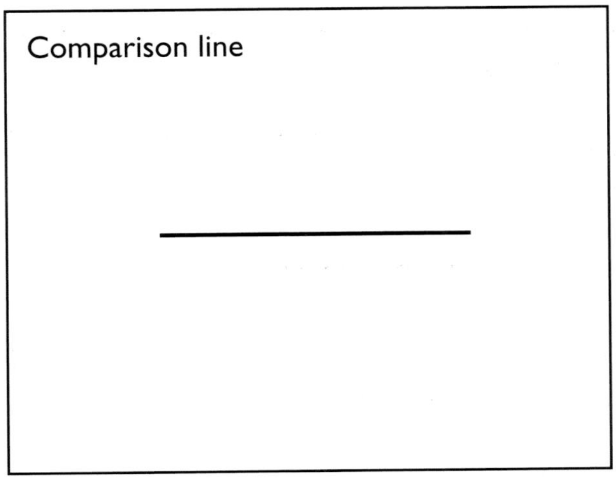

▶ Lesson notes p.61

Psychology storytime

Story 1

'Why do you want to be a vegetarian?', Katie's Mum asked angrily, as she slammed a plateful of bangers and mash down on the table in front of Katie.

'All of my new friends are vegetarian', Katie replied sulkily, cautiously prodding a sausage with her fork.

Katie's Mum sighed loudly and rolled her eyes.

'So you don't have any strong feelings yourself about not eating meat?', she asked.

'Not really', Katie replied sheepishly.

'Well, there's nothing else coming if you don't eat that', her Mum said, nodding towards the full plate.

As her Mum turned her back, Katie picked up her knife, cut off a piece of sausage and surreptitiously looked about her before putting it into her mouth.

Story 2

'Why do you want to be a vegetarian?', Katie's Mum asked angrily, as she slammed a plateful of bangers and mash down on the table in front of Katie.

'All of my new friends are vegetarian', Katie replied sulkily, cautiously prodding a sausage with her fork.

'But what about you? Why do *you* want to be a vegetarian?', her Mum countered.

'I think they're right – eating animals is wrong', Katie said, pushing the plate away from her.

'Well, there's nothing else coming if you don't eat that', her Mum said, nodding towards the full plate.

'That's ok,' Katie replied cheerfully, 'I'll make myself a salad'.

Questions

1. *Identify the type of conformity being shown by Katie in each story.*

2. *Explain with key words (e.g., public/private, behaviour/viewpoint) how and/or why each story illustrates that type of conformity.*

▶ Lesson notes p.61

Elaboration ladders–Asch 1

One of the problems with Asch's conformity research is that it lacks ecological validity.

A further weakness of Asch's original research is that the results may have been unique to one culture and one era – a 'child of its time'.

It could be argued that Asch's experimental paradigm is ethically questionable.

Why does that matter?

How would that affect the results/validity?

Can I explain my point with an example?

Have I got evidence?

How could it be improved?

Have I got a counter argument?

How does this affect the main argument?

Use the prompts above to help you **elaborate** the evaluative arguments on the bottom rung of the ladders.

The more you elaborate your points (without repeating yourself), the more marks you get – hence the smiley face at the top!

▶ Lesson notes p.62

Elaboration ladders–Asch 2

Ladder 1

One of the problems with Asch's conformity research is that it lacks ecological validity.

Hint: Explain how/why Asch's task is insignificant compared to other situations we might conform to.

Hint: Explain how this may have affected the results, or why we can't generalise them outside of the study.

Hint: Here you could include research evidence to support your arguments. Or perhaps a counterpoint you may have.

Ladder 2

A further weakness of Asch's original research is that the results may have been unique to one culture and one era – a 'child of its time'.

Hint: Explain what McCarthyism is, and how it is relevant to the time and culture in which the study took place.

Hint: Clearly explain how and why this might have affected the results of Asch's study.

Hint: Explain why it matters, e.g. generalisability, reliability or validity.

Ladder 3

It could be argued that Asch's experimental paradigm is ethically questionable.

Hint: Explain what ethical issues may arise and WHY, e.g. choose one of protection from harm (embarrassment), deception (lack of informed consent).

Hint: Explain why it matters that these ethical issues arise, e.g. trust in psychologists, fairness, etc.

Hint: Any counter arguments? E.g. did the researchers try to overcome/deal with these issues in any way? Do you feel these strategies were enough?

Why does that matter?

How would that affect the results/validity?

Can I explain my point with an example?

Have I got evidence?

How could it be improved?

Have I got a counter argument?

How does this affect the main argument?

Use the prompts above to help you **elaborate** the evaluative arguments on the bottom rung of the ladders.

The more you elaborate your points (without repeating yourself), the more marks you get – hence the smiley face at the top!

▶ Lesson notes p.62

Deconstructing Moscovici et al. (1969) 1

Aim(s)	
Hypothesis or hypotheses	
Research method **Investigation design**	
Independent variables **How were they operationalised?** (turning a psychological concept into a physical reality – see notes)	
Dependent variable **How was it operationalised?** (turning a psychological concept into a physical reality, one which can be measured – see notes)	
Participant population	
Ethical issues	
Results (be detailed but brief!)	

▶ Lesson notes p.63

Deconstructing Moscovici et al. (1969) 2

Conclusions (be detailed but brief!)	
Internal validity	
External validity	

☐ **Hypothesis** – States what the researcher believes/predicts to be true. A hypothesis is a written statement which can be tested. It is written as a statement as oppossed to a question. For example:

'People remember more when they study in short bursts than when studying for longer sessions'

However, there are problems with this hypothesis...

☐ **Operationalisation** – A good hypothesis needs to be written in a testable way, i.e. it is written in the specific way it will be tested. Take the example above, what do we mean by '*remember more*' and '*short bursts*' and '*longer sessions*'? In order to test the hypothesis we need to specify behaviours which can be measured.

'Short bursts' could be operationalised as 3 x 10-minute study sessions.

'Longer sessions' could be operationalised as 1 x 30-minute study session.

'Remember more' could be operationalised as a memory recall test (of a chapter in a book).

So, the *operationalised* hypothesis now reads:

'People will get more questions right on a memory recall test when they study in short bursts (3 x 10-minute sessions) than in longer sessions (1 x 30-minute session).

☐ **Research method** – e.g. experimental, questionnaire survey, naturalistic observation, correlational, case study.

☐ **Investigation design** – e.g. independent groups, repeated measures, matched pairs.

▶ Lesson notes p.63

Spot the deliberate mistakes! Why people conform

Spot the 10 deliberate mistakes in this text outlining the explanations of why people conform.

Normative social influence

It is possible to behave like the majority without really accepting its point of view. Psychologists have called this type of conformity internalisation. A majority may be able to control other group members by making it difficult for them to deviate from the majority point of view, and thus exerting pressure on them to obey. Going against the majority is easy, as demonstrated by Asch's study where participants clearly felt uncomfortable deviating from the majority position. Humans are a social species and have a fundamental need for social companionship and a fear of rejection. It is this that forms the basis for normative social influence.

Informational social influence

In some cases individuals go along with others because they genuinely believe them to be right. As a result, we don't just to comply in behaviour alone, but we also *change* our point of view in line with the position of those influencing. Because this involves changing both our public *and* private attitudes and behaviours, this is an example of *compliance*. Informational social influence is most likely when:

- The situation is unambiguous – i.e. the right course of action is not clear.
- The situation is a crisis – i.e. rapid action is required.
- We believe ourselves to be experts – i.e. we believe that we are more likely to know what to do.

Social impact theory

Latane (1981) developed a theory to explain why people conform in some situations but not in others. There are several principles included in this explanation:

- *Number* – the more people present, the more influence they will have on an individual. However, the rate of increase in impact grows less as each new individual is added. For example, Asch found that conformity rates rose dramatically up to three or four, but not much beyond that size.
- *Strength* – the more important the people are to the individual, the more influence they will have. For example in Perrin and Spencer's research, when the majority were probation officers and the individual someone on probation, conformity rates were relatively low.
- *Immediacy* – each individual can influence others; but the more people are present, the less influence any one individual will have. Thus, we are more likely to listen attentively to a speaker if we are in a large group than if we are in a small group.

► Lesson notes p.64

Conformity examples

Read these examples of conformity, and decide what type of conformity they illustrate, and briefly outline how that conformity could be explained.

Example	Type (compliance/ internalisation)	Explanation (e.g., informational social influence, normative social influence, social impact theory)
Despite knowing the dangers, Lisa smokes because all of her friends do.		
When Brian buys his football tickets before the game, he always joins the queue along with everyone else.		
Many students at Scruffy High School walk round with their top button undone and their ties loosened.		
Sheema was sat in a doctor's surgery that was full of people and noticed smoke billowing in from the next room. No one else around her raised the alarm, so neither did Sheema. She assumed it couldn't have been an emergency.		
Everyone in the sixth form used to think that having to wear a smart uniform was a bad idea. However, the head boy Liam, and head girl Steph, managed to convince most people that it would help them to be more productive in their lessons.		
Brett is not really interested in politics but most of the people at his university are left-wing. Brett often tells people he supports left-wing views.		
Many of Asch's (1956) participants conformed to the obviously wrong majority decision.		
Many of Moscovici's (1969) participants conformed to a minority decision.		

▶ Lesson notes p.64

Milgram's variations

In Milgram's original study, there were two confederates: an experimenter (the authority figure), and a 47-year-old accountant, who played the part of the 'learner'. The 'real' participant always took on the role of 'teacher' and was told that he must administer increasingly strong electric shocks to the 'learner' each time he got a question wrong on the learning task. The learner sat in an adjacent room so that the participant would hear his increasing signs of discomfort and pain. Milgram found that 65% of participants delivered the maximum 450 volts!

TASKS

1. Cut out the studies below. Each describes a variation of Milgram's study.

2. Estimate the percentage of participants you think gave the maximum 450 volts in that variation of the study.

3. Stick onto 'Obedience barometer' on Handout 153.

4. Briefly explain why you think obedience levels have decreased/increased from the original 65%.

5. Using textbooks or the Internet, find out the actual results and compare with your own.

In the *touch-proximity* study, the teacher was required to force the learner's hand onto a shock plate.

In the *experimenter-absent* study, after giving his instructions, the experimenter left the room and gave subsequent orders over the telephone.

In the *different location* study, the experiment was conducted away from the original setting at Yale University, and instead was carried out in a run-down office block in the town centre.

In the *proximity* study, both teacher and learner were seated in the same room. As a result, the teacher was able to see the reactions of the learner.

In the *teacher's discretion* study, the level of shock delivered to the learner was left to the participants' discretion.

In the *two peers rebel* study, three participants (two confederates and one real participant) shared the task of teaching the learner. Teacher 1 read the lists of words, teacher 2 told the learner whether his answer was correct, and teacher 3 (the real participant) administered the shocks. At a certain point in the experiment, the two bogus teachers refused to carry on.

▶ Lesson notes p.67

Obedience barometer

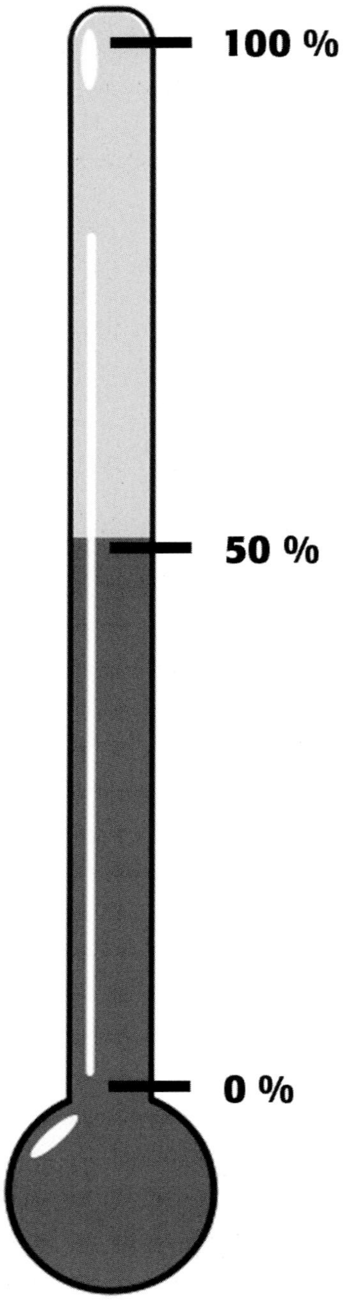

Percentage (%) of Milgram's participants administering maximum shock (450 volts)

▶ Lesson notes p.67

Evaluation skills - Milgram 1

This information will be useful for completing the evaluation exercise on Handout 155. Please bear in mind that the order of the 'points' does NOT correspond to the order of the 'explanations' or the 'evidence'. You need to match them up!

POINTS:

- Lacks internal validity.
- Unethical as it failed to protect participants from psychological harm.
- Population validity is low.
- Not generalisable outside of the research setting (ecological validity).

EXPLANATIONS:

- The study was lab-based, quite contrived, and participants knew they were taking part in a psychology experiment. It is unclear whether obedience rates can be generalised to other more naturally occurring and 'real-life' situations.
- Used only American and male participants, so the extent to which obedience occurs may not be representative of other cultures or the female gender.
- Participants may not have been fooled by the setup because they have come to learn that the true aim of psychology experiments is often disguised. So they didn't really think they were harming the 'learner'.
- Placed the participants under great emotional strain and distress by deceiving them into thinking they might be administering lethal shocks to a fellow participant.

EVIDENCE:

- Orne and Holland (1968) argued that the only reason participants appeared distressed in Milgram's study was not because they believed they were harming the learner, but they were strained by playing along with the experimental setup.
- Rank and Jacobson (1977) conducted a study in a hospital. Nurses were telephoned by a doctor (confederate) who asked that they give a dosage of a drug called Valium to a patient. This order contravened hospital regulations in that nurses were not supposed to take orders from unknown doctors over the phone, and the dosage stated was higher than that advised by the bottle – 89% of the nurses refused to carry out the order.
- Darley (1992) suggests that the experience of administering shocks (even if not real) may activate a previously dormant aspect of an individual's personality such that they feel more able and more motivated to repeat those actions. Their personalities may alter as a consequence of the actions they are asked to perform.
- Using the Milgram experimental procedure, Kilham and Mann (1974) found that 40% of Australian male students would administer the maximum shock voltage, whereas only 16% of Australian female students did so.

▶ Lesson notes p.67

Evaluation skills - Milgram 2

PEE on your essays!

There are many different techniques you can use to evaluate. You may have tried the burger technique (Handout 5, 6 or 142) or the ladder technique (Handout 4, 146 or 147) already. The trick is to practise all of them so that you can develop your evaluative writing in different ways.

PEE-ing on your essays is another technique, and one you may have come across in other subjects at your school.

PEE stands for Point, Explanation, and Evidence. Practise this technique to evaluate Milgram's study.

Step 1 Select one of the 'Points' from Handout 154 (or alternatively write one of your own).

Step 2 Introduce your 'Point' with an appropriate signpost so that the reader/examiner knows what argument you are about to make, for example:
One weakness of Milgram's study is that it lacks internal validity.
It could be argued that...
One problem...
An issue which undermines...

Step 3 'Explain' your 'point'. Explain what is meant by that point, explain how it is relevant and why it is important. You may wish to use ideas from Handout 154. Try to use phrases like:
This means...
This is because...
This is an issue because...
The problem here is that...

Step 4 Use evidence (e.g. Handout 154) to support your evaluative arguments. BUT, don't forget to explain how/why they support the point and explanation – do not simply describe the evidence. Use phrases like:
This is shown by...
This point is exemplified by...
This point is supported by...
Evidence for this comes from...

Extension Can you make any counter arguments to your evaluations?

Can you find any evidence/arguments which do NOT support your point?
Can you find any evidence which contradicts your evidence?
Is there any reason to doubt your evaluation? Has the case been overstated?
Did the researcher have any successful ways to deal with the problems?

▶ Lesson notes p.67

Ecological validity – spot the difference!

Asch	Beyond research setting
Insignificant task – costs nothing to conform	In other circumstances, consequences for conformity may be higher
Moscovici	**Beyond research setting**
There are no passionate views on the colour of different slides	In other circumstances, people may not conform to a viewpoint if they are more passionate about their original opinion
Milgram	**Beyond research setting**
Participants did not believe they were hurting the 'learner' as it was an experiment	In other circumstances, people may not obey when they truly believe they are hurting another person

▶ Lesson notes p.68

Why do we obey?

Milgram's research seems to demonstrate the power of the situation in shaping behaviour, with moral constraints, such as conscience and compassion, being sidelined when the individual is confronted by a powerful authority figure. So, why do people obey? Milgram (1974) offered a series of explanations.

1. Gradual commitment

- Once people obey a trivial, seemingly harmless request, they find it more difficult to refuse to carry out more serious and escalating requests.
- This is known as gradual commitment and can be explained by our human desire to be consistent in our behaviour.
- Evidence to support this explanation of obedience comes from Milgram's research. As participants had already given lower-level shocks, it then became hard to resist the experimenter's requirement to increase the shocks as the experiment continued.
- No shock was ever given in the experiment that was more than 15 volts from the previous level.

2. Agentic shift

- Milgram described the difference between an *autonomous state* and an *agentic state*.
- The *agentic state* is 'the condition a person is in when he sees himself as an agent for carrying out another person's wishes' (Milgram, 1974).
- The *autonomous state* is when a person 'sees himself acting on his own'.
- Milgram argued that when: 1) we are faced with a person who we perceive to be a legitimate authority, and 2) we believe they will take responsibility for our actions – we then enter the *agentic state*.

3. The role of buffers

- A 'buffer' is any aspect of a situation that protects people from having to confront the consequences of their actions.
- Buffers therefore act as mechanisms that protect individuals from the consequences of their actions, making it easier to obey immoral commands.
- For example, in Milgram's research, the wall between the 'teacher' and 'learner' acted as a buffer, protected the 'teacher' from fully witnessing the results of the shocks. When the wall was removed, obedience rates dropped dramatically.

▶ Lesson notes p.69

Resist the influence!

'Emancipate yourself from mental slavery. None but ourselves can free our minds.' Bob Marley

'Conformity is that jailer of freedom and the enemy of growth.' John F. Kennedy

'When someone demands blind obedience, you'd be a fool not to peek.' Jim Fiebig

'Every generation laughs at the old fashions, but follows religiously the new.' Henry David Thoreau Walden 1854

'It is easy to ignore responsibility when one is only an intermediate link in a chain of action.' Milgram

Imagine a world where the whole world conforms to majority influence and obedience. Not only would it be a dull place to live, it would also be a dangerous place to live – as history has already taught us.

Use your notes, your textbooks and the Internet to review studies on conformity and obedience to discover what factors might help us to increase our independent behaviour.

Study	Factor increasing independent behaviour	Brief description/findings
★ Milgram (proximity study)	★ Removal of buffers	★ The 'teacher' and 'learner' were placed in the same room (as opposed to adjacent rooms) so the participant was able to see the consequences of his actions
★	★	★
★	★	★
★	★	★
★	★	★
★	★	★

▶ Lesson notes p.70

Questionnaire

	Agree very much	Agree somewhat	Agree slightly	Disagree slightly	Disagree somewhat	Disagree very much
1 Sometimes I don't feel that I have enough control over the direction my life is taking.						
2 By taking an active part in political and social affairs people can control world events.						
3 It is impossible for me to believe that chance or luck plays an important role in my life.						
4 Many times I feel that I have little influence over the things that happen to me.						
5 Getting people to do the right things depends upon ability; luck has little or nothing to do with it.						
6 Unfortunately, an individual's worth often passes unrecognised no matter how hard he tries.						
7 Capable people who fail to become leaders have not taken advantage of their opportunities.						
8 This world is run by a few people in power, and there is not much the little guy can do.						
9 What happens to me is my own doing.						
10 Most people don't realise the extent to which their lives are controlled by accidental happenings.						
11 People's misfortunes result from the mistakes they make.						
12 There is really no such thing as 'luck'.						
13 The average citizen can have an influence on government decisions.						
14 In the long run people get the respect they deserve in the world.						
15 In my case getting what I want has little or nothing to do with luck.						
16 With enough effort we can wipe out political corruption.						
17 Who gets to be the boss often depends on who was lucky enough to be in the right place first.						
18 Many of the unhappy things in people's lives are partly due to bad luck.						
19 It is difficult for people to have much control over things politicians do in the office.						
20 People are lonely because they don't try to be friendly.						

From: McIlveen, R., Higgins, L. and Wadeley, A. (1992) *BPS Manual of Psychology Practicals*. BPS Books, page 191.

▶ Lesson notes p.70

Locus of control – discussion points

A recent meta-analysis by Twenge et al. *(2004) found that young Americans increasingly believe that their lives are controlled by outside forces rather than their own behaviour. Locus of control scores have become substantially more external in student and child samples between 1960 and 2002.*

Can you suggest any ideas as to why this might be the case? What has changed that might influence American's locus of control?

A recent meta-analysis by Twenge et al. *(2004) found that young Americans increasingly believe that their lives are controlled by outside forces rather than their own behaviour. Locus of control scores have become substantially more external in student and child samples between 1960 and 2002.*

Why have some psychologists argued that a significant rise in divorce rates during this time has contributed to this effect? Why would this influence people to be more external in their locus of control?

A recent meta-analysis by Twenge et al. *(2004) found that young Americans increasingly believe that their lives are controlled by outside forces rather than their own behaviour. Locus of control scores have become substantially more external in student and child samples between 1960 and 2002.*

Why have some psychologists argued that a significant rise in the incidence of violent crime during this time has contributed to this effect? Why would this influence people to be more external in their locus of control?

Twenge et al. *(2004) have reported that externality (in locus of control) is correlated with poor school achievement.*

Why do you think people with a high external locus of control are more likely to do badly at school? Make sure your ideas are fully elaborated and explained when feeding back to class.

Twenge et al. *(2004) have reported that externality (in locus of control) is correlated with depression.*

Why do you think people with a high external locus of control are more likely to have depression? Make sure your ideas are fully elaborated and explained when feeding back to class.

▶ Lesson notes p.71

Essay planning - implications for social change 1

What is social change?

Social change occurs when a society as a whole adopts a new belief or way of behaving which then becomes widely accepted as the 'norm'.

Sometimes, social influence can be a force for positive social change (e.g., Mahatma Ghandi's dissent against the British salt tax in India acted as a catalyst for widespread social reform). At other times social influence may be a force for negative social change (e.g., the Nazi extermination of Jews during World War II was made easier by the tendency for those involved to obey their superiors. Why not type 'social change' into Google and find your own examples?

Discuss the implications for social change of research into social influence (12 marks).

[This is perhaps one of the more difficult essay questions you could face because it is so broad, and you cannot use the simple technique of outlining a study/theory, and then evaluating it. This question requires a little more thought and analysis. This handout and Handout 162 are designed to help you plan this essay.]

Step 1

Use your notes and textbooks to fill in Handout 162. These are designed to help you think about how the social influence research you have already covered might be relevant to social change. The first table is done for you as an example.

Step 2

Use the information in these tables to write a six-short-paragraph essay in the following structure:

1. *Explain one implication of social influence research for social change.*
2. *Provide supporting evidence (+ possible counter arguments).*
3. *Explain one implication of social influence research for social change.*
4. *Provide supporting evidence (+ possible counter arguments).*
5. *Explain one implication of social influence research for social change.*
6. *Provide supporting evidence (+possible counter arguments).*

BUT REMEMBER!

- Ensure that you explain how the evidence supports your arguments.
- Long descriptions of studies are not necessary or creditworthy – you must use studies as a way to discuss the implications of the research for social change.

▶ Lesson notes p.71

Essay planning - implications for social change 2

Implication of research for social change:
Small minorities can influence social change if they are consistent, persuasive, and confident in their message.

Explanation and/or example:
Moscovici argued that minorities are more successful in achieving social change if they adopt these behavioural styles. This is because to cause social change, minorities must convince majority members to change the way they think (internalisation), and when they have attracted enough new supporters, they are then transformed into the new majority.

Evidence:
Moscovici et al. (1969) showed groups of six participants (2 confederates, 4 real participants) 36 blue-coloured slides. Participants were asked to judge whether those slides were blue or green. When the confederates consistently gave the wrong answer (green), they were more able to influence the decisions of the majority in the group.

Implication of research for social change:

Explanation and/or example:

Evidence:

Implication of research for social change:

Explanation and/or example:

Evidence:

▶ Lesson notes p.71

Ethics and social influence research

Ethical issues

- *Informed consent* – Participants should have given their formal agreement to participate based on information regarding the nature and purpose of the study.
- *Deception* – Where possible, participants should not be deceived or misled.
- *Protection from harm* – Investigators have a responsibility to protect participants from physical and mental harm. Normally, this risk of harm should be no greater than encountered in everyday life.
- *The right to withdraw* – Participants should be able to leave the experiment or ask for their data not to be used during and after the study.

Dealing with ethical issues

- *Informed consent* – Give participants as many details as possible regarding the nature and purpose of the study, and ask participants to formally agree.
- *Presumptive consent* – Ask a group of other people whether they feel the planned study is acceptable. We then *presume* that the participants themselves would have felt the same.
- *Cost-benefit analysis* – If deception is involved, it should be passed by an ethical committee who have weighed up the cost (to participants) and benefits (of the study).
- *Debrief* – If informed consent has not been possible, or deception has been used, investigators can ensure participants are fully debriefed about the study.
- *Withdrawal* – Participants should be informed at the start of the study that they have the right to withdraw. That way, if participants do feel they could become physically or mentally harmed as a result of the study, they are able to leave the study before that happens.

Research study	Ethical issue(s)	Ways this was dealt with, or could be dealt with
Asch (1956)		
Moscovici *et al.* (1969)		
Milgram (1963)		
Hofling *et al.* (1966)		

▶ Lesson notes p.72

Discussing ethical issues

Students often have no problem identifying ethical issues in research, but struggle to **discuss** and **elaborate** on why (or why not) those ethical issues are problems. This worksheet is designed to help you practise that technique.

Choose one ethical issue in one study you have looked at in the social influence topic so far. You may already have identified some of these issues on **Handout 163**. Now, fill in the **discussion** frame below:

Identify and explain an ethical issue raised by one study of social influence (e.g. Asch)

The ethics of _______'s study have been questioned . . .

Offer a counter argument, e.g. explain how the issue was successfully dealt with, or, explain any reasons why you feel this ethical issue is not of great concern.

However . . .

Now present a counter to your counter argument, e.g. do the costs (to the participant) outweigh the benefits (of the study) or is there a bigger picture? For example, the effects of ethical issues for the reputation of psychology and the ability to attract volunteers.

On the other hand . . .

▶ Lesson notes p.72

Social psychology dominoes 1

A person's perception of personal control over their own behaviour. Measured along a dimension line from 'high internal' to 'high external'.	**Conformity**
A form of social influence. It is the tendency for people to adopt the behaviour, attitudes and values of other members of a reference group.	**Milgram**
Conducted a series of experiments which highlighted the power of obedience over participants - even if that resulted in the pain of another.	**Independent behaviour**
That which is based on an individual's own thinking, and not distorted by situational pressures around them (e.g., conformity).	**High external locus of control**
A person believes their behaviour is caused primarily by fate, luck or by other circumstances.	**Compliance**

▶ Lesson notes p.72

Social psychology dominoes 2

When an individual conforms publicly, but not privately.	**Informational social influence**
Is the result of wanting to be right, so we look to others to see how to behave and what to believe.	**Buffers**
Anything which can protect an individual from having to see the consequences of their actions. For example, in Milgram's experiment, the 'teacher' was buffered from the consequences of their actions, as they were not in the same room as the 'learner' and therefore could not witness their reactions.	**Internalisation**
Occurs when an individual accepts influence of others both publicly and privately. Essentially, their minds have been changed.	**Social change**
When a society as a whole adopts a new belief or way of behaving, which then becomes widely accepted as the 'norm'. This could be either positive or negative.	**Agentic state**

▶ Lesson notes p.72

Social psychology dominoes 3

When an individual acts for another person rather than acting on their own initiative - because responsibility has been taken away from them by an authority figure.	**Obedience**
A type of social influence whereby somebody acts in response to a direct order from a figure of perceived authority. They may not have acted this way without the order.	**High internal locus of control**
A person believes their behaviour is caused primarily by their own personal decisions and efforts.	**Asch**
Conducted a series of experiments which highlighted the power of normative social influence over participants.	**Normative social influence**
Is the result of wanting to be liked and part of a group.	**Presence of dissenters/allies**

▶ Lesson notes p.72

Social psychology dominoes 4

A strategy one could use to resist pressure to obedience/conformity.	**Gradual commitment**
Once an individual has committed themselves to a particular course of action, it then becomes more difficult to subsequently change their minds (foot in the door technique).	**Locus of control**

▶ Lesson notes p.72

Recognising abnormal behaviour

Recognising abnormal behaviour is essentially a subjective judgement that each of us makes. It is influenced by many implicit values and factors.

This exercise is to help you evaluate how you and your friends recognise and identify 'abnormality' in others. Please read the short vignettes below, which describe different individuals. After reading each one, use the two scales at the end to rate to what extent you think the individual has a psychiatric/psychological disorder and also whether, in your opinion, they should seek treatment. Having rated each vignette, compare your ratings with your friends and discuss any agreements or disagreements in your judgements.

1. Mr Smith has always lived in an isolated cottage. He has six dogs which he looks after. He never goes out of the cottage unless absolutely necessary, and has no friends or visitors.
2. Mr Jones is intensely afraid of heights. He has left a job because it was on the fifth floor, and refuses to visit his daughter who lives in Austria because of the mountains.
3. Mrs Jarvis, who was born in Jamaica, is a follower of the Pentecostal Church and believes that on occasions she is possessed by spirits which make her 'speak in tongues'.
4. Mrs Patel was arrested for shop-lifting two weeks ago. She blamed the tablets (Valium) that she has been taking for the last five years but has recently discontinued.
5. Mr Kahn is a successful executive who has just been told by his GP that he has high blood pressure.
6. Ben is a street musician who recently dropped out of art school. He likes to 'perform' using a variety of vegetables and dead fish!
7. Mrs Lee is a housewife who spends nearly every day at home keeping the house 'spick and span'. Her husband returned home from night work early one night last week and found her dusting at 2:00am.
8. Nadia is 22 years old and a dancer. Although she weighs only six stone, she is continually dieting.
9. Bob is a loner who keeps to himself because he believes that the social security snoopers are out to kill him. Although unemployed he refuses to seek any welfare benefits.
10. Sue is a six-year-old girl who is extremely shy and seldom speaks. She becomes very upset if her parents alter her playroom furniture.
11. Joe is nine years old and wets the bed five times a week. His parents' marriage broke up when he was five.
12. Mrs Black is married with two daughters. Last week she confided to her best friend that she had never experienced an orgasm.

This person suffers from a psychiatric/psychological problem

	Strongly agree	Moderately agree	Do not know	Moderately disagree	Strongly disagree
1					
2					
3					
4					
5					
6					
7					
8					
9					
10					
11					
12					

This person needs treatment for their problems

	Strongly agree	Moderately agree	Do not know	Moderately disagree	Strongly disagree
1					
2					
3					
4					
5					
6					
7					
8					
9					
10					
11					
12					

▶ Lesson notes p.73

Who's calling me abnormal?

Read the examples from the table and decide which of the three definitions (deviation from social norms, failure to function adequately, or deviation from ideal mental health) you think would be most likely to define these individuals as 'abnormal'. Then explain your decision.

	Definition of abnormality	Explanation
1. Man who sits next to you on the bus when plenty of other seats available		
2. Child abuser		
3. Child genius		
4. Born again Christian		
5. Person who talks to their pets		
6. Stressed executives who take time off work		
7. Person in a dead-end job		
8. Person who believes that someone is watching their every move		
9. Person who has to wash their hands every 5 minutes		

▶ Lesson notes p.74

How are the definitions limited by cultural relativism?

General definition of cultural relativism

VERY BRIEF OUTLINE OF 'DEVIATION FROM SOCIAL NORMS' DEFINITION

Explanation of why the social deviation definition is limited by cultural relativism	Explanation of why the social deviation definition is limited by cultural relativism

VERY BRIEF OUTLINE OF 'FAILURE TO FUNCTION ADEQUATELY' DEFINITION

Explanation of why 'failure to function' definition limited by cultural relativism	Explanation of why 'failure to function' definition limited by cultural relativism

VERY BRIEF OUTLINE OF 'DEVIATION FROM IDEAL MENTAL HEALTH' DEFINITION

Explanation of why mental health definition limited by cultural relativism	Explanation of why mental health definition limited by cultural relativism

▶ Lesson notes p.74

Definitions of Abnormality Dominoes I

The individual in question, or those around them? For example, many schizophrenics are unaware of their condition, so do not feel they are not functioning. It is those around them that become concerned. The definition of what 'adequate' means is too subjective - open to debate.	**Definition of abnormality**
Refers to an attempt in psychology to describe what behaviours need psychological treatment. These have changed considerably over history.	**Cultural relativism**
The view that behaviour cannot be judged properly unless it is viewed in the context of the culture in which it originates.	**Cultural relativism (limitation of deviation from social norms)**
Attempting to define abnormality in this way is bound by cultures and times - because norms are different. What is unacceptable in one culture may be acceptable in another.	**Abnormality**
A psychological condition or behaviour that departs from the norm or is harmful and distressing to the individual or those around them. There are different ways to define this.	**Failure to function adequately**

▶ Lesson notes p.74

Definitions of Abnormality Dominoes 2

From an individual's point of view, abnormality can be judged in terms of not being able to cope with day-to-day living.	**Who can achieve these criteria?**
Criticism of deviation from ideal mental health. For example, who actually is able to self-actualise (reach their full potential)? Who doesn't have negative thoughts about themselves from time to time? Does this make you mentally ill?	**Deviation from social norms definition**
Defines abnormality by behaviours which go against the often unspoken rules of a culture or sub-culture.	**Self-actualise**
One of Jahoda's five criteria, if you deviate from this, you are considered mentally ill. It means to fulfil and reach your full potential.	**Cultural relativism (limitation of failure to function adequately)**
What 'adequate functioning' means could be different in different places. For example, a long period of grief might be seen as 'failure' in one culture but normal in another.	**Self-attitudes**

▶ Lesson notes p.74

Definitions of Abnormality Dominoes 3

One of Jahoda's criteria of ideal mental health. Means to have high self-esteem and strong sense of identity.	**Cultural relativism (limitation of deviation from ideal mental health)**
Many of the 'ideal' criteria are culturally bound applying mostly to middle-class Western people in individualist cultures. In collectivist cultures, the emphasis is on the group (not individual goals) - so being able to self-actualise is not a priority.	**Autonomy**
One of Jahoda's five criteria, if you deviate from this, you are considered mentally ill. It means to be independent, able to cope on your own.	**Deviation from ideal mental health**
Defines abnormality in a similar way to physical health. An absence of any five 'ideal' criteria set out would mean that you are abnormal (and mentally ill).	**Susceptible to abuse (criticism of deviation from social norms)**
This definition could be used in order to oppress people in a culture - if you don't agree with the social norms you are mentally ill! This used to happen in Russia 50 years ago.	**Who judges (criticism of failure to function adequately)**

▶ Lesson notes p.74

Biological model - Basic principles

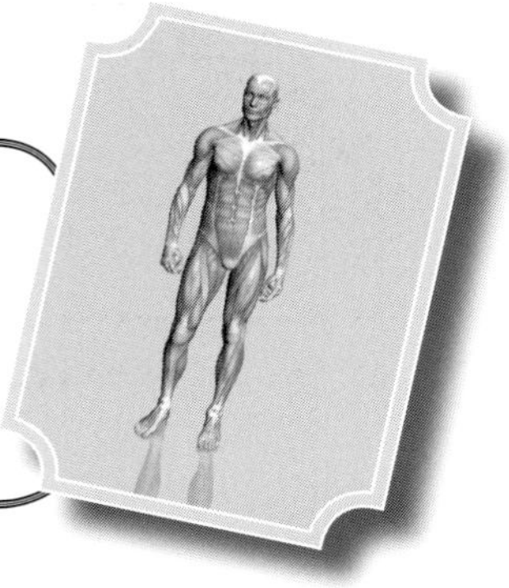

Abnormality is caused by physical factors

The biological (medical) model assumes that all mental disorders are related to some change in the body. Mental disorders are like **physical disorders**, i.e. they are illnesses. Such changes or illnesses may be caused by one of four possible factors: genes, biochemistry, neuroanatomy and viral infection.

Genetic inheritance

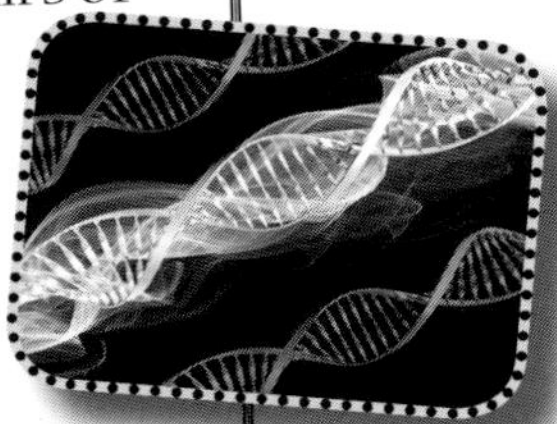

Abnormalities in brain anatomy or chemistry are sometimes the result of **genetic inheritance**, and so are passed from parent to child. One way of investigating this possibility is by studying twins. Pairs of identical twins can be compared to see whether, when one twin has a disorder, the other has it as well. This provides us with a ***concordance rate*** – the extent to which two individuals are similar to each other in terms of a particular trait. There are low concordance rates for some mental disorders (e.g. phobias) but relatively high concordance rates for others (e.g. schizophrenia). Many of the genes responsible for abnormal behaviours are the product of **evolutionary adaptations** in our ancestors, despite the fact these traits are no longer useful.

Certain genes lead to abnormal biochemistry and/or abnormal neuroanatomy

Genes tell the body how to function. They determine, for example, the levels of hormones and neurotransmitters in the brain (**biochemistry**). High levels of the neurotransmitter serotonin are associated with anxiety, whereas low levels have been found in depressed individuals. Genes also determine the structure of the brain **(neuroanatomy)**. Research has shown that schizophrenics have enlarged spaces (ventricles) in their brains, indicating the shrinkage of the brain tissue around these spaces.

Viral infections

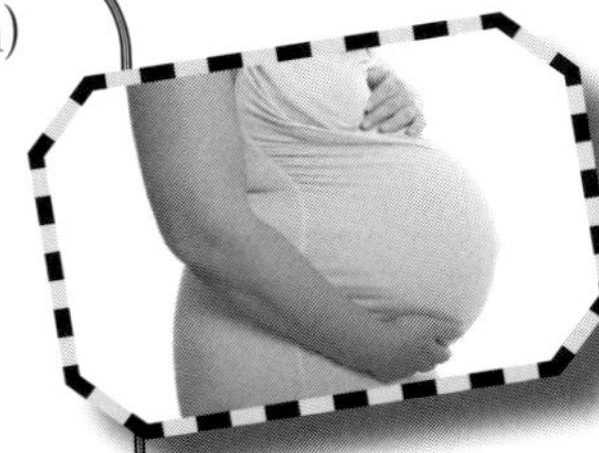

Research suggests that some disorders (such as schizophrenia) may be related to the ***exposure to certain viruses*** *in utero* (i.e., in the womb). For example, Torrey (2001) found that the mothers of many people with schizophrenia had contracted a particular strain of influenza during pregnancy. The virus may enter the unborn child's brain, where it remains dormant until puberty, where other hormones may activate it, producing the symptoms of schizophrenia.

▶ Lesson notes p.74

Biological model

Connect 4

Genetic inheritance:

Link...

Biochemistry and neuroanatomy:

Link...

Psychopathology, e.g. schizophrenia:

Link...

Concordance rates:

▶ Lesson notes p.74

Psychodynamic approach – the bigger picture I

ID -

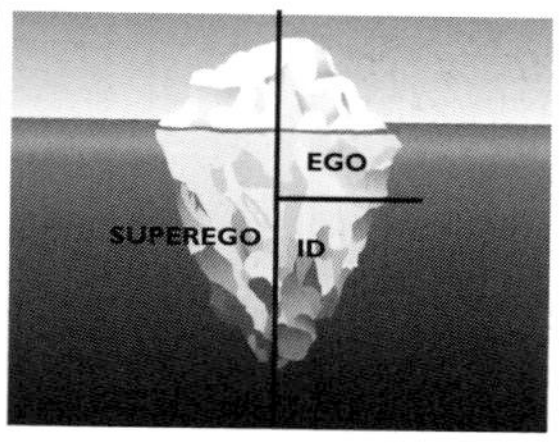

EGO -

SUPEREGO -

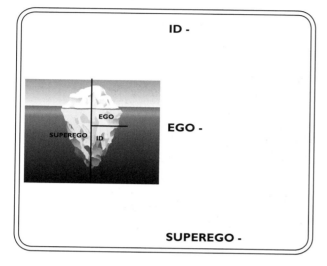

Childhood experiences

Ego defences

Repression

Regression

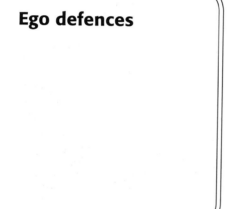

Mental disorder

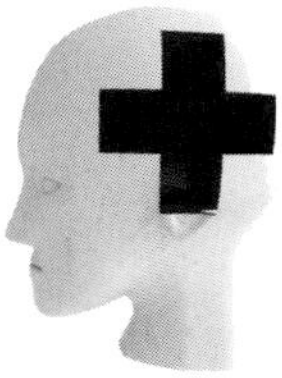

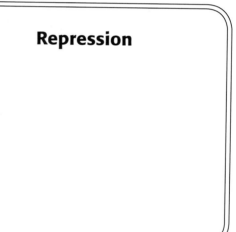

▶ Lesson notes p.75

Psychodynamic approach – the bigger picture 2

Conscious mind

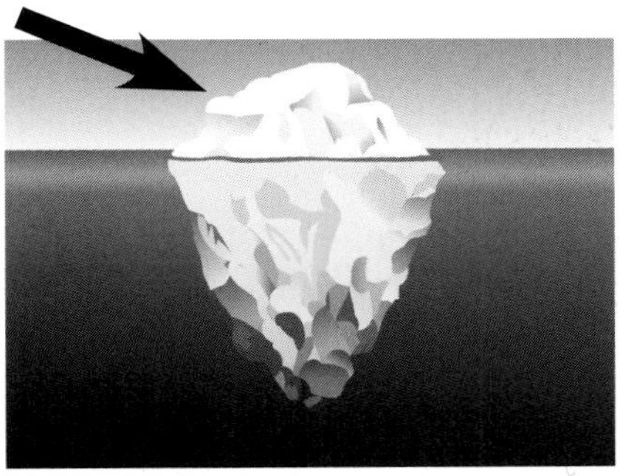

Unconscious awareness

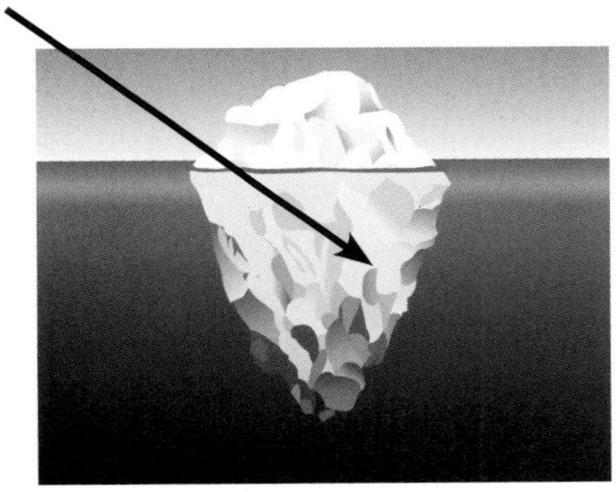

Conflict

▶ Lesson notes p.75

Explaining abnormality using the behavioural model

Remember that the behavioural model suggests that abnormal behaviours are learnt as a result of external events, and can be learnt via the principles of:

- Classical conditioning
- Operant conditioning
- Social learning theory

Use your textbook (e.g., p 188 of *The Complete Companion*) or your notes to explain how the abnormal behaviours below may have been learnt.

☛ Many years ago, as a child, Rick used to visit a dentist who thought anaesthetic was just for sissies. The dentist has a large grandfather clock in his waiting room. Years later, Rick still feels uneasy and a little anxious whenever he hears the tick of a grandfather clock.

☛ Alana is extremely scared of spiders. Whenever she sees a spider, she freezes and often screams. She has been like this for as long as she can remember. In fact, when she was younger she can remember her mother reacting in exactly the same way.

☛ For most of the week, Bryan is in a depressed mood. As a result, he has been taking a lot of time off work and he is worried he may lose his job. His wife, Jane, is very understanding and when he is feeling depressed, she tries to cheer him up by cooking him his favourite meals and trying to convince him what a wonderful man, husband and father he is. However, this doesn't seem to make much difference.

☛ Laura has an unhealthy relationship with food. She has an extremely low daily calorie intake (around 600 calories) and often refuses to eat her dinner. Her mother feels her behaviour may have been influenced by the magazines she reads. They often highlight the 'amazing' bodies of slim celebrities and include derogatory remarks about celebrities who have put on weight.

☛ Nicola also has an unhealthy relationship with food but doesn't read the magazines like her friend Laura (see above). Over two years ago she was slightly overweight and went on a diet. In the beginning she got a lot of lovely comments from her friends about how great she was looking because of her diet. She is now two stone underweight, and receives a lot of attention from her friends who think she has a problem and believe she has an eating disorder.

☛ Robert was an underweight eight-year old who had always been very reluctant to go to school. Every school night he ate little and even that was vomited up later. He twitched and became more and more anxious as the evening wore on. When he couldn't get to sleep he would cry, and his mother would come and sit with him and tell him comforting stories. In the morning Robert got up early and paced up and down, or sat in a corner, occasionally rushing to the toilet to be sick. When it was time to go to school he had to be pushed out of the house, though often his tears and complaints of feeling unwell led his mother to relent and allow him to stay home – it didn't matter greatly as the boy was unlikely to get much out of school in the state he was in.

Try to explain this phobia of school using both classical conditioning and operant conditioning.

▶ Lesson notes p.76

Faulty thinking strategies

The cognitive model assumes that thinking, expectations and attitudes (i.e. cognitions) direct behaviour. Mental illness is the result of disordered thinking. The issue is not the problem itself, but the way you *think* about it.

For example, Beck *et al.* (1979) argued that depressed people make errors in their thinking and processing of information from the world. Some of the common faulty thinking strategies are listed below:

All or none thinking (dichotomous thinking) – A tendency to classify everything into one of two extreme categories, e.g. success and failure.

Arbitrary inferences – Drawing negative conclusions without having the evidence to support them.

Overgeneralisation – Incorrect conclusions are drawn from little evidence (e.g., a single incident).

Catastrophising – Where relatively normal events are perceived as disasters.

Selective abstraction – When a person only pays attention to certain features of an event, and ignores other features that might lead to a different conclusion.

Excessive responsibility – Excessively taking responsibility and blame for things which happen.

Read the case study of a depressed patient below:

'I can't bear it. I can't stand the humiliating fact that I'm the only woman in the world who can't take care of her family, take her place as a real wife and mother, and be respected in her community. When I speak to my young son, Billy, I know I can't let him down, but I feel so ill-equipped to take care of him; that's why he frightens me. I don't know what to do or where to turn; the whole thing is too overwhelming… I must be a laughing stock. It's more than I can do to go out and meet people.'

(Frieve, 1975)

- Highlight areas of this passage that you feel illustrate faulty thinking strategy.
- Identify the faulty thinking strategy you feel the woman is using.
- Explain why you think the quote illustrates that bias.
- Extension: Do you think faulty thinking strategies are the *cause* or *effect* of depression?

▶ Lesson notes p.77

Cognitive model of abnormality - evaluation and elaboration

Your exam essays are marked out of 12 and there are 6 marks available for evaluation. Many students miss out on evaluation marks because they do not *elaborate* their comments and evaluations in sufficient detail to get the full marks.
Here are the marking bands for Evaluation: (Rudimentary = 0–1 marks), (Basic = 2–3 marks), (Reasonable = 4–5 marks), (Effective = 6 marks).

Your task here is to match up the evaluation points from the left, further and further to the right in order to increase your evaluation marks (remember though that you would only have time for 2–3 evaluation points).

Rudimentary	Basic	Reasonable	Effective!
■ One problem with this model is cause and effect.	◆ These therapies concentrate on challenging and changing the faulty thought patterns of their patients.	★ For example, it may not consider how life events or family problems may have contributed to the mental disorder.	✿ As such, this lends support to the fact that abnormal behaviours are the result of faulty thought patterns, as opposed to conditioning (behavioural model) or unconscious drives (psychodynamic model).
■ Another objection to the cognitive model is that it blames abnormality on the patient and assumes they are responsible.	◆ For example, Gustafson (1992) conducted a study which found that irrational thinking processes were displayed by many people with psychological disorders such as anxiety disorder, and depression.	★ For example, an individual with depression may develop negative thinking *because* he is depressed rather than the other way round.	✿ It could be that the original disorder is caused by biochemical factors such as the under activity of neurotransmitters – with negative thinking being the *effect*.
■ A positive aspect of the model is that it is supported by research studies.	◆ Often, the model overlooks situational factors. That is, events in the life of the individual that they cannot control.	★ This shows that people suffering from mental disorders *do* exhibit faulty thought patterns.	✿ Thus there *is* evidence to support the main underlying assumption of the cognitive model of abnormality.
■ The model has also led to the development of successful therapies for treating disorders.	◆ That is, it could be that faulty thinking may be the effect of mental disorder, rather than the cause of it.	★ This focus has been shown to be much more effective than concentrating on immediate behaviours (as the behavioural model would) or deeper meaning (as the psychodynamic model would).	✿ This is because the cognitive model assumes the disorder is simply in the mind of the patient, and that recovery lies in changing that – rather than what is in their environment.

▶ Lesson notes p.78

Comparing models of abnormality

Use your knowledge of the four approaches demanded by the Specification to place a tick or a cross in each of the boxes below. Please note that there may be more than one tick in each row.

M = Medical/biological, B = Behavioural, P = Psychodynamic, C = Cognitive

	M	B	P	C
Treatment requires that the sufferer develop insight concerning the cause of their abnormality	☐	☐	☐	☐
Treatment focuses upon the removal of specific, clearly-defined features of a condition	☐	☐	☐	☐
Treatment is expensive	☐	☐	☐	☐
Approach is scientific	☐	☐	☐	☐
Approach is rejected by more 'client-centred' approaches	☐	☐	☐	☐
Approach believes that cause of abnormality may be linked to parents	☐	☐	☐	☐
Treatment takes a long time	☐	☐	☐	☐
Successful treatment requires the active involvement of the patient	☐	☐	☐	☐
Emphasises mental processes	☐	☐	☐	☐
'Cure' involves identification of 'irrational' thoughts	☐	☐	☐	☐
Approach to treatment raises ethical concerns	☐	☐	☐	☐
Treatment places power in the hands of the therapist and not the client	☐	☐	☐	☐
Treatment is directed at underlying causes of abnormal behaviour	☐	☐	☐	☐

▶ Lesson notes p.78

Case study for a biological therapist

Read the following case study and imagine that you are a psychologist who believes in the biological model of abnormality.

- In trying to understand Adam's behaviour, what evidence would you focus on and select from this case study and why?
- What caused him to behave like this? Provide one explanation (from a biological point of view) for his behaviour.
- What assumptions underlie your explanation?
- What therapy would you offer him?

Slouching in the wide chair in the therapist's room, Adam was unconvinced. He had come for help only after his GP recommended that he see a therapist. The apparent reason was his inability to sleep at night. He did not see the point of talking about his childhood or the other problems that he had been experiencing recently, but eventually, after some gentle questions from the therapist, he agreed to talk.

When Adam was only seven, his mother, whom he loved very much, died suddenly and over the next few years his time was spent living with either his father or his aunt. His father drank a great deal and could not get through the day without a large amount of alcohol. At the same time his father had great mood swings and had even spent a few weeks in the local psychiatric hospital, where he was diagnosed as having manic-depression. As his father seldom had a job for very long, there was never enough money to pay the bills on time and they lived in a very run down part of town. There were times when his father couldn't look after Adam and so he would then go and live with his aunt.

In spite of this difficult upbringing, Adam did well at school and after his A levels went to university. He got a part-time job working in a pub. However, he was also aware that sometimes he felt depressed for no particular reason but at other times he felt really elated and full of energy and excitement. While at university he began to feel very self-conscious with people whom he thought were in authority over him (like his boss, the lecturers and even some of his peers). He always felt slightly inferior and was very sensitive about things such as his clothes because they weren't the 'designer label' that many of the others wore. Being a member of the rugby team helped his self-esteem but after a serious head injury he was advised not to play for the rest of the season.

One day at the start of his second year he started going out with an attractive girl who was on his course. To his amazement they soon fell in love, although Adam could not believe that an intelligent and charming girl could fall for him. Adam became increasingly stressed as the end of year exams approached, especially as his girlfriend did not seem to find exams and revision hard. Like his father, Adam turned to drink to help him deal with the stress. Although he passed his exams, he still kept on drinking as he found that it made him feel less self-conscious and more relaxed, especially in the company of his peers.

One evening, after Adam had been in an elated mood for several days and after he had been drinking more heavily than usual, he had a violent argument with his girlfriend. He accused her of being unfaithful and almost went to hit her, when he somehow managed to stop himself. He was so appalled at what he might have done that he decided to get some professional help.

▶ Lesson notes p.79

Spot the mistakes!

Spot the 10 deliberate mistakes in this text outlining treatments associated with psychoanalysis....

Repression and the unconscious mind

As a therapy, psychoanalysis is based on the idea that individuals are aware of the many factors that cause their behaviour, emotions and general health. Some of these factors operate at an unconscious level, and are the result of regressed memories or resolved conflicts from childhood. During psychoanalysis, the therapist attempts to trace these unconscious factors to their origins and then help the individuals deal with them. The therapist uses a variety of different techniques to uncover repressed material and help the client deal with it.

Free association

One such technique is known as free association, in which the patient expresses thoughts exactly as they occur, even though they may seem unimportant or irrelevant. Freud believed that the value of free association lies in the fact that the associations are driven by the conscious factors which analysis tries to uncover. This procedure is designed to reveal areas of conflict and to bring into consciousness memories that have been repressed. The patient helps interpret these for the therapist, who corrects, rejects, and adds further thoughts and feelings.

Therapist intervention

Therapists often listen carefully as their patients talk, looking for clues and drawing tentative conclusions about the possible effect(s) of the problem. Patients may initially offer resistance to their therapist's interpretations (e.g., changing the subject to avoid a painful discussion), or may even display *transformation*, where they recreate the feelings and conflicts and transfer these onto the therapist (e.g. acting towards the therapist as if he was they despised parent).

Working through

Psychoanalysis is a brief form of therapy. Patients tend to meet up with the therapist four or five times a year. Together the patient and therapist examine the same issues over and over again, sometimes over a period of years, in an attempt to gain greater clarity concerning the causes of their neurotic behaviour.

▶ Lesson notes p.80

Using systematic desensitisation

Desensitisation hierarchy

This is *a series of imagined scenes, each one causing a little more anxiety* than the previous one.

Construct a desensitisation hierarchy using the diagram below which consists of five 'events' that a behavioural therapist might use to help a patient with a phobia of spiders.

Low anxiety level

High anxiety level

How does it work?

Step 1: Patient is taught how to relax their muscles completely. (A relaxed state is incompatible with anxiety.)

Step 2: Therapist and patient together construct a desensitisation hierarchy – a series of imagined scenes, each one causing a little more anxiety than the previous one.

Step 3: Patient gradually works their way through desensitisation hierarchy, visualising each anxiety-evoking event while engaging in the competing relaxation response.

Step 4: Once the patient has mastered one step in the hierarchy (i.e. they can remain relaxed while imagining it), they are ready to move onto the next.

Step 5: Patient eventually masters the feared situation that caused them to seek help in the first place.

Apply your knowledge!

Alana has an extremely anxious reaction to spiders. She completely freezes if a spider is in the room, no matter what the size. She even struggles with plastic and cuddly toy spiders.

Explain how a behavioural therapist might use systematic desensitisation to help Alana with her fear of spiders. (6 marks)

▶ Lesson notes p.81

